5

GERHART HAUPTMANN: THE PROSE PLAYS

GERHART HAUPTMANN

The Prose Plays

Margaret J. Sinden, 1915 –

UNIVERSITY OF TORONTO PRESS

To

BARKER FAIRLEY

*that I may at least acknowledge a debt
which I can never hope to repay.*

Preface

ANYONE looking at a list of Hauptmann's works such as that given by C. F. W. Behl and Felix A. Voigt in their book, *Gerhart Hauptmanns Leben: Chronik und Bild* (Berlin, 1942), will be impressed at once both by the bulk of his writing and by its variety. It contains some seventy items, of every conceivable *genre*, and inspired by contemporary life, by history, literature, legend, mythology, and by religious and philosophical works of very different kinds. Not all that Hauptmann wrote, however, is of the same quality. For almost twenty years after the appearance of his first play in 1889 he devoted himself primarily to prose drama and a long novel, *Emanuel Quint*, in which he portrayed men and society in a realistic manner and with outstanding success. But the very openness and impressionability which made him sensitive to the world around him and formed the basis of his rich and shaded pictures led him also, and increasingly as the years went by, to enter fields less suited to his genius. From the period immediately preceding the First World War until his death he wrote mainly poetic drama, novel, *Novelle*, and verse epic, and he placed ever greater stress, in all his works, on the depiction of irrational forces in man and the universe through the media of symbol and vision, of meditation and mythology. He never lost himself entirely. His gift for the presentation of complex human beings and of the spheres in which they move asserted itself in a number of fine verse plays, and he wrote one or two interesting pieces of descriptive and narrative prose. But wherever his new manner predominates, his work is inferior. Some of his verse plays are as strained and unconvincing as the others are forceful and alive. His late prose writings tend to be inept and sensational. And although there are beautiful passages in *Der grosse Traum*, the long, visionary epic which he intended as his supreme legacy to mankind, clear and radiant scenes and fearful accounts of suffering and destruction, there is also much that is forced, repetitive, and simply obscure. The current tendency to glorify anything that smacks of mysticism and mythology has recently led critics to attribute a value to such works which, on the whole, they do not deserve. Hauptmann's truest insight into the wonders of the universe is to be found in the score of prose and verse plays and in the three or four novels and stories which reveal him, not as a prophet or a magician, but as a humanist with unparalleled gifts of observation and with a deeply Christian love of his fellow-man. The present volume is devoted to a close examination of what seem to me the finest of his prose plays. I hope to follow it with a similar analysis of the best of the plays in verse.

I should like to express here my sincere gratitude to the Humanities Research Council of Canada for their generous assistance in the publication of this work. Quotations from Hauptmann's works, unless otherwise specified, are from *Das gesammelte Werk* (Fischer Verlag, Berlin, 1942), and are reproduced by permission of C. Bertelsmann Verlag, Gütersloh, who now hold copyright.

                                                           M.S.

Contents

Preface   vii

I.   Introduction   3

II.   Early Plays   14

III.   Historical Plays   53

IV.   Middle-Class Plays   99

V.   Plays of the Common People   149

VI.   Epilogue   219

Index   235

GERHART HAUPTMANN: THE PROSE PLAYS

I. Introduction

GERHART HAUPTMANN was born in Salzbrunn, Silesia, in 1862, and *Vor Sonnenaufgang*, his first important play, was written and acted in 1889. The dates establish him at once as a close contemporary of Strindberg, Chekhov, Wedekind and Schnitzler, of Shaw, Wilde, Rostand, Gorki and Hofmannsthal—in a word as a member of the outstanding generation of dramatists who, carrying on the pioneer work of Ibsen, brought forth the great flowering of the European stage that marked the last years of the nineteenth century and the beginning of the twentieth. And the work of these men is related not only because of its high quality, and not only because they were writing during the same years, but also because—although some of them fled from certain aspects of the world around them—they were fully cognizant of the state of the society in which they lived, of the personal, social and economic problems of their fellows, and of their thinking. All their plays, in one way or another, reflect the great changes in man's conception of himself and his environment that are characteristic of the latter half of the nineteenth century, the changes evident in the work of such men as D. F. Strauss, Marx and Darwin, Huxley and Renan, Taine, Freud and Forel, Nietzsche and Bergson.

Such an accomplishment seems all the more remarkable in view of the undistinguished and, in a broad sense, reactionary, drama of the three or four preceding decades. In one country after another, during these years, we note the same two phenomena: the persistence of an outworn verse tragedy, usually with a subject matter from the remote past; and the strong predominance of a type of facile society drama which has been a constant stand-by of the European stage from Kotzebue through Scribe to Mr. Terence Rattigan, but which only in such periods of degeneration is esteemed as well as popular. Ibsen, working in the fifties in the theatres of Bergen and Oslo, found himself directing mainly vaudeville and Scribe, and, in an attempt to provide Norway with a truly national drama, concentrated his own creative efforts for years on the composition of uninspired historical tragedies before, single-handed, he worked his way through to the plays about contemporary life which made him the master of the next generation. The only Russian playwright whom historians consider worthy of mention between Ostrovski and Chekhov is Count Alexei Tolstoi, who dramatized ancient chronicles. In England Tennyson, like Shelley and Byron and Browning before him, tried his hand at elevated verse drama, and with even slighter success. And though Robertson and Jones and Pinero were making first attempts at honest, realistic works, the English theatre subsisted mainly on adaptations of French salon comedy and melodrama, and on native burlesque. In France itself Augier, Dumas *fils*, and above all Becque dealt more seriously and capably with contemporary problems than most other dramatists of the age, but the work of the first two was limited in its scope, and even French audiences were slow to appreciate the sombre and unflinching realism of Becque, though they filled the theatres to watch the plays of the clever and sensational Sardou.

The scene in Germany was equally uninspiring. In the years between 1850 and 1880 or 1890 she was changing, more rapidly than any of her European neighbours, from a group of loosely federated states to a united nation and from a feudal and agricultural country to one dominated by capital and industry; and not only her dramatists, but her poets and novelists found themselves unable to keep pace with the developments. The first sixty years of the century had seen, in long and brilliant procession, the plays of Kleist and Büchner, Grillparzer and Hebbel, and the darkness that followed seemed dark indeed. There were no successors of even approximately the same stature. The Duke of Meiningen, whose example was followed eventually by the important Deutsches Theater in Berlin, did something to preserve the dignity of the classics by careful staging and a rigorous training of actors in ensemble work. But for the rest, in Germany as elsewhere, the stage fell into the hands of nondescript writers of colourless historical plays and salon pieces, the latter the inevitable translations or imitations from the French. Enthusiasm for Wagner was growing, but the only link between drama and opera was the common preference for national themes, historical or legendary. Two men only stand a little above their fellows. In Austria, in the seventies, Ludwig Anzengruber wrote comedies and tragedies which brought a new vigour and a new actuality to the long-established Viennese folk drama; but his efforts earned him only opposition from the authorities and neglect from the public. And in the north the worthy Ernst von Wildenbruch gained a not entirely undeserved fame for a series of historical tragedies and for one or two seriously conceived plays about contemporary life.

Yet the failure of even its most conscientious dramatists is a measure of the failure of the era. However admirable the intentions of the writers of verse tragedy may have been, they achieved no more than a pale reiteration of the work of their predecessors. The plays of Tennyson have been called "mechanical exercises in an imitated art."[1] Wildenbruch's first success came in 1879 with *Die Karolinger*, a tragedy written for a Munich contest whose terms stated expressly that, to be eligible, entries must avoid all hitherto unsolved social and political problems. Such authors either merely interpreted history as the moral and emotional struggles of what R. F. Arnold so aptly termed "the upper ten thousand of the past,"[2] or, when they conceived that they had a message for their own day, exalted duty, self-sacrifice and love of the fatherland on the obvious assumption that the European fatherlands of the second half of the nineteenth century were simple, patriarchal states, the main duty of whose citizens was to follow their chieftains to death on the field of battle. Neither the fresh and naïve realism of a Robertson, moreover,

[1]T. H. Dickinson, *Contemporary Drama in England* (London, 1920), p. 28.
[2]*Das deutsche Drama* (Munich, 1925), p. 635.

nor the serious moral purpose of an Augier, a Dumas or a Wildenbruch could make their *drames bourgeois* a basis for a new theatre. For not only was their vision gravely limited by a tendency to sentiment and melodrama, but they looked at the world through spectacles, fashioned originally, it is true, in a search for justice and humanity, but fashioned by an earlier generation for earlier scenes.

A brief look at two of the plays in which they are sometimes supposed to have broken new ground, Robertson's *Caste* and Wildenbruch's *Die Haubenlerche*, will reveal this common and traditional outlook. Both plays are based on one of the oldest problems of European middle-class literature, marriage between classes; in both we find the same treatment of the lower classes as either idyllic or comic, and of the upper as either noble and unprejudiced or frivolous and superficial; both have as leading figures pure idealists who are tolerated and even admired as long as the dramatist can prove that there are really no major problems for them to solve; and in both, finally, concessions are made to the labour movement in the form of two characters, a prosperous young worker who is too intent on earning his living to be bothered with social and political talk, and a worthless older man who bemoans the exploitation of the proletariat because he would rather complain than work. The general assumption of all such plays is that if only individuals will work hard, mind their own affairs, keep their wives and daughters out of the hands of seducers, marry within their own class and not be dazzled by rank or wealth, all will be well on the stage and in the world. One German dramatist of the older generation, Hebbel, had known better. In his powerful *Maria Magdalene* (1853), it is precisely the attempt to adhere rigidly to such over-simple precepts which leads to tragedy. But the only dramatist who paid attention to *Maria Magdalene* for many years was Ibsen. The play, however, was Hebbel's only bourgeois tragedy and, as such, easily overlooked. More surprising is the fact that, during this same period, a series of great novelists were keeping pace with or anticipating the scientists and the thinkers. Yet the historical dramatists seem never to have heard of *A Tale of Two Cities* or of *War and Peace*; the writers of plays about contemporary life remained unmoved by *Les Paysans* or *Crime and Punishment*, by *The Return of the Native* or *L'Assommoir*.

By the mid-eighties, however, the combined impact of a new civilization, a new learning, and a new fiction was becoming so great that for many men a corresponding reform of the theatre seemed one of the most urgent needs of the age; and their hopes were primarily for prose plays which would deal with contemporary life with the same breadth, exactness and daring as the novel. Translations of Ibsen began to appear and there were a few performances. In 1886 Tolstoi added fuel to the fire with his grim tragedy of peasant life, *The Power of Darkness*. In 1887 there followed *The Father*, the first of Strindberg's drastic studies in sexual antagonism. In the same year, in Paris, Antoine established his Theatre Libre, and proceeded to act Ibsen's plays, *The Power of Darkness*—which Augier and Dumas predicted would fail—and the many new French, Russian, German and Scandinavian plays which were quickly forthcoming. In 1891 the appearance of Archer's translation of Ibsen and a performance of *Ghosts* shook England with such effect that the hitherto faltering steps of Jones and Pinero were strengthened, and it was possible to conceive that there would some day be an audience for Shaw. In Germany, where, as we have noted, not only the drama was languishing, but the novel and the lyric, there were cries for a revolution of all *genres*. There is nothing to be gained by discussing here in detail the manifestos of such men as Georg Conrad and the Harts, Bleibtreu and Henckell, Alberti and Bölsche—they were one in their faith in the new sciences and in their demand for a literature which should reflect an industrial and scientifically minded civilization, directing its eyes especially to the proletariat and to the problems of the relations between the individual and his environment.[3] But mention should be made of Arno Holz, who made a special mark by his insistence

---

[3]An excellent account of the various critical proclamations is given by T. M. Campbell in his introduction to *German Plays of the Nineteenth Century* (New York, 1930).

on the proper technique for the new art, namely photographic and phonographic reproduction. And it should be noted also that in Berlin the efforts to reform the drama culminated, in 1889, in the formation by a group of enthusiasts of an organization called the Freie Bühne. Its members hoped, like Antoine in Paris, to present new and experimental plays, and they began their activities in October of the same year with a production of *Ghosts*. By the beginning of the nineties both the need and the desire for a new drama were as evident in Germany as in England or France. And rarely have the hopes of a group of men been more abundantly answered than by the plays of Schnitzler and Wedekind, and, above all, of Hauptmann.

To explain the need, however, does not explain Hauptmann's ability to meet it. Critics have seldom failed to note, and quite rightly, that to some extent he appreciated and was stimulated by the heralds of the new régime who were working in Berlin, where he lived for a good part of the eighties. In 1884 there appeared an anthology of poems, the purpose of which was indicated in its title, *Moderne Dichtercharaktere*. Hauptmann sympathized with the rather uncertain efforts of its contributors to write realistically about factories and modern city life, and he later called them "Fleisch von meinem Fleisch." From 1887 he sometimes attended meetings of a literary society called Durch, whose members had shouldered the mantle of the anthologists, and who came together to read new works and to discuss the problems of a new literature. And through this connection, early in 1889, he met Arno Holz, who was not only continually expounding his methodological theories, but who read aloud to him a series of sketches called *Papa Hamlet*, minute descriptions of scenes from everyday life, which he had just completed with a friend, Johannes Schlaf. Hauptmann acknowledged the impression the little work made on him by dedicating to the pair his first play, *Vor Sonnenaufgang*, and it will be necessary to say more about this presently.

Yet we should not place too much stress on such influences. Not only had Hauptmann less formal learning than most of his predecessors in the German drama, Lessing or Schiller or Kleist, but also, although he did some desultory reading from a fairly early age, it was a long time before he became primarily interested in literature, to say nothing of drama. There is, to my knowledge, no evidence that he knew the pale efforts of his elders, although in his early twenties he tried some historical plays himself. And it is interesting to note that, as late as the winter of 1884-5, when he was attending the University of Berlin as an occasional student and listening to lectures from the historian Treitschke and the physiologist Du Bois-Reymond, he seems to have been completely unaware that under the same roof and at the same time the future leaders of the Freie Bühne[4] were gathered in the seminar of Wilhelm Scherer, a highly popular professor of German literature and a critic with advanced ideas. Contact with literary circles like Durch and with theorists like Holz helped Hauptmann to discover his genius. But more important for his development was the direct impression made on him by economics or pathology, or, eventually, by great contemporary literature itself. And most important of all, for he was of a deeply impressionable nature, were his wide contacts with the society of his day, with people of all classes and of the most varied convictions. He wrote *Vor Sonnenaufgang* when he was twenty-seven. Fifty years later he stated that his work had not yet exhausted the experiences of the first quarter-century of his life. To appreciate his prose plays, it is not enough to know something of the state of the German drama before him and of the agitation for reform; we need also some understanding of the scenes of his early life and of his manner of reacting to them.

Salzbrunn, where he was born, was a small resort town. But it was a town which offered him a wider variety of experience than one might at first sight expect. His father was the owner of a fashionable hotel, Zur Preussischen Krone, and within its walls he found a veritable cross-section of the society of his day. The town, moreover, lay on the edge of an industrial region;

---

[4]Max Halbe, *Scholle und Schicksal* (Munich, 1933), p. 352. These included Otto Brahm and Paul Schlenther, its first director and its leading critic.

miners and weavers lived in its lower part, and he knew their quarters and played with their children. Then, at the age of twelve, he was sent with an older brother, Carl, to the *Realschule* in Breslau, where they lived with a series of families—once with a small carpenter, and again with the pastor of the local prison— and where he was free, once school was out, to roam the city. The school itself gave him his first real introduction to the Prussian spirit, for most of its teachers were former army officers, fresh from their triumphs in the war against France. He hated its regimented life, and left when he was fifteen. From then on, for many years, his movements form something of an Odyssey, where wandering itself is more important than any imagined goal. He spent a year and a half with an uncle on a great estate called Lohnig, working from dawn to dark with the peasants and the day-labourers. He had thoughts of becoming a sculptor, and spent two winters at a newly established art academy in Breslau and a winter in Rome. He lived in Dresden and in a small village on the Elbe, making some attempts to write. He joined Carl and a group of friends in Jena, where the biologist Haeckel was the hero of the day, and where he heard lectures on art, literature and science. He lived in the teeming Rosenthal quarter of Berlin, taking lessons in acting, and there also, as has been noted, attending some lectures. Finally, in 1885, he married the daughter of a wealthy merchant, Marie Thienemann, two of whose sisters were already married to his two brothers, and after a brief sojourn in a Berlin apartment near an overhead tramway, the young couple withdrew to the relatively isolated suburb of Erkner, where, amidst the sand and the fir trees, Hauptmann's life, for the first time in many years, acquired some measure of stability.

But even then there were frequent diversions, trips to the city, summers on the island of Rügen, winter weeks in Hamburg where his oldest brother Georg was living with his parents, who had had to give up the hotel some time before, and, most important of all, in the summer of 1888, a lengthy stay with Carl and his wife Martha in Zurich. For in Zurich the air was vibrant with new discoveries and with a desire for reform. Men of all professions and persuasions, from the most pragmatic scientist to the most irrational religious fanatic, were proclaiming the coming of a new era. Carl was immersed in the study of philosophy and psychology: their friend Alfred Ploetz, just back from the United States where he had been investigating the possibility of founding a co-operative community, had now turned to bacteriology. Hauptmann himself became deeply interested in the work of the psychiatrist Auguste Forel, director of the city's hospital for the insane, and, in his free moments, a strong opponent of the use of alcohol and an advocate of the rights of women. In the streets one could catch sight of Gottfried Keller, Switzerland's great liberal novelist, and of Arnold Boecklin, whose paintings were a startling combination of the natural and the fantastic. In a cemetery nearby Ulrich von Hutten lay buried, and Georg Büchner, both of them German reformers who had found sanctuary in Switzerland. The first women students of Europe sat in the lecture rooms of the University, among them refugees from Poland and Russia, and one of them, Josepha Kodis-Krzyzanowska, was a frequent visitor in Carl's house. Gerhart, who had been reading more intensively in the past year or so than before, had already some knowledge of Ibsen and Tolstoi, and both the presence of the Russian students and his interest in the work of Forel fired him with enthusiasm for Dostoievski. He was by no means treading entirely new ground —indeed, some of his literary friends from Berlin were also with him in Zurich. But here science and literature were felt to be one in a great ferment of activity. These months proved the climax of his contacts with the most advanced thinking and writing of his time.

Hauptmann, then, knew north and south before he wrote his first play, he knew city and suburb and country, and people of all occupations and classes. Moreover, from his earliest years, he had encountered widely different interpretations of life. His mother's people, who either worked on the land or were officials in the service of Salzbrunn's local ruling house, were conservative

in their ways and in their political and social convictions, and
were leaders in Silesia's Herrnhut community of pietists. His
great-grandfather on his father's side had been a weaver and then
a waiter before he became a hotel-owner. His father, who had
been in Paris in 1848 and had helped to man the barricades, was
a liberal and progressive man, an agnostic, and, in the eyes of
his in-laws, "ein roter Demokrat." And if his mother's family
found it difficult to understand the attitude of his father, they
found the ideas of Carl and Gerhart and their friends more incomprehensible still. This variety, both of men and of opinions,
was to be reflected in Hauptmann's best work.

Das Abenteuer meiner Jugend,[5] a long autobiography which is a
rich source of information about the details of Hauptmann's
early life, tells us also something about his characteristic reactions
and the growth of his sensibility. The members of his family,
he writes, were given to self-assertion and to frequent, impassioned arguments, and he himself soon became accustomed to
formulate his thoughts in the same manner; his imagination
became a forum in which all questions were fought out by the
shades of his friends and his family. "Wer wüsste nicht," he
adds, "dass Eristik das innerste Wesen des Dramas ist. Also war
es das Drama, als das ich das Leben zu leben gewöhnt ward.
Anders verstand ich das Leben nicht." Even as a child, moreover,
his life alternated between intense activity and dreaming, and
in the first Breslau years the dreams began to take on definite
contours, for as school became more and more unbearable, he
took to recreating for himself his "real" life, the life of the hotel
with its courtyard and store-rooms, its garden and salons. During
his months in Lohnig, where he worked in a state of semi-
exhaustion from dawn till twilight, the world about him stamped
itself on his mind with a strange lucidity that seemed to make it
part of an inner vision. From this time on he formed the conscious
habit of observing his surroundings, absorbing them in their most
precise and fleeting manifestations. Often, in the following years
in Breslau, he rose in time to watch the city stirring into life,

[5]First published in 1937.

and in Hamburg, in 1887,[6] he rode boat and omnibus, early
in the morning and late at night, trying, with senses more lucid
than in daylight and with passionately excited mind, to see
things as if he had never seen them before.

In all this we have a further clue to the origin of his work.
In 1889, in a comedy called *Die junge Welt*, his fellow-dramatist
Frank Wedekind portrayed him as a literary detective, spying
on his friends and recording their every gesture in a note-book.
And he did make notes. But for years he had been creating scenes
in his imagination, picturing the movements of people in definite
surroundings and developing their characteristics in dialogue:
his memories, as his own words confirm, and not his note-book,
were the real source of his inspiration. "Ich sehe Leute auf der
Strasse," he said later to C. F. W. Behl, "Dann werden sie sofort
zur Erinnerung. Ich vergesse sie vielleicht wieder eine Zeitlang.
Und dann wird die Erinnerung plötzlich ganz scharf und klar—
und dann kommt die Gestaltung gleichsam von selbst."[7] And
many years later, discussing what he had tried to achieve in his
plays, he used the image of a tree in Gallowayshire, Ireland,
which began to grow on a wall, but stretched roots downwards
until they were firmly lodged in the earth.

[6]According to *Das Abenteuer meiner Jugend* and Behl and Voigt's *Chronik*. Willy
Krogmann, in *Gerhart Hauptmann Hamburgensis* (Hamburg, 1946), adduces sound evidence for placing the date somewhat later.
[7]*Zwiesprache mit Gerhart Hauptmann* (Munich, 1948), p. 100.

II. Early Plays

THERE IS LITTLE in Hauptmann's first, sporadic literary efforts to indicate that he was aware of the specific nature of his genius. He wrote a few poems as early as his years in Lohnig, and by 1888 he had completed a small volume of verse which he published under the title *Das bunte Buch*. He wrote a fragment of an epic in hexameters called *Das Hermannslied*, and three historical verse tragedies, only one of which, *Germanen und Römer*, has survived. And he wrote a Byronic verse narrative called *Promethidenlos*, based on a sea voyage he had made from Hamburg to Naples in 1883. The works are for the most part imitations of the Romantics, of the early Heine, and of the popular historical novels of Wilhelm Jordan and Felix Dahn. What reading Hauptmann had done, it is evident, was leading him in wrong directions.

By 1887 he seems to have decided that literature, not art, was to be his vocation—he was possessed by the desire to write, he says of his weeks in Hamburg—and to have turned his thoughts to some extent from the past to the present. In the spring of that year he wrote a good, realistic sketch of peasant life entitled *Fasching*, and in the same spring he wrote *Bahnwärter Thiel*, a story set in a community on the Spree, about a railway worker who murders his brutal second wife because marriage with her is threatening the destruction of his soul. The work is a masterpiece in its portrayal of the simple and yet profound nature of the hero and in its vivid descriptions of hamlet and forest. Hauptmann's feet were at least on the right path. But month followed month and there was no successor to *Thiel*. Clearly, his real awakening was still to come.[1]

[1] Among notes made by Hauptmann between 1886 and 1888 or 1889 Walter Requardt ("Erkner im Leben und Werk Gerhart Hauptmanns," dissertation, Hamburg, 1951)

There is very strong evidence for believing that it came during his months in Zurich. He found himself at this time, he writes in the autobiography, thinking of his earlier literary efforts and wondering why, for the most part, he had been writing about far-away scenes and people, and trying, like a vampire, to suck blood from the poets of the past. And then he happened to read Tolstoi's *The Power of Darkness*. The Russian play impressed him by its earth-bound life and made him remember scenes from his boyhood which he had, he thought, forgotten— the lower village, with its wretched miners' and weavers' huts, the fashionable upper part of the town, the newly wealthy peasants of the nearby coal-mining district—and he began to see a vision of plays which he himself might write:

Meine Knabenzeit, die mir so gut wie entschwunden war, tauchte wieder auf, und in der Erinnerung an sie machte ich fast von Minute zu Minute neue Entdeckungen. Das ganze Ober-, Mittel- und Nieder-Salzbrunn entfaltete sich. . . . Aber vor allen Dingen die Dorfstrasse, die Weberhütten und die Bergmannsquartiere, diese das Ärmlichste vom Ärmlichen. . . . Auf der einen Seite von Salzbrunn die fürstliche Welt, auf der anderen das Industrie- und Grubengebiet von Waldenburg. . . . Die reichen Kohlenbauern von Weisstein drängten sich ein. . . . Ich habe ein Stück" Die Weber" geschrieben. In Zürich regte sich bereits sein embryonales Leben zugleich mit dem eines Bauerndramas, dem ich den Titel "Der Sämann" zu geben gedachte.[2]

We do not know precisely when Hauptmann began to write *Der Sämann*, the first of the two plays which he glimpsed in this vision. There is a story, which has become almost a tradition, that it was Holz who first moved him to do so by suggesting that they collaborate in the writing of a play as he and Schlaf had collaborated in the writing of *Papa Hamlet*. The story has amusing variations. According to Paul Schlenther, Hauptmann fled at the suggestion to his parents in Hamburg, and returned

has discovered a number of prose fragments and a list of projected works, highly interesting inasmuch as they contain the germs of many of Hauptmann's subsequent stories and plays. At the same time they are further evidence that the dramatist was mainly preoccupied during this period with narrative prose and that he was still only feeling his way towards a realistic portrayal.

[2]For a similar account of the origin of *Vor Sonnenaufgang* see C. F. W. Behl, *Zwiesprache mit Gerhart Hauptmann* (Munich, 1948), p. 45.

with an almost complete manuscript which, on the advice of Holz, he named, not *Der Sämann*, but *Vor Sonnenaufgang*.[3] According to Holz, it was not he who proposed collaboration, but Hauptmann.[4] And according to Hauptmann himself, the play was not written in Hamburg, but in Erkner, in the early hours of the morning.[5] Whatever the details may be, it is clear that Zurich had given him the deep sense of a changing world which permeates many of his prose plays—to say nothing of his major novel, *Emanuel Quint*—and concrete ideas both for *Vor Sonnenaufgang* and for *Die Weber*, though the latter was not to be written for another three years. And his experience there left a quite specific mark also on other early plays, on *Das Friedensfest* and on *Einsame Menschen*. Hauptmann's memory, it would seem, was not deceiving him, and we must associate his first real discovery of himself as a dramatist with his visit to Switzerland.

Once he had found himself, he wrote rapidly and without pause. The Freie Bühne acted *Vor Sonnenaufgang* for the first time on October 20, 1889, and they were able to follow it with *Das Friedensfest* on June 1, 1890, and with *Einsame Menschen* on January 11, 1891. The first play brought Hauptmann both intelligent appreciation and notoriety. *Einsame Menschen* established him in the eyes of the theatre-going public as an author of some repute, and the state theatres were opened to him, though not, as we shall see, once and for all. And public opinion was right. The three plays were not only written in quick succession, they mark a rapid advance to mastery.

I

The setting of *Vor Sonnenaufgang* is a Silesian village, a farming community in the not too distant past, now a centre of the coal-mining industry. The action takes place in the house and

---

[3]*Gerhart Hauptmann, Leben und Werke* (6th ed., Berlin, 1912), p. 50.

[4]*Johannes Schlaf* (2nd ed., Dresden, 1909), p. 22.

[5]Behl, *Zwiesprache*, p. 69. An entry in Hauptmann's diary for January 1889, also indicates that during his sojourn in Hamburg he was not working on a play but on a novel. (Printed by Requardt, *Erkner im Leben und Werk*.)

courtyard of one of the former peasants, Krause, who has acquired sudden wealth through the discovery of coal under his fields, and who has become in consequence, together with his family, thoroughly degenerate. When the play opens he is a confirmed alcoholic who has drunk his animal strength into a sub-animal state of brutality. He spends most of his time in a nearby tavern and we see little of him. More in evidence are his second wife, a vulgar, blatant woman, and another debased peasant, an idiotic young man named Kahl who is her lover and who is also accepted by the family as the fiancé of the younger of her two step-daughters, Helene. Closely associated with this group are two people, Helene herself, who has only recently returned home from a Herrnhut boarding-school, where, at the wish of her dead mother, she has been brought up, and Hoffmann, the husband of the older daughter, a mine owner and speculator, and a man more polished than his in-laws, but also, if we consider the extent of the damage he does, more corrupt. The two remaining major characters come from the world without. One is a serious young economist named Loth, who has strong socialist leanings and iron convictions about the importance of heredity. And the second, who stands, a cool observer, on the fringe of the action, is a doctor, Schimmel-pfennig, who is working among the peasants and miners, collecting information and money, both of which he hopes to use some day to improve the position of women in society.

The action is very simple. Loth comes to the village to investigate conditions among the miners, finds that Hoffmann, a former school-mate, is staying with his father-in-law, visits him, and is invited to remain for a day or so. He falls in love with Helene. But when he learns that marriage with her would give his children alcoholic ancestors, he leaves at once. Helene, who was already unhappy at home, and whose eyes have been sharpened by Loth to the dangers of her blood and environment, shoots herself. In the meantime her sister has given birth to a dead child.

Vor Sonnenaufgang is based on Hauptmann's direct and personal observations. But, as we should expect, he was influenced in the organization and interpretation of his material by the example of those who had written on similar themes before him—the evidence suggests Ibsen and Tolstoi—and he was intent also on satisfying what his literary friends in Berlin and his scientific friends in Zurich expected from a modern dramatist. He did not succeed at once in integrating completely these varied elements or in presenting them in a way that was fully compatible with his particular temperament and with his deepest convictions. There are discrepancies and weaknesses in the play which the critic must note and seek to account for. Yet it has also great strength and promise—evidence that in many ways the impulses that prompted it were closely related and helpful to one another. The setting, for example, was one which Hauptmann knew well and which at the same time, as his contemporaries wished, reflected a highly important social problem—the effects of industrialization on a former agricultural community. It lent itself also to the tracing of hereditary and environmental influences on the characters. And it gave the dramatist an opportunity of developing his gift for writing the spoken language. The dialogue must have made the heart of Arno Holz dance for joy. The broad peasant dialect, the student banter that Loth, Hoffmann, and the doctor have retained from their school-days, the stuttering of the sub-normal Kahl, the nasal humming of Frau Krause's affected ladies' companion—Hauptmann's sensitive ear was able to reproduce these and a dozen other cadences, not, as yet, without an almost too deliberate stress on detail and on idiosyncrasies, but with a fidelity and a range of tone that the German drama had not yet known.

In the matter of structure also Hauptmann showed a natural gift for complying with the demands of current dramatic criticism, which rejected as untrue to life the plot devices—the intrigues, chance meetings, and unforeseen discoveries—which were the stock-in-trade of the *salon* pieces of a Scribe, and which had been imitated in Germany. *Vor Sonnenaufgang* manages

without them. And here Hauptmann had distinguished models
in the plays of Ibsen. He must have learned much from the older
dramatist about the art of beginning with a ripe situation and of
precipitating the catastrophe by a mere incident. He may even
have learned that a particularly effective incident is the arrival
of a stranger. And Ibsen must have helped him also to master
the technique of analytic exposition, of revealing the past gradu-
ally and of building tension by this means rather than by action
and counter-action proceeding in the present and before the eyes
of the spectator.

Yet if Hauptmann was an apt pupil, he was also independent.
Ibsen sometimes avoids plot in the present only by relegating
it to the past, and this is particularly true of *The Doll's House*,
with which we know Hauptmann was familiar. In the Nor-
wegian play plans and misunderstandings of bygone years have
formed a knot which has to be explained and untied in the course
of the action represented on stage. The information that Hauptmann gives us is of a very different kind: we learn of the ruthless
way in which Hoffmann has acquired his wealth; we hear that
Loth, some time ago, spent two years in prison for political
heterodoxy; we are told that Kahl, who shoots for sport about
the house and yard, once hit a peasant; the doctor relates that the
first Hoffmann child inherited the alcoholic tendencies of his
mother and grandfather and killed himself on a broken schnaps
bottle. Such details do not, in any sense, reconstruct a story.
They help to reveal character and they make the general situation
vivid and clear. More and more, as the play advances, they con-
vince us that, the people and the circumstances being what they
are, a tragic end is inevitable. Even by comparison with the
works of Ibsen, to say nothing of those of the older generation
of French and German dramatists, *Vor Sonnenaufgang* moves
away from any traditional use of plot in favour of characterization and of the painting of milieu. The shift is significant in
more than one respect. Professor Ernst Feise, making similar
observations, has noted that it means that Hauptmann was far

more interested than Ibsen in proving that his characters are determined by heredity and by early environment.[6] But it is also an anticipation of the strength of Hauptmann's mature work, which, as we should expect from his intense interest in observing the scenes and the people around him, lies in good part in the revelation of human nature in its most individual manifestations and in its most intimate connections with the surrounding world, whether this world is natural or man-made, physical or spiritual, as concrete as houses and economic conditions or as intangible as the shifting light on the early morning sea. "Was man der Handlung gibt," he wrote later, "nimmt man den Charakteren."[7] *Vor Sonnenaufgang* is a first expression of this conviction.

It was one thing, however, for Hauptmann to concentrate his attention on character and situation, and another for him to portray them with complete success in this, his first play, and just at these vital points the precepts of his friends and his own experience sometimes diverge and sometimes conflict. He chose his general setting, we have noted, both because he knew it and because it provided him with material for a lesson on social conditions. When he came to elaborate the details of character and incident his conception of what he ought to be teaching frequently interfered with his sense of reality and gave the play unlifelike and exaggerated notes foreign to his later work. The first act, for example, contains what must be one of the most improbable supper-table conversations in all dramatic literature, a scene which Hauptmann intended to be awkward and painful, but which became more painful than he designed. Even the beginning puts some strain on our credulity, and it is not easy to listen to Frau Krause discussing imported wines in heavy dialect, to hear of Kahl's sadistic forays against mice, pigs, and larks, to accept the naïvely angry protests of Helene and the

---

[6]In the course of a comparison of Ibsen's *Rosmersholm* and Hauptmann's *Einsame Menschen, Germanic Review*, 1935, p. 159.

[7]Hauptmann wrote no connected dramatic theory, but a collection of aphorisms and brief utterances was published for the first time in the *Grosse Gesamtausgabe*, XII (1922), and reprinted in 1924, under the title *Ausblicke*.

superior, sardonic glosses of Hoffmann without feeling that we cannot take all of this seriously and that something or someone is being parodied. Then, as the wine is passed, Loth launches into a lecture on the evils of drinking, citing as a warning the beast-like peasant whom he has seen in the adjacent tavern. Kahl stutters as well as he can through his laughter that that must have been the old man, Helene leaves the table in tears, and Frau Krause follows, furious because her step-daughter is such a prude. Through all of it Loth remains undisturbed and uncomprehending. He cannot be allowed to perceive the truth until the last act. But the full horror of the situation has to be impressed upon the spectator. The result is that we must either consider Loth a fool or dismiss the whole scene as unconvincing and clumsy.

Less improbable is the brief glimpse that Hauptmann gives us, at the beginning of the second act, of the besotted Krause, as Helene tries to get him into the house and has to struggle against his unfatherly embraces. But the incident was undoubtedly intended as a drastic protest against the dishonest decorum of older dramatists. And the last act was certainly written in re-action to their parlor scenes, which were as decorated and artificial as the lacquered and crochet-covered furniture amidst which they were set. In Hauptmann's parlor, at the end, Loth sits waiting for news of the birth of the baby, which is dangerously delayed, and Hoffmann, Helene, or the doctor join him for a moment's respite and to report on the progress in the bedroom above. It was during this part of the play that the theatre scandal which enlivened its first performance almost reached the status of a riot, and a forceps went waving through the air. The reaction of a modern reader is apt to be simply that the scene is forced and unnatural.

Yet there is a vividness of setting in the play and a wealth of realistic incident which indicate that these strained scenes are only the errors of a beginner, and that there is nothing basically wrong in Hauptmann's conception of his task. He is able to evoke a wonderful sense of space and locality and to make them active elements throughout the whole work. The low peasant *Stube*, disfigured by modern furniture, speaks of the changes which have disrupted the community. The busy courtyard gives us a glimpse into the life of the whole house. Beyond it lies the street, where the miners pass in silent rows, and beyond that again are the fields, where anyone who wishes to stroll by the brook or under the trees must watch for cave-ins caused by the mines below. The latter areas cannot, it is true, be adequately represented on the stage, even by the most skilful of sets, but they are vividly present in the consciousness of the characters. And if the action of the first and last acts leaves something to be desired, that of the second, third, and fourth is, on the whole, admirable. Early in the morning, in the courtyard, we watch various members of the family begin their day, and Loth and Helene meet and talk by the dove-cote. Then follows breakfast, and Hoffmann tries to persuade his guest to give up his investi-gations, provoking Loth, in consequence, to such admirable statements of his beliefs that Helene, who has admired him from the beginning, is swept away by a vision of a new and happier existence, and half confesses that she loves him. After a love scene in the garden arbour, during which she makes timid and vain attempts to tell him the truth about her family, we have an engaged couple. This is the main thread, and it may seem that it has been spun rather quickly. But there are woven about it so many living incidents—the activities of the servants, for example, the departure of Kahl, who has been spending the night with Frau Krause, the attempt of Hoffmann to persuade Helene to take charge of the coming child and to show a little tenderness for him, the unfortunate father, the visit of the doctor, in whom Loth recognizes another school-friend—that when the curtain falls on the fourth act we feel, not that the attachment between Loth and Helene has been formed in an improbably short space of time, but that we have grown deep into the world portrayed and that the whole situation lies rich and heavy on our hands, with catastrophe about to break at any moment.

If we turn from problems of situation and incident to those of characterization, we can make similar observations. Krause, Frau Krause, and Kahl make up something like a group of specimens for demonstration purposes, and there is no need to labour the point that Hauptmann, in painting them, was intent on making his colours thick, bright, and unmistakable. Loth and Schimmelpfennig, moreover, are intended as *raisonneurs*; they interpret for us, discuss, and draw conclusions. Yet it would be too much to say that any character in the play is a mere type, or that the only function of Schimmelpfennig—to say nothing of Loth—is to mediate between the peasants and the audience. Hauptmann's sense of life is always greater than his desire to rationalize. He was to do his most effective teaching, not by isolating certain facts and features of his scenes, but by engaging the sympathy of the spectator for characters whom he drew as fully as possible, without ceasing to indicate the causes of their suffering. And some of the characters here have an individuality and a complexity which is more than the dramatist needs in order to sustain his thesis. There is the old peasant Bleibst, for example, crippled for life by Kahl's gun, who sits in the courtyard at the beginning of the second act, sharpening his scythe, surly and suspicious at first when he catches sight of the towndweller Loth, but eloquent and friendly when Loth offers him money, and placid in his attitude to the transgressors around him. "Amool wiil jedes," he says of a maid who has just been dismissed for improper conduct, adding, for he has seen the departing Kahl, "au de Frau."

Loth and Hoffmann too are characters in their own right, although here the thesis of the play prevented Hauptmann from developing fully the complex figures he envisaged. Loth comes to life not so much through his convictions as through his love. Indeed he confesses to Schimmelpfennig that his work had become mechanical and that his love for Helene has filled him with a new joy and faith. The force of his emotion is amusingly revealed in a long speech in which he begins by protesting that he is by no means intoxicated, that he does not even find Helene particularly beautiful, and ends by declaring that she is the loveliest

girl whom he has ever seen. Unfortunately, before the words
are cold on his lips, and with only a trace of regret, the need
for joy and faith leaves him, and he departs. We accept his
transformation from a rigid theorist to an ardent lover, but we
find it difficult to imagine the lover reverting so quickly to his
former state. With Hoffmann Hauptmann is rather more successful. He begins by painting a striking picture of a hypocrite
and a ruthless egotist, a man who advocates "practical" action
because he hates and fears socialism, and who talks to Helene
in sentimental tones about his suffering in order to mask his
sensual desire. Then, as the play proceeds, we see more and more
deeply into him and understand that he is not only despicable
but pitiful, a weakling who has need of bolstering his self-
confidence by frequent drinking and whose jovial welcome of
Loth, while it is intended to disarm a potential enemy, springs
in part from a desire to be respected by his former classmate.
We even agree with Schimmelpfennig when he claims that
Hoffmann's finer sensibilities have not been entirely blunted by
his environment and that he suffers from his wife's immoderate
drinking as much as such a man can suffer—"so viel er überhaupt
leiden kann." The analysis is penetrating and convincing and
Hoffmann is far more than the *nouveau-riche* industrialist whom
the play required as a foil for the social reformer Loth.

The greatest freedom of characterization, however, is found
in Helene. She has an integrity and a freshness, and a young,
puzzled, and inarticulate but strong repulsion from the life
around her that mark her as an individual rather than as a character
portrayed in accordance with scientific theories. Indeed, according
to science, in spite of her upbringing in Herrnhut, she ought not
to have the strength that she has. Schimmelpfennig describes
her as doomed to degradation. "Nimm ihr nicht das . . . Wenige,
was du ihr noch übrig lässt," he warns Loth, when the latter is
considering briefly whether, although he cannot marry her, he
ought not to make some attempt to save her, and by "das
Wenige" he means alcohol and an affair with Hoffmann.
Hauptmann has taken care to give us one or two details which

might support the doctor's opinion. "Aber du warst doch sonst keine von den Zimperlichen," says Hoffmann as Helene, in imitation of Loth, refuses wine; and she herself confesses that she had at one time felt an attraction to someone—and she can mean only Hoffmann—before she realized the kind of a man he was. But our main impression is that science is wrong and that she is strong in her youth and purity; and this impression is substantiated by the fact that she does not resign herself to sinking into the morass surrounding her but commits suicide. In her case Hauptmann does not merely give us more than his theory requires, he contradicts it. His science and his direct observation are at loggerheads.

It is not possible to read *Vor Sonnenaufgang* without rejoicing that the author was able to paint such a figure as Helene. But the fact that her character runs counter to the main thesis of the play does not mean simply that he was too enthusiastic about his heroine; it puts the whole tragedy out of joint. What we ought to feel at the end of the play is a sense of the havoc wrought by rapid social and economic change, horror at the spectacle of the older Krauses, disgust and anger with Hoffmann, the opportunist, and pity for Helene, whose finer nature is bound to be destroyed by her physical heritage and her environment. The Krauses and Hoffmann evoke the required reactions. But if we pity Helene it is because she is unfortunate enough to fall in love with a cold theorist who chooses to masquerade for a day as St. George and then deserts her. And our main emotion is not pity for the victim but anger with the inhuman sociologist.

Some such confusion is no very remarkable state of affairs in a first play and there is nothing to be gained by dwelling on it as such—as a measure, that is to say, of Hauptmann's failure. But it can be very illuminating to try to discover why a specific young author gets into a specific predicament, and the problem, in this case, is worth a little further consideration. Hauptmann set out to portray the importance of the laws of heredity and environment together with certain abuses of the economic system, and not only to portray, but to explain and discuss.

Loth exchanges stories of social injustice with Helene; he and
Hoffmann repeatedly recall the activities of the student socialist
club to which they once belonged—Loth as its head, Hoffmann
as a half-hearted "corresponding" member—and they debate
more than once about the situation and rights of the miners;
the doctor enters at some length into the more purely physiological aspects of the degeneration among the peasants. There is
no doubt that some of this discussion is interesting, both for its
own sake and for the light it throws on the characters. But
before long we begin to feel that there is too much talk, that it
is rather boring, and that the theories of the young agitator
are preventing him from seeing the truth, at least as far as Helene
is concerned. We realize that Hauptmann is simply recording
what he has heard from others, and in a way that indicates that
he has little of the genius of an Ibsen or a Shaw for the direct
method, for argument or controversy as such. To the extent
that he was attempting to build his play on discussion, the writing
of it cannot have given him great satisfaction.

Nor does he seem to have derived much pleasure from the
portrayal of those characters whom I have called specimens.
His powers of observation, it is true, stood him in good stead,
and he produced figures not easily forgotten. But he kept them
in the background. Ibsen, or Shaw again, would have made more
of them, would have portrayed them in a sharp and dry light
and with mocking and appreciative vehemence. Hauptmann
lacks the combination of intellectual zeal and emotional detachment which makes such treatment possible. Nor could he
approach his degenerates as Tolstoi might have done. *The Power
of Darkness* is certainly to some extent responsible for the forbidding aspects of Hauptmann's peasants and for the seriousness
with which he regards them, and he and Tolstoi are alike in their
need to enter emotionally and sympathetically into the lives of
their characters. But they seek this identification by different
means and their values are different. The very contrast between
the settings of the two plays is significant: cold and mud surround the Russian *izba*; fruitful nature and the freshness of

early dawn still prevail in the Silesian courtyard, in spite of the menacing scenes beyond. For all the sombre gloom of his first play, Hauptmann's joy in the world and his interest in the fate of human beings here and now are greater than those of Tolstoi. And he cannot find his way to the hearts of his characters by pitying them as members of the desperately sinful race of man. Neither here nor at any later time does he exalt characters who, like Tolstoi's Akim, talk in admiring rapture about the beauty of confessing one's sins. His true Christians, like his true humanists, through whom he was to discover his own approach to the world, are silent in love and in understanding of the natural laws of life. He made this discovery as early as *Einsame Menschen*. In the meantime specimens of degeneracy seem to have struck him as theoretically important, but as distasteful and repellent and not as tragic.

Looking at the work of Hauptmann as a whole, Paul Fechter argues that he was continually trying to escape from the depressing scenes which, as a naturalist and sociologist, he felt bound to paint, into realms where he could allow his fancy and his sentiment free play.[8] I do not believe that such considerations help us very much in the interpretation of the later works. Hauptmann rapidly left dogmatic naturalism behind him and with it the sense of dismal repulsion that we find in his first plays. His escapist works, moreover, are usually so poor that we cannot feel that the pressure behind them is very great. But Fechter's theory throws valuable light on the early plays and particularly on the problem of *Vor Sonnenaufgang*. Hauptmann's attempt to portray the Krauses and Loth represents a narrowly scientific outlook on the world, which does not attract him greatly. The peasants appear repulsive, the sociologist rigid and pedantic. And it would seem that, unconsciously, he recompensed himself for his unpleasant task by painting the courtyard and Helene and the love scenes of the third act. To call such scenes escapist would be an exaggeration. But they reflect an optimism characteristic of the early Hauptmann and they

[8]*Gerhart Hauptmann* (Dresden, 1922), pp. 49, 61.

reflect a feeling of the value and beauty of life which was to remain with him always, and which was not satisfied by the criteria of the psychologist or of the professional reformer alone.

II

If we look from *Vor Sonnenaufgang* to the works that followed it, we realize that it must have taught Hauptmann two things. He must have understood, first of all, that he had found in realistic prose drama a field eminently suited to him, for he did not begin to move away from it until 1894. Yet he must also have been conscious of the lack of integration in his first play, for he did not venture again at once into the larger arena which it suggests, but turned instead to smaller, more specifically domestic canvasses. In making this decision, he may have been influenced, once again, by the example of Holz and Schlaf, who in the summer of 1889 were planning their play *Die Familie Selicke*.[9] In *Das Friedensfest* and in *Einsame Menschen*, in any case, Hauptmann painted middle-class people of the kind most thoroughly familiar to him from his own family life and he concentrated on problems which arise from marriage itself and from the relations between husband and wife and parents and children.

Das Friedensfest was written in the fall of 1889 and acted for the first time in June of the following year. Its setting is an isolated villa outside Berlin where, some thirty years before the beginning of the play, Dr. Scholz, a man of wide interests, but despotic and eccentric, has brought his bride, a woman much younger than himself. The household, as we learn in the course of the action, is unhappy from the first. Quarrels are frequent and violent. Frau Scholz, narrow-minded as a girl, becomes a carping,

---

[9]According to the *Chronik,* Hauptmann did not read *Die Familie Selicke* until February 1890, some two months after the completion of his own play. However, he saw Holz and Schlaf during the preceding summer, and Holz, as has been noted, was much given to the discussion of his own works. His emphasis on the importance of a strictly naturalistic dialogue for the new drama may also have strengthened still further the impression already made on Hauptmann by *Papa Hamlet*—the language of *Das Friedensfest* is even more carefully true to life than that of *Vor Sonnenaufgang*.

self-righteous wife. Her husband begins to drink heavily and develops a persecution mania. The effect of all this on the children, two boys and a girl, is disastrous: they too nag and tear at one another and at their parents. Auguste, the daughter, remains unmarried and becomes martyred and embittered. When the father finds that he cannot dominate the boys he disowns them and turns them out to face the world as best they may. The elder, Robert, finds a routine office job and resigns himself cynically to the fact that he and his family are nervous degenerates. The younger, Wilhelm, pulls himself together, studies music, and even becomes engaged to marry a girl of a warm and happy disposition, Ida Buchner. But his self-control is not easily maintained, and when the girl's mother urges that they should all spend Christmas in his home, he consents only with great reluctance and apprehension. Frau Buchner does not realize how serious the situation is. She does not know, for example, that on his last visit home he heard his father uttering some vicious gossip about his mother and struck him, and that both men thereupon left the house intending never to return. At the point where the plays begins the attempt at reconciliation is under way. The ladies and Robert have been together for a few days. Wilhelm is due to arrive at any moment.

Chance brings the doctor home, a broken and dying man, on the same evening. For a moment it looks as though Frau Buchner may achieve even more than she had hoped for. Dr. Scholz forgives his penitent son and there are words of peace all round. But Robert, who envies his brother the yellow-haired Ida, reveals his jealousy in a brusque rejection of a gift she has brought for him. A word of reproach for his rudeness plunges the whole family into the familiar recriminations. As the quarrel grows more violent the doctor fears that he may be struck again and collapses. By this time Frau Buchner has lost her initial optimism and is unwilling to allow her daughter to become a member of such a family. Robert too warns Wilhelm that, if he marries Ida, their lives will become like those of the older Scholzes. And Wilhelm himself has lost hope. He has already become aware that, within these walls, he speaks to Ida with an impatient sharpness that might well grow when they are established in a home of their own. But the girl is undaunted, and through her faith in him he finds the courage to try once again and to walk beside her, composed and erect, to stand at the bed of his dead father. Whether their marriage will take a course different from that of the older pair is a difficult question. Clearly the author would like to hope that it will.

If we had Hauptmann's first two plays, and these alone, before us, we should probably be tempted to deal with *Das Friedensfest* in a very summary fashion. It has many of the virtues of *Vor Sonnenaufgang*, the same realism of character, situation, and setting, and the same skill in revealing the past and in maintaining tension in spite of the slightness of the action. And it has the additional virtue of being a quieter work; Hauptmann no longer finds it necessary to shock the spectator by the lurid and exaggerated scenes which he introduced into his first play. But in other ways his second work seems of slighter inherent value and less promising than his first. He is still writing from the viewpoint of the psychiatrist making a study of nervous degeneration as he had formerly done of alcoholic, and the neurotic Dr. Scholz and his family are even more depressing than the uprooted peasants. Wilhelm's struggles and suffering are intended to give the picture depth and magnitude. But when we hear him accusing himself, because he has struck his father, as though he were a Karl Moor and had murdered a saint, we are more likely to interpret such undue self-castigation as evidence of his illness and to hope that some one will soon send for a doctor than to lose ourselves in his guilt and pain. *Das Friedensfest*, moreover, lacks the wide scope and the variety of characters that impress and interest us in *Vor Sonnenaufgang*. The buoyant Ida and her mother are introduced, like Helene, to give the play warmth and hope. And this time there are no contradictions; Ida, as the saviour of the most attractive of the afflicted, is cast in her proper role. But the sweetness and light represented by the Buchners is a little too deliberate to be convincing, and too conventional to achieve the desired effect. Towards the end of the second act, when the great argument which forms the climax of the play is already under way, the voices of the two outsiders are heard from the adjoining room singing "Ihr Kinderlein kommet." Robert, after a brief struggle with his "better" nature, bursts out involuntarily, "Kinderkomödie!" The spectator is inclined to agree with him. Hauptmann was so intent on setting the healthy to rescue the sick that he did not realize that his means were insufficient. The play remains a mass of petty introversions, of lamentation, and of bickering, and the total effect is cramped and dismal in the extreme. Considered on its own merits, or as a successor to *Vor Sonnenaufgang, Das Friedensfest* has little to recommend it or to suggest that Hauptmann was making progress towards the solution of the difficulties that he encountered in his first play.

If, however, we look in two directions, not only backward but forward to *Einsame Menschen,* we find ourselves bound to modify this adverse criticism. *Das Friedensfest,* though it may not be evident at first glance, contains one or two interesting new developments. Dramatic action or conflict, for one thing, is limited in *Vor Sonnenaufgang,* and what there is of it is rather miscellaneous in nature. Suspense is built mainly on the gradual revelation of a desperate situation and there is little struggle, either inner or outer. Helene, to be sure, hopes and despairs. But none of the others, not even Loth, share in her doubts and her perplexity. Frau Krause storms briefly at her step-daughter and at a maid. Loth and Hoffmann argue. But the outbursts are few and the arguments are interludes on which nothing depends, comments, at most, on the state of affairs in the family and in the community. The pattern does not change radically in *Das Friedensfest.* Analytic exposition remains as important here as in the earlier play. But Hauptmann has achieved increased excitement by dropping his *raisonneurs* and by limiting discussion. The entire dialogue is carried by people completely and emotionally involved in the situation presented, a major part of it by the Scholz family. When Robert and Wilhelm relate the past they are telling the story of their own lives to Ida and her mother; when they interpret the present, they are talking of their own fate. And the tension is higher than in those scenes where the detached Schimmelpfennig imparts similar information to the newcomer Loth. Inner conflicts, moreover, play a considerable role in *Das Friedensfest*. It is true that the respect which Hauptmann still owed to materialistic determinism prevented him from allowing his characters to engage in any decisive, once-and-for-all encounters with themselves, or with fate. But they are all aware of the difficulties facing them and make some attempt to overcome them. Even Auguste has moments when she tries to be gentle, and Wilhelm's whole life has been a series of struggles against the influence of his blood and of his environment.

It was the attempt to portray the peculiar temperament of the Scholz family, however, that led Hauptmann to the most important innovation of the play, to a realization of the emotional tensions, the latent or barely controlled conflicts evident to sensitive ears even in relatively quiet, every-day conversation. He had known, we have noted, from an early age, a combination of strong egotism and nervous inflammability in his own family. He was now able to catch the familiar expressions and tones and to heighten and intensify them in the portrayal of his excitable and unstable characters. Common to the language of all is a note of strain and persecution, and a readiness to receive every word as provocation. And each individual has his own variation on this basic theme: the voice of Robert is weary and cynical, that of Auguste abused and petulant; the mother speaks with a plaintive self-righteousness, Wilhelm in quieter, self-reproachful tones, broken at times by flashes of scorn and bitter anger. Any one of them, moreover, has only to sound his own note to start a quite involuntary reaction in the others. Robert need only remark to his mother that the house, since the arrival of so many guests, is becoming "ungemütlich," for Auguste to retort, "empörend." Ten seconds later, without logical connection, she is picturing herself as a handmaiden sacrificed to the needs of her old mother, and Robert is mocking that she would have married fast enough had their mother given her the money to attract suitors. And the word "money" starts Frau Scholz on one of her characteristic tangents. "Geld," she says, advancing towards Robert with outstretched hand, "Da, nimm ein Küchenmesser! schneid mir's 'raus! schneid mir doch das Geld aus der Hand!" Or again, when Robert approaches his mother with a question about Frau Buchner, of whom he is suspicious, she ignores his words in order to express her own anxiety about the intentions of her husband: "Wenn ich lieber wüsste, was der Vater . . . was will er denn eigentlich? . . . so lange hat er mich nich nötig gehabt. Man war doch wenigstens sei eigner Herr. Nu wird's wieder schön losgehen, das Gekujeniere."

There is, of course, except from the viewpoint of the psychiatrist, too much of this nervous tension, too much pricking and slashing in the play, and it is partly because of this that the general impression is cramped and dreary. But the dialogue, within its narrow limits, is constantly agitated and impassioned. And the skill Hauptmann acquired, in *Das Friedensfest*, in depicting the taut emotions and the uncontrollable outbursts of anger that destroy the Scholzes stood him in good stead later, when he had to portray the lives of more normal people, the fine and subtle conflicts which, he believed, mark the existence of every living being, the ceaseless, unvoiced arguments that proceed within the heart of an individual, or the daily battle for supremacy that is fought between a man and his nearest and dearest.

In the matter of characterization also Hauptmann made some progress, a progress which seems to stem from the same source as that just described, namely from his own home. A comparison of *Das Friedensfest* with semi-autobiographical works, with *Das Buch der Leidenschaft*,[10] for example, indicates that Hauptmann not only learned from those very close to him how to depict high emotional tension, but bestowed on the figures of his play experiences and characteristics of members of his own family. Certainly, the Scholzes are not the Hauptmanns, any

[10]Published, as a novel, in 1929.

more than they are the Müllers or the Wedekinds, though the
general situation of the play is based on stories told the dramatist
by a friend, the musician Max Müller, and by Frank Wedekind,
whom he met in Zurich in 1888.[11] But Hauptmann used his
knowledge of his own people to give life and colour to the
tales related to him by others. Frau Scholz particularly has
inherited from his mother memories of a happy childhood and a
genuine though overly possessive love for her children, which
do much to redeem her in our eyes and to make her a reasonably
plausible character. Similarly, Hauptmann's sister has tinged
the figure of Auguste, and Carl that of Wilhelm. Hauptmann's
suburban neurotics are not as vivid and startling as his peasants;
and there is no one character in *Das Friedensfest* better done
than Hoffmann. But, generally speaking, the people of the second
play have greater depth and complexity than those of the first.

The basic trouble with *Das Friedensfest* is its theme. A play
depicting lives so completely isolated and introverted could
not be much more interesting—and then only by virtue of better
and more sensitive writing—than a psychiatrist's report on the
same topic. And Hauptmann first heard Wedekind's story at
the time that he was visiting the psychiatric wards of Auguste
Forel in Zurich. But he had learned something in writing the
play, and he took full advantage of it, and made up for what
he had lost, in his third work, *Einsame Menschen*. Here also
Zurich plays an important role, for both internal and external
evidence suggest that it was based in good part on the intellectual
and domestic difficulties of his brother, in whose house he lived
during his visit, and whose family life was suffering under the
stress of his attachment to Josepha Kodis-Krzyzanowska.[12] But
Hauptmann had known most of its characters for years, either

---

[11]See A. Kutscher, *Frank Wedekind* (Munich, 1922); and F. W. J. Heuser, "Personal
and Literary Relations of Hauptmann and Wedekind," *Modern Language Notes*, 1921,
as well as the same author's "Gerhart Hauptmann and Frank Wedekind," *Germanic
Review*, 1945.

[12]It is interesting to note that the first sketch for the play was written in August 1890,
when Hauptmann was holidaying in Bad Flinsberg with his brother and his sister-in-law,
and was called *Martin und Martha*. The play was completed by November of the same
year.

from his home or from his sojourn, as an adolescent, in Lohnig. *Einsame Menschen* is still closer to his own experience than either *Vor Sonnenaufgang* or *Das Friedensfest*, and it gives us a broader picture than the latter. It paints a middle-class household, but one whose windows are open to the world, past, present and future. Above all, Hauptmann was no longer trying to demonstrate. He did not discard his knowledge of psychology or sociology, but he used it, in a way that was to prove eminently suited to his particular genius, to interpret and to understand before he drew his moral.

III

The framework of *Einsame Menschen* is provided by the radically different interpretations of life, the old, orthodox, pietist outlook that Hauptmann had experienced in Lohnig and the new social and scientific opinions that he had come in contact with in Jena, in Berlin, and above all in Zurich. The Lohnig world in its most convinced form is represented by Herr and Frau Vockerat, a well-to-do Silesian farmer and his wife, and in its gentler aspects by their daughter-in-law Käthe, whose dead father had been a parson and who has been educated in a Herrnhut *Pension*; the world of the new enlightenment is reflected in Anna Mahr, a Baltic German studying in Zurich and in a young man named Braun, a painter, self-styled radical thinker, and advocate of practical, social action. Between them stands Johannes, Käthe's husband and the Vockerats' only son. He has been intended by his parents for the ministry, but he has outgrown, he believes, the world of his fathers, and he is occupied in writing a book which is to establish him as a follower of Darwin and Haeckel and as a pioneer in the search for the bright and brave new world—the "nagelneue Epoche"[13]—which was the hope of his whole generation.

Einsame Menschen is based, like Hauptmann's earlier plays, on a ripe situation, and its plot is equally simple. In a villa in the Friedrichshafen suburb of Berlin, as the play opens, the young

---

[13]Hauptmann's own term.

Vockerats' first child is being christened. The grandparents, present for the occasion, are effusively happy. But Johannes, who has consented to the ceremony only for their sakes, is taut and irritable, and Käthe, always timid with her learned husband and still weak from the birth of the baby, reacts with frightened anxiety to his every sign of disapproval. Nor is the situation improved by the presence of an aged pastor and of Johannes' friend Braun, who is openly scornful of this compromise with convention. Into this tense atmosphere comes Anna Mahr, an acquaintance of Braun, who is visiting Berlin between semesters; and she remains to precipitate disaster. Johannes, it is true, is happy because in her he finds a friend with whom he can discuss his work. But Käthe, although she becomes fond of Anna, is afraid of her, and grows increasingly weak and listless; while Frau Vockerat, who has remained to help, is alarmed both by Käthe's condition and by her son's preoccupation with another woman. After a week's stay Anna starts for the station, but is persuaded by Johannes to return. It is in vain that Braun tries to make his friend face the now evident truth that he is not bound to Anna by their mutual philosophical interests alone, and that he must choose between her and his wife. And it is in vain that Anna, more discerning and more honest than Johannes, decides at the end of a second week that she must go. In the meantime Frau Vockerat has sent for her husband, and before Anna is out of the house he arrives to overwhelm his son with reproaches of sin and ingratitude. As Johannes hears the whistle of the train carrying Anna away, he rushes out of the house in despair to commit suicide.[14]

Even from an outline of the action it is possible to perceive something of the difference between Hauptmann's second play and his third, and the change is still more evident if we compare

---

[14]The manner of Johannes' death is not entirely clear. Braun, coming through the garden, hears a boat being unchained. But a few moments before, revolver in hand, Johannes has threatened to shoot himself, and the sharply apprehensive, "Es riecht nach Rauch hier, nicht?" which Käthe utters just before it is discovered that Johannes is missing, seems to indicate that he has taken the revolver with him, rowed out onto the lake, and shot himself.

for a moment the two sets of characters. In place of the eccentric and diseased Dr. Scholz we find in *Einsame Menschen* the narrow but capable and affectionate Silesian farm owner, in place of the lightly sketched *jeune fille* Ida Buchner the wife and mother Käthe, and in place of the carping, egotistical Frau Scholz the assured, warm-hearted Frau Vockerat. We have in Braun something like a Robert with the poison extracted, and in Johannes, instead of a hero dominated by the single nightmare of a bitter childhood, one whose character reflects a considerable variety of experience and whose thinking is affected by that of the age in which he lives. The figures of *Einsame Menschen* are no longer specimens chosen to demonstrate a specific thesis, they are no longer isolated from the world around them, and Hauptmann no longer dislikes them. He has achieved simultaneously both fuller characterization and a more sympathetic understanding of his people, has found, for the first time in the drama, his true focus. With this the conflict in the creative process which we noted in the first two plays seems to be resolved; he shows no tendency, in his third tragedy, to seek refuge from a grimly realistic world in idealized characters. And with this also the techniques and the gifts which were only partly effective and realized in his first two works—his use of analysis, his accuracy of observation, his sensitivity to the human voice, his ability to link individual and environment—acquire a new and vital significance. He succeeds in creating a world of time, of space, and of people which we can accept without feeling impelled to question the validity of his assumptions and presuppositions, or, if this is unwise even with the richest of poets, within which we can live, inquire, and extend our experience almost indefinitely, in much the same way that we can live within the worlds of Shakespeare and of Molière.

The first claim on our affections, if we turn to consider the characters, is probably made by Käthe, who is veritably caressed throughout the play with a series of pet names—Käthchen, Käthel, Kathinkerle, Käthemiezel—and whom Johannes, in a moment of passion, calls a golden child—"du goldenes Geschöpf

. . . du tiefes Märchenherz." And she deserves all the fondness bestowed upon her. Never throughout the play does she show any desire to monopolize her husband or to think in terms of her claims upon him as a wife, and only once does she complain, crying out that she is, after all, a human being, and that she can no longer bear Anna's and Johannes' talk of the new woman and of the limitations of the average German housewife: "Ich weiss ja nun, wie ganz dumm und beschränkt ich bin. Sie haben mir's ja gesagt, Tag für Tag. Sie haben mich ja nun glücklich so klein und erbärmlich gemacht, dass ich mir selber zum Ekel bin." But for the rest she defends Johannes, to herself, to Braun, and to his parents: "Wir kennen ihn ja. Wir wissen ja, wie gut er im Grunde ist. . . . Hannes wirft sich nicht weg. Ich . . . habe Hannes nichts zu verzeihn." To the last moments of the play her love for him remains clear and pure, and when, at the end of the fifth act, the old Vockerats bring her in from the bedroom where she has been hiding in the dark like a hurt animal, she speaks, in her perplexity and suffering, a last moving declaration of her loyalty and faith: "Übrigens, ich bin doch gut durchs Leben gekommen. Die Fanny Stenzel, die hat einen Pastor geheiratet. Aber wenn sie auch noch so zufrieden und glücklich ist, glaubst du, dass ich mit ihr tauschen möchte? Nein, wirklich nicht." Yet this simple, childlike purity, this self-effacement, the best qualities, one might think, of her Herrnhut upbringing, are at the same time her tragic limitation. For Johannes needs a wife with more positive traits and above all with the assurance that he himself lacks, and Käthe can only retreat. Hauptmann has wonderfully illuminated her predicament through her difficulty in expressing herself. Formerly, by her own confession, she was a chatterbox, and on rare occasions she is still able to speak freely, in almost lyric flashes, about her childhood or about the little boy next door. But her marriage to Johannes has made her increasingly inarticulate, especially towards him, and the pitifully gentle remonstrances, the choked "ich genüge dir nicht," with which she responds to his outbursts of anger and despair, only infuriate him further and complete their alienation from one another. We do not see them together, after the third act.

The older Vockerats are of sturdier material, more practical, more dogmatic, more certain of themselves and of their world. The father in particular is secure in his relations both to earth and to heaven, to his manure piles, his after-dinner stories, his wife and his church, and though his words are marked by the soft emotionalism of the Herrnhut disciple, his fundamentalist conceptions of the nature of man and of God are rigid, absolute, and unswerving. His wife's range is wider, not intellectually— Darwin is to her a silly man who has destroyed her son's faith and happiness—but emotionally; and women, Hauptmann tends to think, have too much regard for life to condemn as quickly as men. She asks Anna to leave, but she does so less on moral grounds than because she fears for Käthe and because she dreads a clash between father and son, and when she perceives Anna's suffering she utters no reproaches but pleads—"Eine Frau zur Frau"— for the lives of her nearest and dearest. The picture of the world in which Johannes, until now, has been unable to find the support he desires is completed by the figure of Braun, a man with a radically shaven head and a downy moustache who lounges through life with the help of a set of phrases and slogans which he cannot trouble to defend, contradicting Johannes, contradicting himself, arguing that Johannes' book is purely theoretical and therefore useless. As a harmless Mephisto to Johannes' crippled Faust, he provides an excellent foil for his impatient friend.

There has been general agreement that all of these people, Käthe, Braun, and the father and mother, are both intensely alive and completely fitted to their roles in the total economy of the play. With Anna and Johannes, although no one, in discussing them, would speak of a reversion to the level of earlier works, critics have been less uniformly happy. Some of the objections that have been raised are probably unnecessary. But the serious representatives of the new generation offered problems of presentation and of comprehension which the other characters did not, and problems which Hauptmann did not always solve easily and completely.

The question of Anna is the simpler. To cite the doubts of Wilhelm Heise, whose analyses of Hauptmann's plays are unrivalled in their sympathetic penetration, the dramatist has not made it clear what kind of a woman she is. Braun characterizes her as egotistical and as ruthless in pursuit of her aims. Braun of course, believing as he does when he says this that Anna has separated him from his friend, is embittered and hardly a reliable witness. But it is clear that Anna has the instincts of an *Erzieherin*, that she has put in some fruitless work on Braun in the past, and that she is intent on shaping Johannes in her own image, at least to the extent of making him more independent. She urges him, after one of his normal quarrels with Braun, not to run after the artist and apologize. She even goes so far as to imply that his marriage was mere youthful folly: "Er war noch Student . . ." she says to Käthe, "Du warst noch sehr jung. . . ." Heise finds it particularly difficult to understand why, since she realizes how Käthe is suffering, she does not carry through her plan to leave after the first two weeks of her stay. Yet she is sincere beyond all question when she tells Johannes, in the end, that she must go for the sake of his wife; she acts on a high and selfless plane in refusing to write him or to see him again; and she is too sensitive to the feelings of others to attempt to defend herself when Frau Vockerat asks her to go.[15] A woman with such contradictory features is, according to Heise, not feasible.

The main difficulty here lies surely in Heise himself. Hauptmann understood better than some of his critics what may happen to a woman when she moves into fields formerly considered the province of men; and even when the arguments concerning Anna are thus starkly marshalled pro and con and abstracted from the emotional tensions of the play, the details do not make up an impossible whole. Anna has been bred in a hard school. She speaks once of parents dead in Siberia. She has had to stand alone, in a new position, in a changing world, with little money.

[15]*Gerhart Hauptmanns Dramen* (Leipzig, n.d.), III, pp. 23 ff.

And her cry, "Ach! Freiheit!! Freiheit!! Man muss frei sein in jeder Hinsicht. Kein Vaterland, keine Familie, keine Freunde soll man haben," is one of heroic and yet bitter resignation. It is not at all incredible that in the twofold warmth of a family life new to her and of her love for Johannes she relaxes and lets herself float a little too far on the waves of a dangerous happiness, or that, understanding Käthe's limits, she cannot always refrain or feel that she ought to refrain from moving towards the possession of the man whom she loves. Hauptmann was never given to underestimating the power of hearth and *eros* even on enlightened and clear-sighted people and even at a time when women in universities were a new and strange phenomenon.

It is true that Anna's character and problems are indicated rather than fully developed. And for this there are two reasons, one of which lies in the very nature of drama and the other in the stress which Hauptmann chose to place on his particular theme. Robert Petsch, in his admirable dramaturgy, makes an important correction of a long-standing error. The not uncommonly held notion that a dramatist can give a full and rounded portrait of each of his characters is, he argues, fallacious, and minor figures, because of the limited length of a single play, are necessarily types.[16] True, if Petsch had been reading more Hauptmann and less Schiller he might not have envisaged the use of "types" as the only alternative to full characterization, for a type is a person with conventionally accepted attributes, whom we already know and recognize, and with Hauptmann every man is a new man, a complex, inexhaustible mystery. "Das Leben auch nur eines Menschen ist unerschöpflich," he once wrote, "man kann, um bestimmte, zusammenhängende, übersichtliche Formen zu erreichen, kaum mehr tun als der Chemiker, der einen Faden in eine gesättigte Lauge taucht, damit sich Kristalle daran absetzen."[17] And Voigt has reported that he was in the habit of making little sketches—"Handzeichnungen" he calls

[16]*Wesen und Form des Dramas* (Halle, 1945), pp. 280 ff.
[17]From a fragment, "Aus dem Tagebuch eines Edelmannes," printed in *Ausblicke* (Berlin, 1924), p. 125.

them—of writing scenes which he probably never intended to use in the final form of the play on which he was working, but which helped him to know his characters, and to see how they would act in different situations.[18] But we must agree with Petsch that, in listening to a given number of people for two or three hours, no matter how significant and revealing their words may be—and it is the business of the dramatist to make them so— we cannot learn all things about all of them. In presenting secondary characters Hauptmann could suggest a full and complicated being, he could indicate, in Anna's case, a fate as rich and tragic as that of the central figures, but even he could only suggest, could only indicate; he could not develop all figures equally. Moreover—and this is the second point—the major stress of the play is on the Vockerat family and on the breakdown of their middle-class ideals of marriage, faith, and a settled career in the service of church or state. And we see Anna most clearly in her reaction to their problems, to the life such a family is accustomed to lead, and its attraction for her. We know her less well as a student devoted to philosophy and as an emancipated woman with her eyes turned towards the future. And it could not have been otherwise unless Hauptmann had decided to make the play hers to the same extent that *Rosmersholm*, for example, is Rebecca West's. Yet to compare her with Rebecca raises again a point worthy of note. Little as we understand of Anna's relations to her work or to her friends in Zurich, we know that, as an enlightened woman, she remains humane. Both her experience and her learning seem to have enabled her to understand the profound differences that separate the older generation from the younger and the world of one individual from that of another. "Sie werten anders, als Ihre Eltern werten," she says to Johannes, "Ihre Eltern werten anders, als Frau Käthe wertet. Darüber lässt sich gar nichts sagen, meiner Ansicht nach." And in order that Käthe may not perish, she resolves to go. We noted a moment ago that the appearance of women at

---

[18]"Die Schaffensweise Gerhart Hauptmanns," *Germanisch-Romanische Monatsschrift,* Jan. 1951, p. 94.

universities did not startle Hauptmann into believing that one
half of the human race was about to change beyond recognition.
And, in spite of the fact that she is not completely developed,
I should be inclined to back Anna, as a representative of the new
woman, against Rebecca or Strindberg's Miss Julie or Shaw's
cigar-smoking Vinnie Warren, who—especially when we think
of the sinister free-thinker, the power-mad tigress, and the
brothel owner with whom they are respectively associated—
appear to reflect male perplexity and terror rather than a quiet
approach to reality.

The objections raised against Johannes are more valid and of a
different kind. No one, to my knowledge, has ever complained
about the lack of light thrown on him, or accused Hauptmann of
making him incomprehensible. But many have claimed that
he is not worthy of his position at the centre of the play and that,
in his case, even after all is understood it cannot be forgiven.
This is a problem to which there is no simple answer. It was
not easy, for one thing, for Hauptmann to present a man of
his temperament, at a moment of crisis, in a way that would
arouse our sympathy. Johannes is an only child. He has been
a brilliant boy, and often ill, hence universally admired and
carefully fostered. In theory he has been taught to be unselfish;
in practice he has been regarded as the centre of his world. And
he has moved from a realm of fixed conceptions and values to
one of rapid change in all fields. All of this has produced a man
who is idealistic, and warm in his love for Käthe and his parents,
but dependent, rash, unstable, and above all nervous and highly
strung. Both his acute sensibility and the sense of duty with which
he has been imbued by his pious teachers make him question
where others do not, and suffer in a way of which others would
be incapable. We hear that the sight of children teasing a drunkard
upsets him, and he confesses that at one time he was ashamed
to look a worker in the face because the man probably had less
to eat than he, and that he wanted to cut himself off from his
past, give away all that he owned, and live in voluntary poverty.
But precisely the same qualities bind him to those who have

loved and cherished him and make him responsive to the world of his childhood, to the white wine and candles of the christening ceremony and to the emotionally powerful cadences of the pietist faith.

We find him, then, at the beginning of the play, living in an uneasy compromise. He has married a woman who is a younger and gentler version of his mother and has taken upon himself the responsibilities of domestic middle-class life. But he is doing nothing towards the support of his household—they are living on Käthe's rapidly diminishing capital—and he is writing a "psychophysiological" book which is to establish him as the most modern of the moderns. He tries to perpetuate this compromise by refusing to recognise the full implications of his attraction to Anna, answering Braun that it is only her friendship he desires. True, he asserts that from now on he will be the judge of his own conduct; and when Anna, in the twilight hour in which she announces her resolve to depart, tries to steel him for the future by impressing upon him that, if they separate on their own initiative, they are acting on a high plane worthy of the new enlightenment for which they both hope, she seems to be having some degree of success. But at a word from his mother his precariously held illusion of self-determination is shaken, and with his father's reproaches his image of himself falls, sullied and broken, forever. Under the strain thus increasingly imposed upon him his nervous instability expresses itself in ever sharper outbursts of temper which, paradoxical as it may seem, are harder on the spectator than on his family. They have known him in calmer moods. We see him only at a time of crisis. At the beginning of the play he can still pull himself together and apologize for his rudeness: "Kinder, ich bin etwas gnatzig gewesen. Seid fidel! Ich bin's auch." Later it is only in conversation with Anna, and not always then, that he can utter a single word without irritation. And it is not easy to bear with a character whose tragic weakness manifests itself in this way. Audiences are prone to respond to irritability by becoming, in their turn, impatient and annoyed.

There are other obstacles to our sympathetic understanding of Johannes. Hauptmann presents him as a man of advanced ideas, and we might well feel a greater admiration for him if we heard a little more about his thinking. It is possible that we are more exacting in this respect than the audiences of 1891, and that the mere names of Darwin and Haeckel caused Johannes' contemporaries to see a halo about his head which has dimmed with the passing of time. It is true also that Hauptmann had had enough of lengthy discussion in *Vor Sonnenaufgang*; what interests him here is to show the effects of new theories and conditions on the emotional lives of his characters, to paint, in Johannes, a restless, sensitive individualist who breaks from a narrow way of life but has not the fortitude to walk the less sheltered roads opening to the future. Professor Feise has suggested that the dramatist found it difficult to define a light towards which his hero was only dimly groping.[19] Yet when we have made due allowance for all this, the fact remains that the references to Johannes' work and ideas are not only few, but at times even slighting. No one could listen without distaste to him reciting to his mother, in pompous tones, Goethe's "Was wär ein Gott," or boasting of the twelve-page bibliography which he has assembled for his book; and no sooner does he begin to expound his vision of new and higher relationships between men and women to Anna than he checks himself, suspecting that she is smiling, and never touches on the question again.

Hauptmann would probably have done better by his hero in this and in other respects if personal reasons had not made his touch somewhat uncertain. The portrait of Johannes, for one thing, reflects a certain amount of self-castigation, for he was himself as a young husband unpractical, restless, and unduly concerned with real or fancied illnesses. It reflects also his attitude towards his brother Carl, whose marriage, we have noted, was the major inspiration of the play. And for Carl, if we can trust *Das Abenteuer meiner Jugend* and *Das Buch der Leidenschaft*, Hauptmann felt both admiration and resentment; admiration

[19]See note 6.

of the brilliant older brother who was, throughout his boyhood
and his early manhood, his mentor and his sponsor, and resentment of the superiority which this sponsorship implied and of
the fact that it was Carl who was the main hope of the family.
There would be no need to probe this sore spot were it not that
the same uncertainty was transferred to Johannes. His creator
has a distinct tendency to place him at one moment on a pedestal
and, at the next, to jerk it, none too gently, from under his feet.
In this one case Hauptmann's concern with the people and the
problems of his immediate environment did not prove a completely unmixed blessing. But the flaws in the character of
Johannes are of small account in comparison to what has been
gained.

Hauptmann's advances in characterization go hand in hand
with the perfection of his dramatic methods. The revelation
of the past proceeds, in *Einsame Menschen*, brilliantly and naturally
as never before. Much of it we owe to the easy loquacity of
Frau Vockerat, whose disappointed hopes constantly lead her to
contrast past and present. She need only listen to Johannes
reciting Goethe's pantheistic poem to be reminded of the day
when, as a student of theology, he preached his first "trial"
sermon. But all the others do their share. It can hardly be maintained that in this play the characters change or develop during
the course of the action. For that we must wait until later works,
although Hauptmann was never as interested in tracing change
as in fathoming depths and shades. But he succeeds in showing
how his people have grown, and he makes them appear to
become more and more complex as we learn more about the
experiences which have shaped them. The most striking innovation in the use of analytic exposition is the immediate effect
of all these accounts and recollections on Johannes. For not only
has he never outgrown the influence of his early life, which
both holds and repels him to the moment of his death, but we
see the past being used as a fetter to bind him or as a goad to
spur him on. Frau Vockerat's memory of his sermon is only
one instance of this. At a critical moment in the last act his

father overwhelms him with a sense of shame and ingratitude
by speaking of the long hours his parents have spent at his bed
when he was ill, as a child. Braun charges him with having driven
away his former friends by renouncing his ideals of social action
in favour of pure science. Anna offers him her mother's ring in
the hope that it will give him the courage to face the lonely
years to come. Analysis has become more than a technique for
the propounding of sociological theories; it is an immediate
and vital part of the conflict. In the *Ausblicke* Hauptmann wrote
that a play that is not exposition from first to last is not completely alive, lacks what he called "die letzte Lebendigkeit."
And he wrote further that every man is engaged in a constant
attempt to come to terms with his own past: "Immer wieder
werden Episoden aus dem grossen Epos des eigenen Lebens vom
Gegenwartsbewusstsein dramatisch geformt." *Einsame Menschen*
is a first striking formulation of these convictions. The struggle
in Johannes' case, of course, is heightened by the fact that he
lives in a changing world. But if, according to the critic Friedrich
Schlegel, there is in every life a novel, according to Hauptmann
there is a drama, and one of its most important constituents is a
man's struggle to assert his own position in relation to the forces
that have shaped him as a child.

The phrase "die letzte Lebendigkeit" might be used also to
describe what Hauptmann, after the partial success of his first
two plays, now achieves in his dialogue. *Einsame Menschen* has
the apparent spontaneity of casual conversation, carrying us
along easily at one point, halting, half revealing at another,
breaking, at yet another, into dispute and argument, and catching
everywhere the individual rhythms that can be observed in
Das Friedensfest. But the language here has greater contrast,
variety, and richness of tone. Johannes has the same taut nerves
and the same explosive nature as the Scholzes. His voice takes
on a sharp edge and flares up within the first half dozen phrases
that he speaks. But about it, like an orchestra in contrast with a
rebellious soloist, play the voices of the others, the gentle, diffident
pleading of Käthe, the assured, motherly note of Frau Vockerat,

the easy, quietly confident tones of Anna. And, within their range, the individual voices too may change. The keynote of all Braun's utterances is negation, but he is gentler with Käthe than with the others, he doubts rather than scoffs. Johannes is less bitter with Anna. Nothing better illustrates the sympathy which he feels for her from the beginning than the fact that his first words to her have nothing of their customary tension. He points out over the garden, when he is left to entertain her, explaining that a park with a high wall is his ideal of a place to live, and when she comments "Epikur," he chimes in with an assenting, "Ganz recht, ja." Moreover, it is not Johannes alone who is responsible for the outbursts that frequently bring the tension of the play to the breaking point. Käthe, we have noted, is shaken by a moment of impassioned protest and threatens to leave the house. Frau Vockerat breaks into anger or shrill, ecstatic prophecy, proclaiming, with a refrain of "Seht Ihr! seht Ihr!" that this godless house will crash in the night. And the tempo and mood of the dialogue are sometimes changed or relieved by a wonderful ability to let people talk their hearts out, unconscious, perhaps, of what is happening in the hearts of others. We think of Braun's voluble landlady who appears briefly in the first act, with her tale of the drunken husband whom she has sent packing: "Adolf! sach ick, jeh du man in Jottes Namen bei deine Brieder, sach 'k . . . Sieh du, sach 'k, wo du wat herkriegen dust, und denn jag' et dir man immer feste durch die Jurgel, sach'k. . . ." Or we remember the long effervescent speech of Herr Vockerat that breaks into the stricken silence of the end of the fourth act, his outbursts of joy, punctuated by questions about his grandson and instructions about the disposal of the food that he has brought with him. Hauptmann's contemporaries were inclined to value his dialogue chiefly from the point of view of its faithfulness to nature. To us, it does not seem surprising that a man who could use colloquial prose to express such shades, undercurrents, and sharp contrasts of emotion should one day be able to use verse with the same power.

With the same skill that he shows in characterization and in dialogue Hauptmann makes us conscious of the house and of the locality in which his people live. All five acts play in the combined dining and living room of the villa, but we are as vividly and constantly aware of what is going on in the rest of the house and outside it as if we had lived there for years. In the adjoining bedroom the baby sleeps, from the hall the vegetable woman announces her arrival with the cry, "die Grünfrau," and Frau Vockerat, pausing on her way to the kitchen with a cup of soup in her hand, which she has offered Anna to strengthen her for her journey, can hear someone ascending the stairs, the maid, she thinks—happy that life has become normal again —going up to collect the washing, in reality the returning Anna. Beyond the veranda is the garden from which Anna brings in ripe grapes to decorate the breakfast table and beyond that again the lake where she and Johannes float while he reads to her from his book. From the nearby station we hear the whistle of the trains, and on a Sunday hikers from Berlin disturb the suburbanites with their lusty singing. Not a detail of what might seem a static background but is bound up with the action and with the mood or emotions of the characters. The house itself, in its semi-isolated position, outside the metropolis but near enough to feel its breath, is a vivid symbol—as vivid as the visitors from Silesia and from Zurich whom it shelters within its walls—of the compromise Johannes tries and fails to maintain.

In *Einsame Menschen* Hauptmann established certain characteristics which were to prove more or less common to his good prose dramas, however greatly he changed and developed in future. He depicted people who are in no way extraordinary and whose fate is not unusual, and illuminated through them the sometimes quiet but intense and unceasing struggle which, he thinks, marks the everyday relations of all men. He stressed the nervous and emotional rather than the volitional or intellectual aspects of his characters, and he chose as a hero a man who is passive rather than active. Into this shaded and complex drama he drew all the factors which, as he saw it, influenced the lives of those whom he was painting, heredity, upbringing, surroundings, and the conditions of the broader social scene—the questions, in this case, of the position of women, of new relationships between the sexes within marriage and without, of the demands of life as opposed to the pursuit of pure knowledge, of the position of art in society, and, above all, of the new philosophy with its faith in science and nature and its championship of the free, inquiring individual. In all of this he was both developing what we may perhaps most aptly term his creative impressionism, and utilizing recent scientific attempts to interpret man as a physical organism and as a member of society rather than as an expression of transcendental forces, divine or ideal. He was furthermore bringing to the drama areas and kinds of human experience which are often considered the province of other *genres*. Goethe, for example, or Henry James would have considered Johannes the ideally passive and receptive hero of a novel. Hauptmann saw him as a man engaged in struggle. And he was conscious of his purpose. "Immer mehr 'Undramatisches' dramatisch zu begreifen," was one of the main axioms that inspired his work.

There are still critics who would deny both the validity of this aim and Hauptmann's success in achieving it. Petsch calls *Einsame Menschen* "traurig-lyrisch" rather than "tragisch-dramatisch."[20] And it is true that the struggle which grips the characters is less startling than that which rages among the demi-gods of Schiller or Kleist, that it is even quieter than the conflicts in the plays of Strindberg or Ibsen, who, like Hauptmann, were intent on portraying men as they saw them in the world around them. It is also true that the play is a little youthfully sentimental, that its characters are seen—perhaps Hauptmann was reacting from the Krauses and the Scholzes—through faintly rose-tinged glasses, and that what we feel at the end is not so much a sense of utter and crushing destruction as pity and sorrow. It is true, finally, that Hauptmann was greatly concerned

[20]*Wesen und Form des Dramas*, p. 8.

with the expression of feelings. But his struggle has force and intensity, and there is hardly a line of the play where the emotions expressed are not part of the conflict, are not uttered under tension and under circumstances which make them clash with those of others, whereas in pure lyric emotion is absolute and sufficient unto itself. And if the basis of tragedy is a perception of the inevitability of suffering, together with a sense of loss that outweighs all our attempts to account for it, then *Einsame Menschen* has this basis. Johannes' suicide may be a mercy killing, but the forces that destroy him, gently formulated as they are, are inexorable, and he is incapable of survival in any real sense. And the dramatist is not merely recording objectively and with mild regret; he is deeply shaken.

By the time he wrote his third play Hauptmann had come to see that it is not only obviously unpleasant influences which may destroy a man—schnaps or an unbalanced father—but a whole complex of seemingly less invidious forces, including love itself. We feel *Einsame Menschen* as a tragedy not only because it reveals men as moulded and determined, but because it reveals them as so moulded and determined that even with love and goodwill they cannot break through the walls of their own beings to help and to understand others. In naming the play Hauptmann may have been influenced, directly or indirectly, by Nietzsche's belief that the pathfinders of humanity are always solitary,[21] but it was assuredly not only because of the plight of Anna and Johannes that he called it *Einsame Menschen*. The isolation of individual from individual is portrayed not merely in the hopelessly frustrated arguments between the adored son and his parents, but also in the misunderstandings between Käthe and Johannes, in the distance which, for all their womanly understanding of one another, separates Anna and Frau Vockerat or Anna and Käthe, and in the gulf which is apparent in the end even between Käthe and the older Vockerats, who will never be able to see to the heart of her suffering.

It is significant for the interpretation of the play that the two

[21] See the edition of the play by Evans and Feise (New York, 1930), pp. xxvii-xxx.

people who understand this isolation in all its consequences are Käthe and Anna, the provincial wife reared in a Herrnhut boarding-school and the emancipated woman of the world with struggle and privation behind her. We have already had one occasion to note Anna's formulation: "Sie werten anders, als Ihre Eltern werten. Ihre Eltern werten anders, als Frau Käthe wertet. Darüber lässt sich gar nichts sagen, meiner Ansicht nach." In the last moments of the play Käthe speaks in a like vein to her father-in-law: "Ich ärmliches Wesen habe Hannes nichts zu verzeihn. Hier heisst es einfach: Du bist das—und nicht das." It is equally significant that both women, in the face of this realization, are willing to withdraw, to sacrifice themselves for the sake of others, and that their willingness is of no avail. Their words are a confirmation on Hauptmann's part of a certain relativity of standards and values impressed upon him by his observations and by contemporary scientific theses. But the nature and actions of those who speak them make them more than that. Käthe and Anna, mourning the destruction that they cannot prevent, are Hauptmann's earliest representatives of the enlightened understanding and the humane Christian love that are the fundamental basis of this interpretation of the world and of his tragedy.

III. Historical Plays

IF WE NEEDED anything more than the evidence of *Einsame Menschen* to demonstrate how completely Hauptmann had now found his feet, we should find it in *Die Weber*. For, with his successful study of middle-class life behind him, he was able to return with assurance to the broader type of canvas that he had attempted in his first play, to study once more a problem involving whole communities of people, and a problem on which economic questions had a direct and all-important bearing.

The theme of *Die Weber* is the 1844 rebellion among the weavers of Hauptmann's native province, which in its day had also inspired Heine's ballad, "Die Schlesischen Weber." In actual fact the rebellion was no more than an incident in a three-century-long tragedy. For generations before the uprising the weavers of Silesia had lived in a state of poverty, working at home on hand looms and completely dependent on local "manufacturers" who provided them with yarn and marketed the finished product. Matters became only rather more unbearable for them than usual in the early 1840's, when men and nature alike seemed to be against them: crops were poor, foreign tariffs were crippling the export trade, machine looms were being introduced elsewhere more quickly than in Silesia, and the manufacturers were taking advantage of the resultant unemployment; starvation wages, if any, were the order of the day. The brief hunger riots which ensued were quickly put down and conditions remained much as they had been before. We are reminded of Aristotle's dictum that poetry is more philosophical and hence truer than history when we consider that this minor rebellion inspired both Germany's most famous revolutionary poem and her finest revolutionary play.

Hauptmann had thought of writing some such work, we have noted, in 1888, in Zurich. In April 1891, three months after the first performance of *Einsame Menschen*, he made a ten-day trip to Silesian villages in the Eulengebirge, intent on refreshing his boyhood memories of the weavers and on talking to eye-witnesses of the revolt. With the help of what he saw there, and with that of written sources, particularly Alfred Zimmermann's *Blüte und Verfall des Leinengewerbes in Schlesien*,[1] he set to work in the same spring. The play appeared in book form less than a year later, early in 1892. Why Hauptmann undertook it at precisely this time, and why it did not appear at once on the stage, are questions better answered when we have considered the content and the spirit of the play.

The first act is set in the factory of the manufacturer Dreissiger of Peterswaldau, in the room where the weavers' cloth is inspected and paid for—transactions which are in full swing when the scene begins. The first moments build up a picture of a distress that is radical and universal. A woman begs for a small advance because her husband is ill; a man utters his dismay when he is told that he will be docked because his cloth is lacking in weight. "Ieberall hat's was," remarks one old man, known to all as Vater Baumert, "Wo eemal's Armut is, da kommt ooch Unglicke ieber Unglicke. Da is o kee Halt und keene Rettung." The employees of the house, above all the inspector, Pfeifer, are of a different opinion, and they do not hesitate to speak their minds. The weavers, they charge, are lazy, improvident, and drunken, and they have too many children. Only one young man, Bäcker by name, answers their taunts and calls the coins doled out to him not a wage, but a miserable alms. There have been signs of trouble recently; young men have been singing a song called "Das Blutgericht," and when Bäcker continues to protest, Dreissiger is summoned. But the weaver holds his ground. His money is thrown at him and falls on the floor, and he waits until an apprentice picks it up and places it

[1]Breslau, 1885.

in his hand. In the ensuing silence a starving child falls fainting to the floor—vivid evidence of the justice of Bäcker's charges—and the young man departs. Dreissiger expatiates at length on his troubles, his risks, the difficulty of selling cloth. Yet he is willing, he says, to engage more men in order to alleviate the distress. He leaves Pfeifer to announce the conditions—lower wages. The weavers have hardly heard the words of their employer. They are incapable of thinking of anything but the next copper, the next mouthful of food. There is whispering and grumbling at the end of the act, but there are no plans, no thoughts of action; there is no beginning of a plot.

Nor does the second act bring any definite resolve. It broadens the picture by showing us conditions in the weavers' homes. Vater Baumert and his family rent one or two rooms in a hut owned by an older weaver, Ansorge. In one of them we see Baumert's wife, who, though she can no longer dress or feed herself, is crouched as always over her spooling wheel, his idiot son, his two emaciated daughters, and a four-year-old grandson, all of them hungry in a house where there is not a morsel of food, only drying potato peelings which they hope to exchange presently for a little buttermilk. A brief visit from a neighbour tells another story of hungry children. Ansorge, who is unemployed except for a little basket-work, is afraid that he is going to lose the hut; and, shack as it is, its every nail and board have cost his father a sleepless night or a hungry day. Finally Baumert returns, and with him is Jäger, a former son of the village who is now in the army, well fed and clothed, and with money in his pocket and a bottle. Puzzled and bewildered Baumert and Ansorge question this man of the world about their plight. In answer Jäger points to the wealth of the manufacturers, their roast meat, their carriages, their splendid houses. He has a copy of "Das Blutgericht":

> Ihr Schurken all, ihr Satansbrut,
> ihr höllischen Kujone,
> ihr fresst der Armen Hab und Gut,
> und Fluch wird euch zum Lohne . . .

The naïvely rhetorical phrases, painfully spelt out, fire his listeners as though they were divine confirmation of the injustice of their suffering. Baumert lifts his arms in a rage and Ansorge stammers that they will endure it no longer. There are still no plans. It is not in the nature of these people to contemplate violence.

But the third act brings the despair and the unrest to the breaking point. A day or so later there is a chance gathering in a tavern. Dreissiger's announcement that he will take on more workers brings a few older weavers in for a rare glass of schnaps. A commercial traveller, mainly concerned with addressing the inevitable gallantries to the innkeeper's daughter, finds time to raise an eyebrow at an elaborate funeral procession passing outside. The church, he is told, encourages this profitable custom. Then a peasant and a forester come in, and become the target of complaints against outmoded feudal restrictions. Once again the traveller raises an eyebrow. According to the papers, the distress among the weavers has been exaggerated. At this Hornig, a pedlar who knows the district thoroughly, launches into an account of conditions not portrayable on the stage, of children rolling in manure, of men eating reeking glue or dying, naked, on cold stones. The government investigators, he charges bitterly, have not seen these things because they were afraid to soil their shoes by venturing beyond the main streets. Before his tale is at an end Jäger and Bäcker come in with a group of young men summoned by the authorities for inoculation. With Jäger's money to provide them with schnaps they are noisy and defiant. An old blacksmith adds fuel to the fire by his memories of the French Revolution. An aged weaver begins to speak in tongues, to call on the jaws of hell to swallow their tormentors. The time for an explosion has come and the gendarme, entering to forbid any further singing of "Das Blutgericht," touches it off. The young men scoff at him, and then set out, singing, for Dreissiger's house, sweeping the older men with them, even Vater Baumert who, somewhat abashed at his own courage, explains as he leaves, "A Junges kann manchmal, und a Altes muss."

They intend, as far as they know what they intend, to ask for higher wages.

The ensuing tumult is well under way when the fourth act begins in Dreissiger's house. Dreissiger has guests, the local pastor and his wife. The former is scolding a young theology student, the tutor of the sons of the house, who has clearly been defending the hungry weavers. The inspector of police arrives to promise his full co-operation. On his heels apprentices bring in Jäger, defiant as ever, even towards the pastor: "Ich bin Quäker, Herr Pastor," he explains blandly, "ich gloob an nischt mehr." The gendarme takes him off, hands bound, and Dreissiger makes a momentary attempt to resume the social evening. But shouts from without proclaim that Jäger has been freed. The coachman advises flight; he has the carriage ready at the back door. The pastor tries to breast the storm and is jeered at and, it seems, beaten. As the front door is battered down Dreissiger and his family flee. There is a pause and then, silently and timidly, the weavers fill the room. There are still some who do not wish destruction, among them Ansorge, who strikes his head with his fist, asking himself how he got here. Then he reaches a startlingly simple conclusion—"Nimmst du m'r mei Häusl, nehm ich d'r dei Häusl" and joins the rest in devastation. From here the course is already set for the machine looms in the nearby village of Langenbielau.

There, in a room of the weaver Hilse, on the following morning, the last act takes place. Hilse and his family, just completing their devotions, know nothing of the rebellion as yet. The news is brought by Hornig and a doctor—tales of destruction, of bales of cloth damming a stream, of wine found in cellars and flowing freely, and of the procession on its way. Old Hilse is shocked; among the other weavers the pietist belief that one must endure the troubles of this world for the sake of the next has all but vanished—the troubles have been too many; but it is still strong in him. His daughter-in-law, who has watched four children die from starvation, is jubilant. Between the two stands the son, undecided. The bells of the hamlet begin to ring, and in a moment the rebels are in the house, proclaiming food for all and a new life. Baumert brings a chicken as evidence, a gift for the wife of his old friend, which is rejected. The cry "Militär" summons the vistors to help their fellows. The daughter-in-law goes with them. The son has picked up an axe and is mechanically testing its edge. Shots ring out and Hilse is warned to move from the window where he has begun to work, for the weavers are charging the soldiers. The son rushes out. Hilse remains, in the place, he says, where God has set him, working and praying. Once again there are shots and he falls to the floor. As the curtain goes down his terrified, deaf wife and his small granddaughter are calling his name, in vain. The final antithesis of the play has been reached, the bullets of the state have rewarded its most obedient servant. There was no need for Hauptmann to portray the quelling of the revolt. He had left its most poignant symbol before us.

The story of *Die Weber* has been told at length because no short summary can give an indication of its nature and of its effect. To say that its subject matter is a brief and spontaneous, though violent hunger demonstration virtually sums up the action but does not tell us how Hauptmann managed to build a play on such a slender basis. To say that he gives a detailed picture of the conditions responsible for the revolt suggests, even if we know his earlier plays and even if we give a few representative details, a work that is static and descriptive rather than dramatic. Only when we begin to understand the roles played by the numerous characters, to feel the cumulative effect of the concrete pictures and incidents, to experience the growth of the bewilderment and despair and exaltation which sweep the weavers to unpremeditated action, can we begin to appreciate what Hauptmann has accomplished. He had already extended the bounds of the "dramatic" to deal with a type of hero formerly considered unsuitable for drama and had fused conflict and analysis of the past. In *Die Weber* he explored still further possibilities and dramatized history in a new way in order to show the part played in it by economic conditions and by the people. There was at one time a curious tendency to see the play as a series of five variations on a theme, with only the fourth pitched at a somewhat higher key. Such an interpretation cannot be sustained once the reader has surrendered himself to the work and forgotten traditional dramatic technique. True, unless Hauptmann was to falsify his sources, there could be no rising action in a conventional sense. But he made intensity of exposition take its place; he multiplied the scenes of distress, adding detail to detail, picture to picture, voice to voice; he showed us an old man carrying in a cloth the carcass of a pet dog which hunger has forced him to have butchered, a child crying with hunger, a woman shrieking that she would be content if she had swine fodder for her children, until we, like the sufferers, can bear it no longer, until we too are emotionally ready for the outbreak.

The tension thus roused in the spectator is accentuated by a steady rise in excitement among the weavers. Hans Rabl, in a fine analysis of the action of the play,[2] has pointed out that each act begins a little further above what he calls the "absolute zero" line: at the beginning of the first act the weavers accept their fate passively and without hope; at the beginning of the second, they question; in the third, they protest; and, as the fourth opens, the angry, clamorous mob stands outside Dreissiger's house; in the fifth, finally, we move once again at a rapid pace through the whole scale of reactions, and patient submission and intoxicated rebellion stand face to face. Moreover, although there is no single incident in *Die Weber* comparable in importance to the family quarrel in *Das Friedensfest* or to the arrival of the older Vockerat in *Einsame Menschen*, there are moments of conflict, of contrast, or of outcry which, like waves on a steadily mounting flood, mark vividly this rise in mood. Bäcker's defiance is a first warning flash of the storm to come; the reading of the song, at the end of the second act, whips the emotions of one group of weavers to the breaking point; and the whole third act is a series of disputes between the various patrons of the tavern which reaches its climax at the moment when the gendarme, mocked and insulted, forbids the singing of "Das

[2]*Die dramatische Handlung in Gerhart Hauptmanns Webern* (Halle, 1928).

Blutgericht" as he retreats into the street, with the weavers on his heels. And again and again there are incidents—the departure of Baumert, in the wake of the others, almost embarrassed at the excitement which draws him after them; Hilse's son, rushing out with his axe when he realizes that blood is flowing; the sudden fanatical surge of rage that shakes Jäger when he thinks of the judges, the upholders of the law, who have asserted that the weavers deserve to suffer because they are too lazy to work—incidents which reveal the power of the emotions that sway the people and carry them, unconscious, uncalculating, and armed with whatever house or garden tools they have been able to pick up, to hurl themselves against the guns of the soldiers. There is nothing static or merely repetitive in *Die Weber*. The power of suffering and of anger mounts in the play, as it had done in the life that Hauptmann was portraying, until it bursts forth in blind frenzy, to be quelled almost immediately by the immensely superior forces marshalled against it. He himself, at a later date, spoke of the total movement of the play as a "dramatic curve," rising with ever increasing sharpness through the first four acts, and falling abruptly in the fifth.[3] As there is no planned action in the work, there is virtually no counter-action, until the end. But when it comes, it is decisive and overwhelming.

The material of *Die Weber* is a spontaneous, mass revolt. And if in order to portray it Hauptmann broke new ground in the sphere of dramatic action, substituting for the plans and resolves of conventional drama a constantly increasing emotional excitement and a series of finely distributed moments of conflict, he had to make like innovations in the choice and delineation of his characters. For in order to remain true to his sources, he had to present a whole cross-section of society, to represent a community by a good score of people no one of whom might be to any appreciable degree more important than the others. The weavers themselves, to begin with, had to be numerous, since the universality of the distress among them was the prime cause of the uprising. And among them there had to be some

[3]C. F. W. Behl, *Zwiesprache mit Gerhart Hauptmann* (Munich, 1948), p. 76.

figures with the additional force or strength necessary to account for the outbreak of the revolt just at that moment; to have portrayed one leader, no matter how representative, would have destroyed the collective character of the action. To these there had to be added characters to represent the whole superstructure built upon the industry of the weavers. Hauptmann judged it wise also to show us one or two men who move among them, know them, and can, if necessary, speak for them, and finally one who represents the supercilious and incredulous reaction of the outside world. Accordingly he painted, beside a group of weavers who are marked mainly by their suffering, a smaller group with a somewhat greater strength or understanding than their fellows: a young man who is a little more aggressive than the others, a son of the village who has returned from military service with some primitive ideas of leadership and some knowledge of the world, a woman whose children have died from hunger, and a blacksmith with memories of "Robspir" and the French Revolution who has been denounced to the authorities by the gendarme. He portrayed industry, the church, and the landed and middle classes by Dreissiger and his employees, by a pastor, an innkeeper, a carpenter, a forester, a peasant, a chief of police. And, finally, in the traveller, the theology student, and the pedlar, he gave us people whose position is relatively independent and who speak, as the case may be, against the weavers or for them.

To make all these various people real and to hold them together took all the skill that Hauptmann had developed in his first works, all his genius in the sharp delineation of character and in the linking of individual and background. He had, moreover, to paint a group portrait the like of which he had not hitherto attempted, even in *Vor Sonnenaufgang*, where we see some peasants, but not many, and only hear about the miners. He succeeded brilliantly in meeting all demands. As far as the general picture and the common characteristics were concerned he was helped by the fact that the situation, with all its complexities, native and foreign—tariffs, competition, new machinery, the unbroken prevalence of feudal restrictions—was, as far as the weavers could interpret it, simple and drastic. For them there are two compelling questions, work and food, and one answer, the wealth of the manufacturers. They are therefore united in their hunger and in their hatred of their employer. But Hauptmann was able to unite them also by their language and by emotional traits fostered by centuries of common experience. Generations of poverty have made them humble and subservient, endless days and nights at the looms have bred in them a puzzled brooding and made their speech slow and pitiful and grave, although their weak frames are frequently shaken by a kind of ecstasy which prepares us for the final outburst of the revolt, and occasionally they try to lighten their sorry plight by a flash of *Galgenhumor*. "Ma muss ebens a Mut nich sink'n lass'n," says an old weaver in the first act with typical, helpless patience, "'s kommt immer wieder was und hilft een a Stickl weiter," only to be parodied by a second. "Ma muss ebens, wenn d'r Hunger kommt, zu a vierzehn Nothelfern beten, und wenn ma dadervon etwa ni satt wird, da muss ma an Steen ins Maul nehmen und dran lutschen." We feel this communal attitude vividly, for example, as the ragged figures appear hesitantly in Dreissiger's splendid rooms, silent, gazing, touching, and then, released from their fears by Baumert's mocking, "Such, such, Feiferle [Pfeifer] 's is a Weberschmann auszuhungern," rushing to demolish the salon. We feel it even more vividly in the doctor's description of the uncanny march to Langenbielau—"Da trottelt eener hinterm andern her wie's graue Elend und verfiehren ein Gesinge, dass een fermlich a Magen umwend't"—a unity of character and purpose that is wonderfully reproduced in the most famous and most memorable of Käthe Kollwitz' illustrations for the play, although her weavers are more angular and aggressive than Hauptmann's.

But the characters are also individuals, chiefly by virtue of Hauptmann's success in visualizing and portraying specific and concrete aspects of the total situation. Not only are the surrounding figures—the pert apprentice in the office, the portly, blustering Dreissiger, the stolid innkeeper—quite distinct in

face and function, but the weavers themselves are lifted from
the common background and distinguished from one another
by a special contour, a slight difference in disposition, or a
connection with a particular instance of the general distress.
Not even Hauptmann could or would lift all figures equally.
There are weavers who only join the others in lamentation or in
defiance. Yet Bäcker and Jäger, though both are young and
cocky, are not to be confused; the latter has returned from the
great world with something of its glibness, and takes the lead
in pulling noses whenever he can find an opportunity to do so.
Hilse and Baumert are both gentle, kind-hearted old men, but
the former is upright, almost rigid in his piety, the latter emotionally more volatile, more easily moved to despair, or to rejoicing at this temporary new world where chickens are to be
had for the taking.

It may be difficult to appreciate fully even the half-dozen
characters of a play like *Einsame Menschen* unless a good production makes us aware of the completely natural reality of the
situations in which Hauptmann portrays them—as they gather
for breakfast, for example, or as the women sit over their sewing.
Here, character and situation are linked with even more telling
effect. We do not forget the very minor figure of Frau Heinrich,
for she comes limping into the Baumert's room with a bit of
glass in her bare foot and tells her story of nine hungry mouths
clamouring for a piece of bread not big enough for two while
one of the girls removes the glass and hunts for a rag with which
to bind the cut. And the giant, clumsy Ansorge, striking his
dazed old head in the midst of Dreissiger's damask and mahogany,
remains in our minds longer than many a man who has much
more to say for himself. There is one incident which may well
make the reader or the spectator uncomfortable and remind him
of a theoretic and pedantic naturalism—the moment when
Baumert loses the supper of dog meat which his starved body
cannot digest. And there is one line which seems to me improbable—Dreissiger's, "Am I a sweater?"—"Bin ich denn ein
Menschenschinder?" The manufacturer is an adept at not seeing

the truth, but the evidence is so overwhelmingly against him, the answer to his question is so obviously "yes," that a man of his seeming intelligence could not ask it and expect, as he does, to be assured that he is not. The exceptional nature of such an incident or of such a line may serve to remind us how far Hauptmann had come since *Vor Sonnenaufgang*. There is otherwise nothing forced or constructed about *Die Weber*. It relies so entirely, it is built so surely, on a sensitive, intimate, and detailed understanding of conditions and of people that Hauptmann was able to give life to his characters both as a group and as individuals and thus to make the play a milestone both as a historical drama and as a drama dealing with the lower classes.

It is worth extending a comparison of Hauptmann's first proletarian play and his second to one or two additional points. In *Vor Sonnenaufgang* he was concerned with demonstrating that radically unfavourable social conditions produce degeneration. In *Die Weber* no one argues except Dreissiger, and his speeches are mainly an attempt to justify his evasion of his human obligations. But the degeneration is evident. Zimmermann, indeed, is quite specific on the question. The mid-century Prussian government, he points out, maintaining on the basis of "natural" economic law that it was sound and healthy to let such classes as the weavers find a new means of livelihood on their own, had overlooked one factor: heredity and early environment had made the nineteenth-century weavers physically and mentally unfit to do so.[4] The same conclusions are to be drawn from the play, whether Hauptmann was guided in this respect by Zimmermann, by other historians or economists writing at the time, or by his own direct observation. His weavers have clearly neither the knowledge nor the energy nor the intelligence to better their situation in the face of the forces opposing them. The revolt is the merest outburst of intoxication and of despair. The position of the weavers is as hopeless as that of the peasants of the first play.

[4]*Blüte und Verfall des Leinengewerbes*, pp. 244 ff.

Yet there is a difference. Hauptmann portrays his people here with the same just focus that he had found in *Einsame Menschen*. He no longer sees a helpless and degenerate group as disgusting or vicious or sub-human. And his glance is all the more sympathetic because in these simple, hungry, weak, but not unkindly people he finds something like a spiritual life, a life which is most clearly marked in the figure of old Hilse, but which is perceptible also in the others. For although hunger plays the main role in firing the revolt, we find the weavers puzzling about the meaning and significance of what is happening to them and giving some expression to a sense of justice and of human dignity which seems to have been fed on the conception that all men are children of God, and which makes them feel that, as such, they ought not to be treated as they are. We find also a longing for a higher, freer form of existence, which Hornig tries to formulate in a phrase that has become famous, his "A jeder Mensch hat halt 'ne Sehnsucht," and Baumert in the words, "Ich wollte ja gerne nich mitmachen. Aber . . . d'r Mensch muss doch a eenziges Mal an Augenblick Luft kriegen." It is true that this spiritual life affects men's attitude to the world about them in different ways: it impels old Hilse, for example, to bear his present troubles for the sake of the joys to come hereafter; but in others it sharpens the sense of injustice here and now. This was a paradox of which Hauptmann was not to show himself fully aware until the appearance of the novel *Emanuel Quint*, which was not completed until almost twenty years later. In the meantime he was noting, with the same sensitiveness he revealed towards the wax-like transparency in the flesh of the women, an emotional and spiritual refinement which drew him towards his characters, and which he saw as one justification for the revolt.

Critics have usually agreed in their analysis of these—they must presumably be called purely human and aesthetic—qualities and virtues of *Die Weber*, and have, accordingly, ranked it high among Hauptmann's works. But the nature of the subject matter made it inevitable that the play should also raise other questions, and even those who admit that Hauptmann at his best does not argue, but portrays, and that he is not interested in economic principles but in the effect of conditions on the lives of his characters, have asked themselves whether he intended such pictures as he was portraying here to have social or economic repercussions, whether he hoped that this play would bring about an improvement in economic conditions. To such questions answers have diverged widely. But on the whole the verdict has been that the play has no social or political bearing, that Hauptmann did not intend it to have any, and that, if it awakens any revolutionary impulse in the reader, he is either naïve or is deliberately misreading.[5] As early as 1892, when public performance of the play was still forbidden, Paul Marx wrote that the ban was unnecessary, since the only people whom it could provoke to revolt would be Silesian weavers, who were not in the habit of going to the theatre: "Aufregend könnte es höchstens auf schlesische Weber wirken, welche selten ins Theater kommen."[6] A quarter of a century later Heise asserted that the effect of the play is to discourage, rather than to promote, action —"entnervend, kraftzehrend, nicht aufpeitschend, zur Tat entflammend."[7] Within recent years Werner Ziegenfuss has claimed that Hauptmann's works—and he makes no exceptions —are written in a purely contemplative vein, that they strive for no social consequence or effect and evoke no such desires, "keine derartigen Tendenzen," in the spectator or the reader.[8] And Professor S. D. Stirk, reviewing Marx's early article, agrees that the nature of the play is not such as to incite revolutionary sentiments in the average spectator.[9]

To deny the validity of such assertions, or even to qualify them, is no simple matter. They arise, for one thing, from wide-

[5] An exception is Elise Dosenheimer, *Das deutsche soziale Drama von Lessing bis Sternheim* (Konstanz, 1949), pp. 106 ff.

[6] "Der schlesische Weberaufstand in Dichtung und Wahrheit," in *Magazin fur Litteratur* (Berlin, 1892), p. 115.

[7] *Gerhart Hauptmanns Dramen* (Leipzig, n.d.), I, p. 14.

[8] *Gerhart Hauptmann: Dichtung und Gesellschaftsidee der bürgerlichen Humanität* (Berlin, 1948), p. 15.

[9] "Aus frühen 'Weber'-Kritiken," *Gerhart-Hauptmann Jahrbuch* (Goslar, 1948), p. 15.

spread and deeply rooted tendencies to separate rigidly "propaganda" and "literature" or to consider political organizations as the sole instruments of economic reform.[10] There is no evidence, internal or external, that Hauptmann was writing at the dictates of any party or that he intended *Die Weber* to help provoke a general revolution in the social order. The play did not, in actual fact, even as a result of its first stormy performances, lead to one act of violence—at the most it sent some Hungarian workers from a theatre singing the Marseillaise. But there are strong grounds for thinking that, when the naïve spectator sees in the play a condemnation of social injustice, he is closer to the truth than Hauptmann's cautious and learned critics; and an examination of the author's own words and of the circumstances under which the play was written will, I think, bear this out. Moreover, the reception of *Die Weber* was not what Hauptmann had hoped for. He wanted reform; the negative reaction of certain sections of the public to his play indicated that there would be no reform without revolution.

Hauptmann's own pronouncements about his motives in writing his play vary somewhat with the years. In 1891 or 92, before the struggle with the authorities and the ensuing public storm had broken, he told Max Baginski that he hoped, through his work, to arouse the active sympathy of those who had means —"das werktätige Mitgefühl in den Gutgestellten." Even the most easy-going of men, he felt, were not without feeling.[11] Clearly he saw social and political reform as two different things, but he did desire the former. Two years later he was more cautious.

I will not deny [he told a New York reporter] that I have hoped that the well-to-do folks who see my *Weavers* may be moved by the appalling misery which is reflected in that work—a misery with which I have been brought into contact and which has moved me strongly. But . . . only the most careful

[10]Cf. Hauptmann's own words to J. Chapiro, "Partei . . . muss wohl jeder ergreifen, nur dass dies Parteiergreifen bei einem selbständigen Geist nie einer Parteipolitik entspringen wird." *Gespräche mit Gerhart Hauptmann* (Berlin, 1932), p. 70.

[11]"Gerhart Hauptmann unter den schlesischen Webern," in *Sozialistische Monatshefte*, I (1905), p. 153.

and painstaking analysis can explain the complex motives which dictate an artist's work. Deeply as I was stirred by the woes of my weavers, for instance, when I conceived the play, once I had set to work I saw nothing but the marvellous material they gave me for creating a great, moving, human drama. In the delight of building up my scenes, for the time being, I forgot all else. Yet, indirectly, *The Weavers* will teach something, I dare say. To the dramatist however, it is of smaller importance, what he teaches.[12]

The play, it should be observed, had in the meantime been forbidden on public stages and had aroused waves of angry protest among the well-to-do. We may therefore grant Hauptmann all the pure creative joy which, he said, went into the writing of it, and still suspect that consciously or unconsciously he was underestimating its social significance in order to get it on the stage. A glance at the policy of his lawyer, Richard Grelling, confirms our suspicion. Grelling, struggling at this time with censor after censor in his efforts to have *Die Weber* released for performance, was also asserting that the play had no didactic tendencies, and there is no mistaking the fact that he was advancing at least some of his arguments with his tongue in his cheek. He sought to impress on the authorities that Hauptmann had portrayed the revolt exactly as it was described in his historical sources, which was true. But he also urged that the play would not impress audiences of the 1890's as connected with their own day, which was only partly true. And he pointed out that Hauptmann had punished his weavers for their sins, that he had set up an anti-revolutionary ideal in the person of old Hilse, and much more in the same vein, which—as the censors realized— was wholly untrue.[13] By the time Hauptmann came to write his autobiography, in any case, he was ready to revert to his original interpretation. "Schopenhauer," he wrote, "[hält] Mitleid für Liebe, Liebe für Mitleid. . . . Diese Art Mitleid wird mir . . . "Die Weber" diktiert haben. Aber ebensosehr der Zwangsgedanke sozialer Gerechtigkeit."

[12]Quoted from F. W. J. Heuser, "Gerhart Hauptmann's Trip to America in 1894," *Germanic Review*, 1938, p. 15.

[13]H. H. Houben, *Verbotene Literatur von der klassischen Zeit bis zur Gegenwart* (Dessau, 1925), I, pp. 340 ff.

The confession that he wrote the play under the hard pressure of his desire for social justice is confirmed when we consider the circumstances of its inception. Hauptmann's first thoughts of the work were inspired by memories of Salzbrunn, which, incidentally, brought before him the contrast between wealth and poverty; and he later visited the villages he portrays. These facts critics generally recognize. What does not seem so widely known is that the plight of the weavers was almost as sorry in the early 1890's as it had been fifty years before, although Professor Stirk, quoting from Marx's article, has remarked that the harvest of 1890 was a failure, and that "the cries of hunger from the Silesian mountains rang through all Germany."[14] They rang indeed to such effect that many who first read or saw the play believed that the misery depicted was based on contemporary newspaper articles. And it seems reasonable to suppose that Hauptmann, after writing two family plays, turned, in the spring of 1891, to the theme that had first occurred to him three years before because he had been reading the newspapers also. But he had no need to rely upon them for his pictures of distress. When he went into the mountains he was not, like the government officials of his play, afraid of soiling his shoes, but went up into the out-of-the-way villages where the work was still done on hand looms, when there was work. Baginski, who visited the villages with Hauptmann, has given a detailed account of what was to be seen there. The ruined huts, he reports, were half buried in the snow, with not a human being, not an animal, to be seen; there was little smoke from the chimneys, for almost no one had wood; few paths were shovelled, for no one had work to take him outside. Within the huts they found people clothed in rags which had been worn so long that they seemed to be grown to them; they saw water dropping down filthy walls, a naked child, ill with fever and covered with a rash, lying on rags on the floor, a woman, in advanced pregnancy, standing among starving children, the older girls pressing their trembling

[14]"Aus frühen 'Weber'-Kritiken," p. 201.

lips together, the younger crying aloud for food.[15] There is no need to labour the point that scenes such as this found direct reflection in *Die Weber*, in *Hanneles Himmelfahrt*, which was written in 1893, and in *Quint*. Hauptmann was assuredly thinking of more than childhood memories when he spoke to the New York reporter of the misery with which he had been brought into contact and which had moved him deeply.

The impression that Hauptmann was writing under the stress of immediate personal experience is still further strengthened by a comparison of the play with the two works that are commonly accepted as its sources. Neither Zimmermann's *Blüte und Verfall* nor Wolff's eyewitness account, *Das Elend und der Aufruhr in Schlesien*,[16] can match the picture of distress painted in *Die Weber*. It is true that Hauptmann represented the course of the revolt and the complex conditions responsible for the suffering as he found them in his historical records. It is also true that the books give details concerning the poverty of the weavers, many of which he wove into the rich texture of his work. Wolff remarks, for example, that he had seen old men walk for miles through the snow, heavily laden, for the sake of a few coppers; Zimmermann reports that the weavers were happy if someone gave them a little buttermilk and that they were driven to eat the carcasses of dogs or horses in their hunger. But both, and especially Zimmermann, are more interested in questions of import and export, of markets and tariffs, and of government regulation and supervision than in lengthy descriptions of poverty and suffering. Hauptmann does not neglect these wider aspects of the problem. But he lessens the importance attached to them by putting them in the mouth of Dreissiger and, in general, he shifts the emphasis of his play from the more remote economic questions to the picture of hungry men exploited by a wealthy employer. We can only suppose that he did so because this was what had been impressed upon him most vividly by his personal

---

[15]"Gerhart Hauptmann unter den schlesischen Webern," p. 201. According to the *Chronik* Hauptmann went to Silesia in April 1891. There is no mention of a second trip. Baginski tells of meeting him there early in 1892.

[16]Reprinted in *Dokumente des Sozialismus*, I (Berlin, 1902).

experience and because he hoped in this way to obtain help for the sufferers.

As far as the weavers themselves are concerned then, there was no great difference to Hauptmann between the world of 1844 and that of 1891. And there are other aspects of the play which give us the same impression. The furniture in Dreissiger's room may be that of the first half of the century, but there are characters who look astonishingly like the author's own contemporaries. There is, for example, the commercial traveller. Wolff has a story about one such who undertook to condemn the weavers a day or so after the revolt, and who, for his pains, was shown the door of the station waiting-room where he was holding forth.[17] He may have had the same superior big-city brashness as the traveller in *Die Weber*, but there is little in Wolff's article to suggest any concrete picture. It seems reasonable to suppose that Hauptmann had seen some such character in real life, particularly when we compare him with others whom he drew from his experience, the gentlemen who frequent the *Stammtisch* in *Michael Kramer*, for example, who set our teeth on edge in precisely the same way. Moreover, the police of *Die Weber*, cringing and submissive and engaged in spying and denunciation, look very much like the police of *Der Biberpelz* and of *Emanuel Quint*. And like observations can be made in regard to Dreissiger. The sources indicate that his prototype had grown wealthy rapidly, that he lived in great luxury, and that he was notorious for forcing down wages. Hauptmann has again filled in this outline from his own experience. The man we see in the play is the counterpart of Hoffmann, the upstart capitalist of *Vor Sonnenaufgang*, and the two view themselves and the world in the same way, regarding themselves as reasonable and not "inhuman," and storming against the workers and against the agitators whom they hold responsible for all their trials. Hoffmann accuses Loth: "Ihr macht den Bergmann unzufrieden, anspruchsvoll, reizt ihn auf, erbittert ihn, macht ihn aufsässig, ungehorsam, unglücklich, spiegelt ihm goldene Berge vor." Dreissiger

[17]*Das Elend und der Aufruhr*, p. 311.

justifies himself, speaking to the pastor, in virtually the same terms: "Da ist ja den Leuten lange genug klargemacht worden, in welchem entsetzlichen Elend sie drinstecken. . . . Schliesslich glaubt es der Weber, und nun hat er den Vogel. . . . Jetzt murrt er ohne aufzuhören. . . . Jetzt möchte alles gemalt und gebraten sein." And Dreissiger's scornful rejection of *Humanitätsduselei*, the pastor's concern for the preservation of the "social peace," have the ring, not of the middle, but of the late nineteenth century. Such terms may be unconscious anachronisms. But if the weavers know nothing of modern labour movements, if they utter no party or class slogans, their opponents are ahead of them. They know all the answers.

It is hardly credible, in a word, that we should have *Die Weber* as we have it today if Hauptmann had not seen starvation face to face and if he had not been thinking, as he wrote it, of his own day. Nor is it credible that he expected it to move spectators to nothing more than "contemplation." It seems probable that the kind of action he hoped for was broadly social rather than directly political. And this brings us to the second point in our consideration of the relation of the play to society. Public reaction to the play belied Hauptmann's hope. The authorities proved as wilfully blind as Dreissiger who, faced with the spectacle of a child fainting from hunger, stormed at the child's parents. When the leaders of German society were presented, in *Die Weber*, with a condemnation of economic conditions, past and present, they denounced and forbade the play.

From March 1892 till October 1893 public performance of *Die Weber* was forbidden in Berlin. When it was finally acted for the first time in the Deutsches Theater in September 1894, the Emperor dismissed the judge of the high court—the Oberverwaltungsgericht—who had released it from police censorship, and cancelled the royal loge. Local police received secret instructions from the Ministry for Home Affairs to delay performances wherever permission to act the play was sought, regardless of the court decision. In one town performances were

given only on week-days so that people of the lower classes
would be unlikely to attend. In others admission prices were
raised in the same hope. As late as 1901 the play had not been
given publicly on any stage in Saxony. In town after town it
could not even be read to an audience. Regimental commanders
"desired" officers to remain away from performances. There
were loud protests in the Reichstag. The Prussian General Synod,
meeting in November 1894, recorded its horror officially.
Newspapers charged that Hauptmann was making propaganda
for the Social Democrats and positively inciting people to
class hatred. *Die Weber*, said its adversaries, portrayed the church
and the state as failures, it showed police being beaten and
soldiers driven away. It was cheap, revolting and theatrical in
the worst sense. Officials in Breslau asserted that the first, dialect,
version was intended to arouse the Silesian weavers. When
Hauptmann submitted the second, relatively standard German
version to the Berlin officials they claimed that he had altered
his language with the deliberate intention of stirring up the
workers in the capital. It might be too much to say that the
play completely failed to evoke the response he had hoped for.
But cultured people expressed the opinion that, though the
work was not dangerous for the enlightened, those less well
educated than themselves might not realize that the picture of
distress was both exaggerated and untrue of their own day. And
it is disheartening to find, in Houben's thirty-odd closely packed
pages recording the affair, only one official, von Bennigsen,
Oberpräsident of Hannover, who admitted that even in the last
decade of the nineteenth century workers were sometimes
exploited: "Es komme ja heute noch vor, dass Arbeiter und
Arbeiterinnen in unglaublicher Weise von ihren Arbeitgebern
ausgenutzt werden."[18] The Social Democrats may, initially,
have been somewhat over eager to claim as flesh of their flesh
a work which, though indicating that the evils of capitalism
were the result of the whole system, put more stress on the simple
need for greater humanity towards one's fellow-man; but the

[18]*Verbotene Literatur*, I, p. 361.

established powers literally made the play into a revolutionary force by refusing point blank to recognize the validity of any criticism or to acknowledge any need for reform.

It would be encouraging if the official attitude of the 1890's could be dismissed as a type of hysteria long since overcome. But when later critics reverse the judgments of the conservative authorities and claim that *Die Weber* is not a criticism of society but great literature and a contemplative study of man, they seem to be misguided, if not to the same extent, at least for similar reasons. Professor Stirk, agreeing with Paul Marx that the play is in no way a revolutionary work, and then adding, "Dass die deutschen Zeitungen in der Ostzone nach Hauptmanns Tode besonders *Die Weber* lobten, hatte wohl seine eignen Gründe,"[19] is clearly of the opinion that the play can be rescued from the Russians only by denying that it contains criticism of a social order still prevailing on this side of the Iron Curtain. But the value of a play does not depend on its remoteness from the immediate problems of the age in which it is written. It depends first and last on the power and understanding of the author. If he is a mediocre man, who has nothing to express or formulate except what has already been expressed or formulated by the average member of the group or society for which he is writing, he will produce a mediocre work, with or without a message, and there are just as many poor plays written by those who profess that they have no axe to grind as by those who admit that they do. But if he is a man of the stature of Shaw, his brilliant paradoxical formulations of social and ethical problems will have a human and aesthetic value which cannot be put to shame by the work of any dramatist known to history. And it is on this level that we must judge *Die Weber*. To wish to save Hauptmann from being grouped with some minor exponent of conventional social or political theories by claiming that his works have no social tendency is to reason by false analogy. It is a fallacy to argue that *Die Weber* is not a propaganda piece but a great and moving human drama. What should be

[19]"Aus frühen 'Weber'-Kritiken," p. 190.

argued is that, because it is a great and moving drama about the suffering caused by laissez-faire economics, it is at the same time one of the most powerful condemnations of that system that the stage has ever seen. It was not necessary for Hauptmann to teach explicitly what he had experienced so deeply. And only those critics who are mainly concerned with the inferior mysticism of his declining years would claim that, for him, the deepest experience is incommensurate with the desire to act.

A note of caution is necessary, however. *Die Weber* occupies a special position among Hauptmann's works, differing even from those which are closest to it, from *Geyer* or *Quint* or *Hanneles Himmelfahrt*, to the extent that, great as is the suffering portrayed, its causes do not seem immutable. Zimmermann uses as a preface for his history a quotation from Montesquieu: "Il n'y a rien de si affligeant que les consolations tireés de la nécessité du mal, de l'inutilité des remèdes, de la fatalité du destin, de l'ordre de la providence, et du malheur de la condition humaine. C'est se moquer de vouloir adoucir un mal par la considération que l'on est né misérable. . . ." And something of this resolute spirit must have moved Hauptmann in writing the play, for he leaves us persuaded that, with some good will and understanding, the situation of the weavers could be improved. All that is needed is direct economic action. Possibly the reception accorded Hauptmann's work had something to do with the deeper pessimism that marks many of his later plays, and with the more complex causes of the tragedies depicted there. This does not mean that his subsequent works are of slighter social significance than *Die Weber*. But he did not again suggest quite such a specific solution for the problems he portrayed.

One word more. *Florian Geyer*, like *Die Weber*, was long misunderstood. But no one, to my knowledge, has denied that Hauptmann wished to teach something through his portrayal of the sixteenth century, namely the need for German unity. Perhaps this lesson seemed more palatable than the demonstration of the desirability of social and economic reform. But it is logical to suppose that a man who finds a message for his own day in events that happened three hundred years before would look with the same searching and critical eyes at the present and the immediate past.

II

Even before Hauptmann had completed *Die Weber* he was planning a drama on a related theme, this time on the critical uprising of 1524-5 which historians, for convenience, call the Peasants' Revolt, though it was by no means confined to the third estate but was almost a national movement, banding together peasants, townsmen, and members of the lower nobility in a loosely defined attempt to curb the power of the church, the higher nobles, and the princes, and by so doing to achieve national unity, religious reform, and better economic conditions. In the summer of 1892 Hauptmann was in Franconia, visiting the cities that had witnessed the rise and fall of the rebellion. But *Florian Geyer* was not to be completed as quickly as *Die Weber*. Hauptmann found it necessary, for one thing, to do a considerable amount of source reading in preparation for it. Then, too, other plays intervened. Late in 1891, while he was still working on *Die Weber*, he had written his first comedy, *Kollege Crampton*. A second comedy, *Der Biberpelz*, and a two-act tragedy, *Hanneles Himmelfahrt*, took a great part of his time during the years 1892 and 1893. Then there were domestic interruptions, as a result of which he spent the first months of 1894 in the United States, and it was not until the summer of that year, after another trip to Franconia, that he seems to have settled down to the actual writing of his second historical play. It was completed in the spring of 1895 and acted in January 1896. But the date of its first performance seems to remove it further from *Die Weber* than is actually the case. For all their differences, the two plays, both experiments in the dramatization of history, first of a local, then of a national action, are so closely connected in theme and in treatment that they seem to belong to one chapter.

The source material from which, in the course of these three or four years, Hauptmann was slowly building up his play was both extensive and varied. In two long articles published in 1942 and 1943 Hermann Weigand has traced the imprint on the tragedy of folk-song and *Meistersang*, of sixteenth-century chronicle and pamphlet, of seventeenth-century comedy and novel, of David Friedrich Strauss's Hutten biography, and of historical works of Hauptmann's own day. He discovered that more than one hundred and sixty passages, chosen apparently without discrimination from works of the Reformation and of the Counter-Reformation, and from Protestant and Catholic historians, are embodied in the play.[20] The documentation from life that marked Hauptmann's first works had become, in *Die Weber*, in part a documentation from historical sources; the process is completed here. *Florian Geyer* suffers no loss because of the change. Documentation from history, like documentation from life, is only the more rational aspect of Hauptmann's creative impressionism. And *Geyer*, like *Die Weber*, is a remarkable example of a new kind of historical drama in which the realistic detail of Hauptmann's pictures of his own time is used in portraying a former era with such skill and sensitivity that the past comes to life on the stage. This does not mean, it should be noted, that the two plays are, like Schiller's *Maria Stuart* and *Die Jungfrau von Orleans*, identical twins dressed in period costumes. Hauptmann is fully aware of the difference in the spirit and in the problems of the ages which he is portraying. And *Geyer*, for all its realism, is a more poetic play than its predecessor; indeed, it is the most poetic prose play that Hauptmann had written up to this time.

The tragedy begins with a *Vorspiel* in the castle of the Bishop of Würzburg, where a scribe is reading aloud to a group of knights the *Twelve Articles*, the demands of the peasants for the abolition of serfdom, for relief from feudal obligations, and for ministers chosen by their own congregations. The glosses of

[20]"Auf den Spuren von Hauptmanns Florian Geyer," *Publications of the Modern Language Association of America*, LVII, pp. 1160–95; LVIII, pp. 797–848.

the knights are bitter and arrogant, but the tide is against them. New adherents, even from their own class, are flocking to the peasant cause: and the Bishop is on the point of flight, leaving his followers to defend his castle.

In the first act we meet leaders and representative figures of the revolt as they gather for a conference in the chapter-house of the Neu-Münster in the town: the knights Stephan von Menzingen and Götz von Berlichingen, the peasants Bubenleben and Kohl, the humanistically minded rector Besenmeyer, Geyer's secretary Löffelholz, Tellermann, the leader of his famous, well-discipled *Schwarze Bande*, and finally, to the cheers of the people, Geyer himself. It is clear that the time is ripe for a final, decisive action, and the mood, as we should expect, is exultant. But the discussion that follows bodes ill for the future. Geyer speaks urgently of the need for order and unity, but knights and peasants are suspicious of one another as individuals and as groups. They cannot decide upon a leader. And when, at the end of the act, those who have been sitting around the council-table plunge their knives into its centre, as a symbol of the heart of the foe, the diversity of their aims is clear: to some the enemy is the Swabian League, to others the church or the great new trading companies, and to still others a specific individual—the Bishop of Bamberg or the Chancellor of Bavaria. Only an undistinguished scribe named Sartorius strikes at the root of the trouble and aims his knife at German disunity—"Der deutschen Zwietracht mitten ins Herz!"[21]

Disaster comes swiftly. In a Rothenburg inn, in the second act, the citizens of the town are celebrating their newly won freedom. But there is again sharp quarrelling between the peasant leaders, and there are rumours of serious disorder among the revolutionary forces in Würzburg. Geyer, who has come for heavy artillery, is in haste to return. Then Besenmeyer remembers that Marei, Geyer's camp-follower, is sleeping, exhausted, behind the stove. She brings grave news. The army of the Swabian League, the main force left opposing them, has won a great victory. More-

[21]In the 1942 edition, in accordance with stage tradition, this line is given to Geyer.

over, the Würzburg leaders have broken their word to Geyer, stormed the castle without cannon, and been thrown back with crippling losses. The *Schwarze Bande*, enticed to join the attack, has been cut to pieces. From now on the downward movement proceeds unabated. The peasants call a general assembly in Schweinfurt, but it is too late. Word comes that allies are rapidly deserting and that the Swabian League is recapturing post after post. Geyer sets out to see what can be done with the disordered remnants of the forces at Würzburg, but before he can reach them the mortally wounded Tellermann brings news of a final battle, lost through the desertion of Götz von Berlichingen. For the peasant leaders there is no possible course but to try to save their own individual lives. But Geyer's thoughts are clearly of death. And, like so many of his followers, he is slaughtered. The last small band he can muster is smashed by the Würzburg garrison and, wounded, he seeks shelter in the castle of his brother-in-law, Wilhelm von Grumbach. Grumbach, once an uneasy associate of the rebels, is now trying to re-establish himself with the victors and is entertaining knights of the League. Betrayed by his own relatives and set upon by drunken members of his own class, Geyer is shot from behind by a mercenary, a religious fanatic whom he had once had to strike for insubordination.

Florian Geyer, like *Die Weber*, and unlike the conventional historical play, is strikingly devoid of action. The few major events, reported rather than shown, serve mainly to cast their shadow over the scene and to account for the falling mood; and the last three acts are no more than a long-drawn-out portrayal of catastrophe, a picture of the slow dying of a mortally wounded body, whose strength suffices only for a few convulsive quivers before it sinks into final quiescence. And, like *Die Weber* also, *Geyer* is long and filled with detail and with the recording of emotion. Again it is Hauptmann's reading of history that is responsible for the changes in the traditional form. In both plays he felt bound to give a faithful and realistic picture of the revolutionary forces and of the world against which they were in revolt, and this meant many characters and many incidents rather than a swiftly moving action. In both he was striving to keep close to his historical records, and the records for *Geyer* did not suggest any clearly circumscribed or decisive struggle, particularly during the last phase of the revolt with which Hauptman deals,[22] beginning at a point where it seems that the peasant forces will triumph because of the sheer weight of numbers and the universal desire for a change of some sort, and portraying the degeneration of the situation, the disunity, and the wasteful frittering away of the army for want of a clearly envisaged purpose. Those who criticize the play because of its lack of action, pointing out that it has a hero who is a potential leader but who never does anything, are attacking the very source from which the tragedy stems. The revolt fails because Geyer is never given a chance, because he has no opportunity to act.

It is obvious, then, that the problems concerning the "dramatic" nature of Hauptmann's plays are more urgent in *Geyer* than ever before. He solved them in part by resources that he had already developed in his earlier works—by his skill in characterization and analysis, and by the recording of emotional intensity and complexity and constant cross-currents and clashes that has been characterized as his dramatic texture. His gift of recording the rubbing of temperament against temperament and the clash of individual with individual is evident, to take only one example, in the council-table scene of the first act, which bristles with a dozen minor conflicts: at one moment the ironic mockery beneath which Löffelholz shelters his deep seriousness flashes out to counter the nonsensical fanaticism of Bubenleben, and at the next the bright rage of Geyer flares at the cowardly evasiveness of Götz von Berlichingen. Nor is the play lacking in lively minor incidents or in moments of sharp tension. Tellermann, heated with wine and with the joy of a triumphant return to his native Würzburg after a ten-year exile, spies a

---

[22]Hauptmann appears at one time to have planned more than one play, perhaps a trilogy, on the revolt.

priest whom he recognizes as one of those who presided while
his mother was being burned at the stake for refusing to admit
her son's heresy, and lashes out at him with fists and tongue
—"ich bin ein heimlicher Ketzer. Meine Mutter selig wollt's
nit gestehn . . . Gott verzeih ihr's"—until he is overcome by
his own fury and falls, almost unconscious, to a chair. The
mercenary, Schäferhans, sword in hand, rushes into the Rothenburg inn in pursuit of Karlstatt, the former colleague of Luther
who is now an adherent to the peasant cause. At the end of the
third act the sick Löffelholz collapses, begging his friends, who
have had to depart without him, not to let him die alone, and
the end of the fourth is marked by the death of Tellermann.
The fifth act, in which, after the long, slow degeneration of
recent events, we are stirred to hope that Geyer may escape
at least immediate death, is particularly rich in such moments.
We watch Grumbach and his lady, anxious to disclaim any share
in the revolt, driving Marei away and encouraging the knights
in the torture of captured peasants. We see Geyer, when he
arrives, almost discovered by one of the celebrants, and wresting
with difficulty a promise of temporary shelter from his brother-
in-law. Then, as Anna von Grumbach indicates his hiding-place,
we see Marei spring out before him, only to be shot, and see
him standing alone, at bay, with the knights advancing on him
from the front and Schäferhans manœuvring for a position from
which he can shoot him from behind.

Such scenes may well remind us of a similar use of incident in
earlier plays, above all in *Die Weber*. They are the natural
expression of the friction, the disorder, and the lawlessness of
the time, and the equal of anything that Hauptmann had done
before. But there is also a mature and refined tension in *Geyer*,
the like of which he had not yet achieved. It is evident particularly
in the scenes where we learn about the two events that determine
—as far as any single events can determine—the outcome of
the revolt, namely the attack on the Würzburg citadel and the
desertion of Götz with the last considerable force at the disposal
of the peasants. The messenger of the Würzburg defeat is Marei,

and her story is told at the end of the second act. Geyer is on the
very verge of setting out with the cannon—in the middle of
the scene the pipers without begin to play their escort—when
Besenmeyer remembers that the girl has been asleep behind the
stove for some time. She has letters, written in Latin, from
Löffelholz, and while Besenmeyer is reading them Geyer asks her,
casually, the natural question, "Was macht der Tellermann?"

> MAREI: Den Tellermann haben sie in die Eisen gelegt.
> GEYER: Was macht der Tellermann, Dirne? Hör, was man fragt.
> MAREI (*trotzig*): Ich hab's gehört.

Geyer tries to catch his breath. He gives the girl wine, he
asks her how Löffelholz is and when she left Würzburg. Then
he repeats the question, and receives the same dreadful answer,
that Tellermann is in chains. Still unable to comprehend, he
tries a slightly different approach:

> GEYER (*schreit sie an*): Wen haben sie in die Eisen gelegt?
> MAREI: Den Tellermann.
> GEYER: Den Tellermann?—Meinen Leutinger [Leutnant]?
> MAREI: Ja, Kapitän.
> GEYER: Wer hat den Tellermann in die Eisen gelegt?

But now there is a diversion. The pale Besenmeyer reports
the victory of the Swabian League. Geyer responds with a
vehement "Gen Würzburg!" The pastor checks him: there is
still more to come. And again, before he in his turn can continue,
Geyer remembers that he still does not know what has happened
at Würzburg. From now on his mind, reluctant to grasp the
first news of the disaster, anticipates the worst. He continues
to question, but he knows before he is told that the *Schwarze
Bande* is no more.

> GEYER (*zu Marei*): Sind unsere Schwarzen dabei gewest?
> MAREI: Ja, Kapitän. Als sie die Hörner blusen: "welche fechten wollten,
> kämen recht," . . . ist kein Haltens gewest. . . . Hat der Tellermann sie Rebellen
> genennet, pflicht- und eidbrüchig. . . .
> GEYER: Und da haben sie ihn in die Eisen gelegt.—Noch eins, Bruder Rektor:
> übel gerannt und übel gefallen, schlecht gewagt, den Sturm verloren?
> BESENMEYER: Ja, Bruder Geyer!
> GEYER: Freilich wohl.

And he begins to take off his armour. The passage, the impact of which grows with every reading, is a masterpiece, both in its gradual revelation to the spectator of what has happened and in its recording of the effect on Geyer. We see the hands of his assailants rising to strike him and watch the blows fall, one by one, and we see him, at the end of the scene, a broken man. The end of the fourth act, where the messenger is Tellermann, is shorter, but equally effective. Delirious, and exhausted, with his clothes in rags and the ragged remnant of a black standard in his clenched hand, he can stammer only disconnected phrases: "Ah! Der Berlinger! Wo ist der Berlinger? Aus dem Staube gemacht—Das Pulver ist nass.—Verfluchtes Gesindel! . . . Kerls, fürchtet euch nit. . . ." But it is enough. A moment later, when the dying and now silent man has been placed on a blanket, and the innkeeper, without saying a word, is hurriedly burning the papers of the peasant council, Besenmeyer asks, indirectly, the question to which they all know the answer—that this is the end.

> BESENMEYER: Was hat er gelallt, Bruder?
> GEYER (leise): Königshofen.
> KARLSTATT: Es sind die dreissigtausend des Götz.
> MENZINGEN (laut): So bin ich am Ende mit allem Meinen.

It does not matter, when we consider the force of such scenes, that we learn of the attack on Würzburg or of the battle of Königshofen only when they are over. And moments like these, together with the disputes in word and deed of which I have given some examples above, form an important element in the play and give it a completely adequate tension. There is no danger of its becoming, as a first glance at a material so lacking in action might suggest, either a pageant with a stress on *in memoriam* or an elegy for a whole community of voices.

With like skill—and a skill which is again reminiscent of that developed in *Die Weber*—Hauptmann overcame the difficulties inherent in portraying large numbers of characters; in this case, knights and peasants, artisans and merchants, officials, clergymen of the most varied ranks and persuasions, scribes and scholars and professional soldiers. We may at times, particularly in reading the play, be uncertain of the identity of a given speaker. But the revolt, for all its complexities, is such a burning issue with all the characters that the unity is preserved and our impression of the whole situation grows and deepens as the work proceeds. The figures themselves are bright, the incidents which bring them into the action effective and, at times, unforgettable. There is, for example, the lively travelling scholar Martin, whom we see hammering green branches over the door of the Neu-Münster chapter-house to welcome Geyer, singing a spring song as he does so, and mocking the theological subtleties that he has shaken from him: "Der Vater ist der Sohn der Jungfrau Maria. Der Heilige Geist ist ein Mensch und der Sohn der Jungfrau." There is the pedlar, hawking with impartial commercial zeal tracts against Luther, or, at his customer's pleasure, against Rome, and dispensations "warm vom heiligen Vater."

There are even more memorable figures, striking both in themselves and in the roles they play. One such is the old woman who appears in the third act, with her son, blinded for his innocent confederacy in the rebellion. The already shaken Geyer is just about to set out for Würzburg to see if anything can be saved there, and she adds to his burden by cursing all heretics, and him in particular, for the injury done to her son by the army of the Swabian League. Another is the old Jewish merchant Jöslein, who worships Geyer because he has promised the same law for all, "auch vor uns Juden." And Jöslein gives an account of the wealthy trading companies of Augsburg which goes far to explain the invectives directed against them elsewhere by Geyer and by Löffelholz: "Haben se mir stinkiger Jud geheissen und Wucherer angeschrien, und rennen doch selber mit dem Juden-spiess. Aber nit im Kleinen. Mein!—Mein! Betrügen hunderte und tausende arme Einleger um ihr saures Geld, fallieren und sind viel reicher dann zuvor. . . . Ich hab niemalen unter Safran Rindfleisch gehackt, Gaiskot in den Lorbeer getan, Lindenlaub in den Pfeffer, noch hab ich Fichtenspäne vor Zimmet verkauft. Aber ein armer Jud muss es ausbaden." The characters are not always shown at a moment of conflict, but there is always conflict in the background; and there is always colour and variety and high emotional intensity. Indeed, the sixteenth century offered Hauptmann a greater opportunity for unusual and picturesque characters than the contemporary or nearly contemporary themes he had hitherto attempted, and he took full advantage of it. Moreover, by keeping so many people in the foreground and vitally connected with the whole, he accomplished once again what he had done on a simpler scale in *Die Weber*: he presented history as the affair of the people and of all people. His triumph is the greater here, where he had to give realistic life to men who had lived two hundred and fifty years ago and to avoid making a mere copy, building a sixteenth-century house with the vision and equipment of a man dwelling in the nineteenth.

Even in his use of means already familiar to us Hauptmann was not, thus, in the writing of *Florian Geyer*, merely marking time. But the play has also notable innovations, and a very important element in its composition is its stress on mood or atmosphere. We have had some evidence already, above all in *Einsame Menschen* and in *Die Weber*, that Hauptmann's strength lies not only in his analysis—be it psychological, social, or economic—but in his power of touching basic human sensibilities and of creating an all-pervading emotional climate in which his figures move and breathe. This appeal to the emotions and this evocation of an atmosphere are more intense in *Geyer* than in any earlier play, almost intense enough to be termed lyrical. They do not invalidate the analysis. But Hauptmann reacted to his material not only as a careful, sensitive observer, but as a man passionately involved in the tragedy he perceived, and he gave his feelings strongly poetic expression. Moreover, he made his evocation of mood serve a genuinely dramatic function. The main characters are torn between two sharply marked emotional extremes: on the one hand they are filled by a strong and exultant hope that the nation is about to be reborn; and on the other they are depressed by weariness and despair, and by horror of the meanness and cruelty which characterize the actions of all around them, knights and peasants alike, for the rebels have rapidly sunk to the level of their opponents. The two moods contrast and conflict with one another and go far to make up for whatever may be lacking in the play in the way of orthodox action and counter-action or of struggle between opposing tendencies in the breast of the hero.

The Bible, with related legends and poetry, and, to a lesser extent, the new humanism—the sixteenth-century equivalents, it may be noted, of Käthe and Anna—are Hauptmann's main sources for the formulation of the first of these two moods. The vision and the ideals, the hope and the longing that fire the rebels at their best moments are most frequently expressed in Biblical terms. The peasants are hungry and thirsty, one of the knights says, but not for bread alone, "aber nit nur nach Brot und Wein, sondern der Herr hat seinen Hunger und Durst gesandt, zu hören sein Wort, lauter, klar und rein...." And the speech of a blind monk, beginning as a mock defence of the church and the princes in the crude style of a sixteenth-century anti-Lutheran harangue, becomes a rhapsody in praise of the new truth which rings with phrases from the Old Testament and the New. Men must beware, he says, of devilish agitators, who talk as though Barbarossa, or even the Saviour, were about to return, and who give no thought to what might happen if one of them did: "Gott helf euch, ihr arme, verblendete Wider-christen!... Wer wird Münster und Dome bauen, wann man Gott in keinem Tempel meh anbeten wird, sondern allein im Geist und in der Wahrheit? Wer wird noch des Fürsten und Herren Geleit brauchen und bezahlen auf der Landstrassen, so man überall sicher ist gleich wie in Abrahams Schoss?..." And he concludes, "Bestehlet und belüget euch! Wenn einer zehn Röcke hat, so reisse er dem den elften vom Leibe, der nur einen hat. So verstehet der Papst, so verstehen die Pfaffen das Evangelium. Aber Gott sprach: es werde Licht!... und so licht ist es worden, dass ich es scheinen sehe, Gott, sei mein Zeuge! durch meine blinden Augen."

The hope that some find in the Bible, others, notably Besenmeyer, draw from the clear spring of human reason: "Ich habe
gelebt und gewirket in der tröstlichen Meinung, uf die einst
Graf Eberhart von Württemberg die hohe Schule zu Tübingen
gegründet hat: graben zu helfen den Brunnen des Lebens, daraus
von allen Enden der Welt unversieglich möge geschöpft werden
tröstliche und heilsame Weisheit zur Erlöschung des verderb-
lichen Feuers menschlicher Unvernunft und Blindheit." But
the main spokesman of the new ideals is Geyer. And on no
occasion does he speak more movingly than at the end of the
fourth act when, with all hope dead, he shakes off for a moment
the disgust and despair that threaten to overwhelm him, and
as Marei helps to arm him, thinks of what he had been fighting
for, resolves to remain faithful to his vision, and paraphrases
and quotes from Ulrich von Hutten's well-known manifesto:

> Von Wahrheit ich will nimmer lan,
> Das soll mir bitten ab kein Mann,
> Auch schafft, zu schrecken mich, kein Wehr,
> Kein Bann, kein Acht, wie fast und sehr
> Man mich damit zu schrecken meint;
> Obwohl meine fromme Mutter weint,
> Da ich die Sach hätt gfangen an:
> Gott wöll sie trösten, es muss gahn;
> Und sollt es brechen auch vorm End,
> Wills Gott, so mags nit werden gwendt,
> Darum will brauchen Füss und Händ.
>   Ich habs gewagt.[23]

Schnall fester, Marei [says Geyer], ich muss das Eisen fühlen. Deutschland
ist ein Land, ist aller Länder Krone, hat Gold, Silber, Brot und Wein genung,
zu erhalten dies Leben reichlich. Aber es ist der Zwietracht kein End. . . . Ich
hab gedacht, ich wollt Wandel schaffen. Wer bin ich, dass ich's gewagt?
Sei's drum: "Von Warheit will ich nimmer lan." . . . Den Helm, Marei!—
"Das soll mir bitten ab kein Mann, auch schafft, zu schrecken mich, kein
Wehr, kein Bann, kein Acht." . . . Die Armschienen fest, ich will mich damit
begraben lassen! . . . "Obwohl meine treue Mutter weint, dass ich die Sach
hab fangen an, Gott woll sie trösten. . . . (*Das Schwert umgürtend*) Es muss

---

[23]David Friedrich Strauss, *Ulrich von Hutten* (Leipzig, 1858), II, p. 121.

gahn."—So, itzt bin ich gefasst. Lebt wohl, liebe Brüder, es müsste wunders zugehen, wann wir uns sollten wieder begegnen. Tut mir Bescheid: Ulrich von Huttens Gedächtnis! Des Sickingen Gedächtnis!

The end of the fourth act, with its evocation of Hutten's resolute and beautiful poem, is the last major expression in the play of the mood of hope and faith. The end of the fifth, as Geyer dies with hatred in his eyes and as his enemies shout in shameless triumph over his dead body, brings the play to a close in a mood of despair and repulsion. And instances of savage cruelty, of coarse and filthy behaviour, of the distortion of religion into fanaticism and superstition, and of the degeneration of men to the point of sadism and obscenity are so frequent throughout the play, and so vividly expressed, that they create an atmosphere which infests it and hangs over it like a foul pall. It is not the killing in battle which seemed to impress Hauptmann most, though what we hear of that is grim enough, and more than once there is an echo of Luther's demand that the peasants be struck down ruthlessly—in the words of the innkeeper Kratzer, for example, "Haben die armen Leute gesungen: 'Nun bitten wir den heiligen Geist', und also singende hat man sie lassen treten unter die Hufe der Gäule, sie darniedergestochen, geschlagen und keinen geschonet." But more frequent are accounts of the torture of the survivors or the captured. We hear of "pious evangelical brothers" parading heads on pikes, of a black devil of a witch thrusting a bread knife into the body of a knight and smearing her shoes with the blood and fat that issue forth, of the commander of the Swabian League himself, aided by other counts and nobles, chaining a man to a tree and building a fire around him, fetching and throwing on wood with his own hands. The gentle Karlstatt, starved and exhausted, cannot force food down as he thinks of the scenes from which he has just fled in Würzburg: "Vor meinen sehenden Augen haben sie einen in Stücke gehauen und einander geworfen mit dem blutigen Fleisch." And we hear not only of deeds that are fiendishly and grotesquely cruel, but of the mean lust of animal baiting. One of the knights who appears in the last act reports that they recently set a captured peasant to attack his brethren, promising him his life if he could kill them and he disposed of five: "Der sechste aber, der wollt nit daran, stellete sich meisterlich, und kamen die beiden in ein Ringen, herum Lottel, hinum Trottel; was spasshaft zu schauen. Und als sie ganz wohl ineinander gemengelt und verstricket, traten sie fehl von ungefähr, rolleten die Böschung hinab in den Graben und versoffen beide." We have some direct experience of such delights as we watch the same knights whip and bully a group of terrified peasants.

We have direct experience also of the perversion of religious feeling in the wild messianic outbursts of Bubenleben, for example, or in the nurse's story which helps to usher in the bitter counter-revolutionary night of the fifth act. The woman is trying to comfort Anna von Grumbach, her mistress, by assuring her that God is ever ready to help. A criminal was just about to be snatched from the gallows, she relates, by a stinking devil with a lashing tale, when the angels remembered that the doomed man had once sacrificed a candle, and intervened; the devil cursed and fled. But the most notable scene in this respect is probably the appearance of the old woman and her blind son in the third act. She regards the litany as a charm to ward off further evil, and its gentle cry to the Lamb of God is mocked and distorted by the curses and jingles with which she accompanies it:

DIE ALTE FRAU: Du gottloser Schelm und Bösewicht . . . Bist selber ein schwarzer Bauer gewest! Hast meinen Sohn beschwatzt mit deinen höllischen, boshaften, teuflischen Lügen, mit deiner verdammten, falschen, bübischen evangelischen Freiheit.
DER ZERLUMPTE MENSCH: Heilige Maria!
DIE ALTE FRAU: Bitte für uns!
DER ZERLUMPTE MENSCH: Heilige Gottesgebärerin, heilige Jungfrau aller Jungfrauen!
DIE ALTE FRAU: Bitte für uns!
DER ZERLUMPTE MENSCH: Du Morgenstern! O du Lamm Gottes, dass du hinwegnimmst die Sünden der Welt!
DIE ALTE FRAU: Bitte für uns—hodie tibi, cras sibi. Sankt Paulus, Sankt Bartholomäus, die zween Sohne Zebedäus, der heilige Sankt Wenzel und der selige Stenzel, die sein gut vors kalte Weh. . . .

The third aspect of the degeneration, finally, may be summed up by another excerpt from Karlstatt's account of the state of affairs in Würzburg: "Stehlen, Buben, Katzbalgen, Huren, Saufen. . . . Junge Kinder und zitternde Greise, Unzucht, Schande und Laster. . . ." Peasants and nobles together behave, in the words of one of the knights in the *Vorspiel*, like mad, drunken swine. The peasant leader Kohl had sworn, charges Bubenleben, that he would sleep in the bishop's silken bed and drink his oldest wine from a golden goblet, "und wenn du voll wärest, so sollte dir müssen der Oberste Hauptmann uf Unserer Frauen Berg die silberne Schüssel vorhalten: darein wolltest du kotzen." And for the knights there is a new game called "das Maislen," "ein neu à la mode Spiel," in Geyer's bitter words, which consists in throwing furnishings and food: "Man schmeisst den Hausrat hin und her, wirft einander mit Kuchenfetzen und beschüttet sich mit unsauberem Wasser." Grumbach and the knights indulge in this sport in the last act and it is one of them, staggering in to clean his face and clothes of the porridge thrown at him by another, who almost discovers Geyer.

The basic cause of the failure of the revolt is the inability of its adherents to see beyond their private interests and opinions. But degeneration of all kinds rides with it, as destructive as the horsemen of the apocalypse, and in this atmosphere the new life that men had thought growing withers and rots. "Hat ein Aussehn gehabt, als sollte der Frühling hervorkeimen allenthalben. ist aber alles wiederum verfaulet in Finsternis," says Karlstatt, and Geyer too has recourse to imagery to express the contrast between hope and disgust which dominates the play. He denounces his confederates passionately for having defiled a holy cause, for having tossed a jewel into a pigsty, and he uses the new game as a symbol of their betrayal: "Den besten Handel, die edelste Sache, die heiligste Sache . . . eine Sache die Gott einmal in eure Hand geben hat und vielleicht nimmer—in euren Händen ist sie gewest wie ein Kleinod im Saustall. Ihr habt das Maislen damit gespielt. Das Allerheiligste habt ihr herumgezerrt uf euren Gelagen, darüber gerülpset und gekotzet mit euren Zechgesellen, es durch eure Lotterbetten gezogen, mit euren Huren und Buben zertreten und beschissen."

Critics have not been blind to the poetry of such passages as Karlstatt's lament for the spring whose young buds have rotted in the darkness. But there has been some tendency to regard them as alien poetic flashes in a primarily analytical and descriptive work, a tendency which was natural in view of Hauptmann's innovations in the dramatic presentation of history. The main attention of his readers was drawn, at first, to his careful documentation and his broad picture of society, and these are important elements of the play. But it is important to realize also that the language is highly poetic, not exceptionally but throughout. Weigand has noted that the prose tends to become a loose, four-beat verse in moments of emotional stress, in the line "Hat Rost am Eisen aber nit am Schwert," for example;[24] and he might have quoted many like passages to illustrate his point— Geyer's "übel gerannt und übel gefallen, schlecht gewagt, den Sturm verloren," to mention only one. Even at its most prosaic, the dialogue is strong and rhythmic, picturesque, and rich in images and in proverbial expressions: "Gott hat uns bis hieher glücklich und wohl geführet. . . . Dannoch will mir das Herz nit fast gross werden und lustig;" "Das Glück schneit mit grossen Flocken;" "Kehricht seid ihr, Kot von der Landstrasse, elendes Gerümpel, das Gott besser hätt hinterm Ofen lassen liegen." Philologists may dispute whether Hauptmann was at all points justified in his adaptation of the language of the period, and laymen complain that he used some phrases that are needlessly obscure. But he was inspired by the power, the colour, and the richness of the writing of an age when poetry and prose were not as sharply distinguished as they were in his own, and he created in his turn a rich and moving and a more poetic prose then he had used hitherto. *Florian Geyer* fuses lyric and dramatic in its evocation of strong, antithetic moods whose expression is condensed and heightened to the point of poetry.

The characters in *Florian Geyer*, in comparison with those of the earlier plays reveal similar changes, above all in Geyer himself and in his closest associates. We have observed that Haupt-

---

[24] "Auf den Spuren von Hauptmanns Florian Geyer," p. 816.

mann felt and possessed his people so intimately that he sometimes wrote scenes about them which he probably never intended
to use in the final form of the play; and we have observed also
that he was able, not only to picture their behaviour in the most
minute detail, but to catch a predominant and characteristic
strain and rhythm in the speech of each. He wrote additional
scenes for *Geyer*, showing his hero at home, in private life.[25]
But it is difficult to conceive that even Hauptmann could picture
a man who lived three centuries before his day in quite the same
realistic way as he did his own contemporaries. And although
the play makes us feel that he knows his sixteenth-century people,
and knows them well, there is less stress on details and analysis
than in earlier works, and more on the predominant rhythm
of each person's speech, on an emotion, a gesture, an attitude
which is typical of the character in question and which leaves us,
in the main, with an emotional impression. The composition
of character, like the language, is more lyrical or, in some cases
more balladesque than before.

We know of Geyer, for example, that he formerly fought
under the French in Italy, that he has a wife who does not
approve of his present course, and that he once sat between
Besenmeyer and Ulrich von Hutten at a banquet in Gotha,
dreaming of the revolution to come. We know also that he is
an excellent soldier, stern, just, courageous, humble, and devoted
to the cause for which he is fighting. Yet we really know him,
not because of what we hear about his background or even because his words or actions illustrate all these qualities, but because
we feel him to be the embodiment of German longing for national
unity and for freedom. Heise has an intimation of this when he
describes him as "die wärmste Erscheinung des Dramas, nicht
ihr Mittelpunkt, doch das Symbol des Ganzen"[26]—although,
as the play's "warmest spot," he is also its centre, to the extent
that any one person can be the centre of an action such as Hauptmann had to portray. And this impression is created because a

[25]Behl, *Zwiesprache*, p. 174.
[26]*Gerhart Hauptmanns Dramen*, III, p. 49.

great part of what he says and of what others say about him is
expressed in poetic terms, in terms of symbol or legend or hero-
worship. This is particularly evident in his paraphrase of Hutten's
verses, but there are many more such memorable passages.
When he speaks of his mission he thinks of himself as a man
awakened by God, and at the gate of Würzburg, straight and
black on his horse and sword held high, he challenges the bishop:
"Hie kehre ich heim, Florian Geyer, in Kaisers Acht und Papstes
Bann, aber von Gott erweckt, erwählet und geführet! Hie
kehre ich heim, Florian Geyer, des Sickingen Freund und der
Pfaffen Feind. . . ." Or again, from the window of the Rothenburg inn he speaks to the crowd of the reawakened emperor
in the Kyffhäuser and pictures himself as a John the Baptist
sent to prepare the way for the new kingdom: "Der Barbarossa
ist auferstanden und wird herfürtreten mit ganzer Macht.
. . . Wir wollen ein deutsch evangelisch Oberhaupt: einen
Volkskaiser. . . . Er soll den Krönungseid schwören. . . .
Und wie der neugewählte König hat Antwort zu geben: 'Ich
will', so sag ich auch, Ich will, ich will, ich will. . . . Dem
Barbarossa will ich den Weg bereiten." His remorse, his sense
of the irretrievability of the golden opportunity, ring like a
dark lament through the third and fourth acts: "Peser le feu,
mesurer le vent, faire revenir le jour passé, c'est chose impossible;[27]
. . . Wo sind meine Dunkelknaben geblieben? Meine schwarzen
Fähnlein, die ich mir gemustert? . . . Es reuet mich fast, es
reuet mich fast. . . . Der nagende Hund liegt mir unterm Herzen,
dieweil ich zu leben hab. . . . Der heimliche Kaiser muss weiter
schlafen. Die Raben sammeln sich wieder zu Haufen." His
final resolution is that, having served God, he will henceforth
serve no lesser master—"Itzt habe ich einer göttlichen Sache
gedient. Itzt dien ich keinem König mehr." And the others
speak of him in like terms. For them he is a noble in the truest
sense—"ein ehrlicher Ritter und Reuter von Adel"—a hero
whose armour may be tarnished but in whose heart justice flames,

[27]Weigand, "Auf den Spuren von Hauptmanns Florian Geyer," p. 800, Esra IV,
4-5, via Moscherosch, *Philander von Sittewald*.

the hand forged by God to the sword of the *Schwarze Bande*. He is the hope, the defiance, the resoluteness, the sorrow, and the bitter resignation of the people, the essence of the emotions that move them, and the symbol of the rebellion, in victory and in defeat.

The irrational aspect of Geyer's nature is further heightened by the attitude and the characterization of those who are closest to him in the play—Löffelholz, Besenmeyer, Tellermann, Marei—for they too are marked, in varying degrees, by the same poetic treatment. Marei, who is Geyer's creature completely and inaccessible to all others, has sometimes reminded critics of Kleist's Käthchen.[28] A *Lagerdirne*, without roots in any known or ordered world, intense, taciturn, and defiant, she might with equal justification remind us of Mignon. Geyer himself best expresses her sombre and yet colourful nature as he dreams, at the end of the fourth act, of the clothes in which he proposes to dress her in the impossible future: she will have three cloaks, he promises, if he is alive a week hence, "einen rosenfarbenen aus Mecheln, einen lombardischen, einen rauchfarbenen aus Brügge. . . . Du sollst dich in gelber Seide tragen, als wenn du einen safrangelben Nürnberger zum Vater hättest." Equally colourful, if less enigmatic, is Tellermann, a man flashing in victory and valiant in defeat, who, though embittered by persecution, is gay and impetuous by nature—"Der Wein ist mir in'n Kopf krochen. Das Glück ist mir ins Herz krochen." And we remember Besenmeyer as we remember a line of poetry or a bar of music, for the warmth that fills his old body and inspires his tongue at the apparent new birth of the nation; and Löffelholz for the intelligence and humour that carry him, ill and with an aching head, through floods of documents to the end—"ich kann nit mit Euch, aber der Tod wird mich finden, kann ich ihn gleich nit suchen." Action in a ballad, said Goethe, is not for its own sake, but is a means of evoking a mood. The characterization of *Florian Geyer* is directed to a considerable extent towards the same end.

[28]Paul Schlenther, *Gerhart Hauptmann, Leben und Werke* (6th ed., Berlin, 1912), p. 131; Weigand, "Auf den Spuren von Hauptmanns Florian Geyer," p. 847.

In many ways, indeed, considered in its relation to Hauptmann's drama in general, *Geyer* points more strongly than most of the prose plays to the plays in verse—the good verse plays, that is, not *Die versunkene Glocke*, but *Der arme Heinrich*, *Die Winterballade*, or *Veland*. It springs from an examination of literature and of history which Hauptmann strove to make as careful and detailed as his examination of contemporary life, and it gives an exact and realistic picture of the Peasants' Revolt. But in the simplification of character for the purpose of creating a predominant emotional effect, in the heightening and intensification of language, and in the evocation of strong and strongly contrasted moods Hauptmann was moving towards the later verse plays. This does not mean that all the verse plays show all these characteristics or that *Geyer* is the only prose drama in which we can trace these or like developments, for with Hauptmann, as every man is a new man, so every play is a new play, a voyage of exploration into unknown territory. In works like *Michael Kramer*, for example, or *Rose Bernd*, he was to reveal an insight into psychological problems which are more complicated and less obvious than those which had attracted the young dramatist, and he carried this mastery into *Der arme Heinrich* and into *Iphigenie*. Most of the verse plays have also a sharper and more definite conflict than *Geyer*. But it is significant that this, the first play in prose based, like those in verse, entirely on material beyond Hauptmann's immediate experience, should show such a combination of exact observation and genuine poetic power. Nothing could better illuminate the close connection between the prose plays and the verse, and the growth of the one from the other.

Yet, although the poetic aspects of *Florian Geyer* are important, both because they form a major element in the structure of the play and because they point to future developments, it must not be forgotten that it is primarily Hauptmann's gifts as an observer that make the work remarkable in the evolution of historical tragedy. It is not, to be sure, a scientific or a Marxian treatise, and if Heise is justified in praising the clairvoyance with which Hauptmann outlines the decisive political currents of the era, it is too much to see in Bubenleben a declassed intellectual and a zealous guardian of the purity of the class struggle.[29] But the dramatist's understanding of the influences that move society, sharpened in his plays of contemporary and near-contemporary life, served him well in his portrayal of an earlier age. *Geyer* gives a vivid impression of the forces at work in the early sixteenth century and an indication of their complexity: the power of the new faith, with its fanaticism as well as its sincerity and its longing for independence; the desire for justice, fighting both against outgrown feudal restrictions and against the imposition of an authoritarian legal system; the new power of capital; and the influence of other lands on German affairs. And although Hauptmann owed much, in his interpretation of history, to his nineteenth-century sources, he was in one respect at least, according to Weigand, ahead of them: he understood better than they the importance for Germany of intervention from without.[30] The question of French support for Geyer arises repeatedly in the play until he finally answers it in words which may well have more weight for a reader of the mid-twentieth century than for one of a generation ago: "Wahr ist's, der Wind wehete stark von West. Sollten wir aber nit unsere Segel spannen, wo wir gen Osten wollen schiffen, allein weil der Wind von Frankreich wehet? . . . Wer nach den neuentdeckten Inseln fahren will, nutzet die Winde, wo sie wehen. Er kann mitnichten immer gradaus schiffen, nur dass er sich selbst Glauben hält und dem Ziele treu bleibe." As a record of the complex and far-reaching nature of historical cause and effect, German drama has nothing to place beside Hauptmann's play: not, certainly, Schiller's *Tell*, with its plain issues and stylized, idealized *Volk*; not Hebbel's portrayal of kings and governors and the devastation wrought among them by the ideal in its course through historical reality; and not the selected and argumentative realism of Brecht. Goethe's *Götz* comes closest perhaps, and not merely because the two authors are dealing with the same period but

[29]*Gerhart Hauptmanns Dramen*, III, p. 47.
[30]"Auf den Spuren von Hauptmanns Florian Geyer," p. 814.

because Goethe, like Hauptmann, was working, though in a far more naïve and spontaneous manner, directly from contemporary documents. And the only English equivalent is Shaw's *St. Joan*.

Not that *Florian Geyer*, although it is less polemical than a Brecht work, let us say *Mutter Courage*, is without its message. It is a plea for unity among Germans, and it is also, by implication, a plea for democratic government, for it presents national and social issues as affecting all classes and as the concern of all people, precisely as they are presented in *Die Weber* and in Hauptmann's plays about the life of his own era. In view of the power of the play and the force of these arguments it seems strange that audiences who applauded Hauptmann's discussion of social or political problems in the works about contemporary life— problems which more often than not reflected no credit on the government—rejected *Florian Geyer*. When it was acted for the first time on January 4, 1896, it failed completely; one typical reviewer termed it "eine hohle Puppenkomödie."[31] It continued to fail until after the First World War. German audiences, it is true, had not experienced until then the mass civilian suffering brought on by war which forms so great a part of the tragedy of *Geyer*. But the failure seems due also to the curious ambivalence of the average patriotic mind, which will sometimes accept criticism on domestic issues but invariably resents it on the level of national, historical affairs. In the 1890's the historical sense of the nation was responding to the resounding drama of Ernst von Wildenbruch; the same Berlin audience that rejected *Florian Geyer* gathered again, three weeks later, and welcomed Wildenbruch's *König Heinrich* with such applause that the play was repeated one hundred times in the next five months. And Wildenbruch, recording the struggles of Henry IV, pitted Emperor magnificently against Pope, and pictured his hero as a ravaged Titan and a radical idealist who, having sought God in His representative on earth and failed to find Him, resigns himself

---

[31]Albert Scholz, "Zur Bühnengeschichte von Hauptmanns 'Tragödie des Bauernkrieges,'" *Monatshefte für deutschen Unterricht*, Jan. 1943, p. 16.

to the maintenance of order and of his own lofty position by power politics. True, peasants and townsmen are introduced, but as the Emperor's devoted children, eager to offer him awe-inspiring sums of money in return for protection. *König Heinrich*, in a word, glorifies and justifies the policies of Bismarck and of Wilhelm II, and its ideals were popular enough to make audiences unresponsive to a play which demonstrated—for all its dream of a "Volkskaiser"—that national affairs concern the nation, that the majority of people suffer in times of calamity, and that they have the power to make their own history.

There is, finally, one other way in which *Florian Geyer* marks a new phase in Hauptmann's work. *Einsame Menschen* leaves us with an ache of pity for people who have the best of intentions but who nevertheless destroy those whom they love. In *Die Weber* Hauptmann's sense of pain at the suffering he was por-traying was balanced by anger with those responsible and by hope of alleviation in the future. *Die Weber* was followed by two comedies and by *Hanneles Himmelfahrt*, a short play about an abused girl who is compensated for her unhappy life by the most beautiful dreams and visions of a better world that Haupt-mann can evoke. The early plays, considered as a group, are thus relatively optimistic. *Geyer* is sharper and harsher in its tragedy than *Einsame Menschen*; and although, like *Die Weber* it points to the need for decency and responsibility in social affairs, it leaves us in hopeless and uncomprehending despair. In the depths of the suffering it portrays it is closer to the works of Hauptmann's middle period—to *Rose Bernd* or *Michael Kramer*—than to his early plays. In its dark and uncompromising ending it is as bitter a tragedy as he ever wrote. Geyer, for his part, crashes to the floor rigid and with his eyes filled with hatred. And from such victors no generosity is to be expected. True, Lorenz von Hutten, cousin of the great Ulrich, picks up the fallen sword and reads the motto, "nulla crux, nulla corona." But the others in the room scream down to the courtyard that Geyer is dead, and the trumpets blare out in shrill rejoicing to mark the end of the national movement and the triumph of particularism and of the old ways.

IV. Middle-Class Plays

Einsame Menschen appeared in 1891. By the outbreak of the First World War Hauptmann had published fourteen plays in prose in addition to those just discussed.[1] Four of these—*Elga* (1896), *Und Pippa tanzt!* (1905), *Die Jungfern vom Bischofsberg* (1906), and *Griselda* (1908)—fall outside the sphere of his best work, either because he was writing too quickly or because he was not so much interested in portraying his characters as in investing them with some symbolic or poetic function, and may be dealt with briefly. *Die Jungfern* is a gentle and rather trite play about the loves of four sisters who live in a quasi-enchanted palace on the Elbe, an attempt at writing a romantic comedy of upper-middle-class life which fails for want of wit and invention; Hauptmann's failings along these lines will have to be considered at greater length in discussing *Kollege Crampton*. In *Elga* and *Griselda* he attempts to portray, not people, but a problem, in both cases that of the daemonic force of sex. The former is a superficial dramatization of Grillparzer's *Das Kloster bei Sendomir*. It was written quickly and in all probability, since Hauptmann had just been awarded the Grillparzer Prize, as a tribute to the Austrian dramatist. But the *Novelle* is a poor piece of work, a melodramatic tale of a middle-aged count who murders his young and beautiful wife together with her lover, and the play is still poorer. In Grillparzer's portrait of Elga we can discern the hand that later drew the enticing and abandoned heroine of *Die Jüdin von Toledo*. Hauptmann's seductress is petty and offensive and his count, with his devotion to passion and melancholy, dull and improbable. Matters are not much better in *Griselda*, a play about a young nobleman who first takes a robust peasant

[1]There is at least one prose play, *Christiane Lawrenz*, written between 1905 and 1907, which has never been published, possibly because, like the later *Herbert Engelmann*, it was "abgeschlossen," but not "beendet."

girl as his wife and then drives her from him by his pathological jealousy of their child. The transformation of the defiant, earthy Demeter into a gentle and gracious lady is strained, the conversation at court, intended to be witty and graceful, is artificial and sometimes vulgar, and the hero, though we glimpse the tragedy of his perversity, is neither invariably compelling nor humanly interesting. Strindberg or Wedekind might have handled such themes. Hauptmann's work lacks the radical quality which shows us one facet of life naked and unconditioned; it is fumbling and uncertain and at times pretentious.[2]

The question of *Und Pippa tanzt!* is more complicated. Most critics would agree that the works just described are not among Hauptmann's best; but many see in *Pippa* a poetic beauty and a mystic depth which make it the finest of the prose plays. And there are grounds for enchantment in the first act, in which Hauptmann is highly successful in evoking the atmosphere of a remote tavern, high in the wilderness of the Silesian mountains, on a cold winter night. Workers from a nearby glass factory play cards with an Italian adventurer who has a beautiful young daughter, and the director himself, bored and dreary and longing for city lights, offers the Italian a large sum if the girl will dance. But before the end of the act it is evident that the play is not going to remain on this level. A young apprentice named Michel enters, clearly in search of some unknown. Then an old worker named Huhn dances with Pippa—an inarticulate monster in pursuit of an elf. Finally the Italian is caught cheating, there is a sharp quarrel, he is shot, and in the confusion the old man manages to pick up the girl and vanish with her into the snow. The work is headed for fantasy and symbolism and it follows this course to the end. Michel rescues Pippa from the glass worker's hut and the two find shelter still higher up the mountain in the house of a wise old man named Wann, who, reading Michel's dreams, places in his hands a tiny model of a gondola and shows him a

[2]The impression that Hauptmann did not know what he was trying to do in *Griselda* is strengthened by two painfully "comic" scenes which Behl found among the paralipomena and persuaded the dramatist to include in the version of the play printed in the 1942 edition.

vision of Venice, the magic south from which Pippa has come. But Huhn follows them and Pippa, drawn to him in spite of her fear, dances once more until she falls dead, leaving her beloved, blinded and insane, to continue his search alone.

In the course of all this Hauptmann allows the human, psychological interest with which the play begins to become thinner and thinner and the plot to grow more and more unrealistic and arbitrary, without achieving the beauty of language, the symbolic heightening of the figures, or the deeper, ideal significance of action for which he was striving. This is not to deny that the play has its moments of beauty, even in the last acts, or that Pippa has a certain mysterious childlike grace and charm. But there is too great a gap between what we see and what Hauptmann wishes to represent. The director is clearly intended as a connoisseur, as the essence of a polished man of the world; he speaks the language of the bourgeois *Stammtisch*, of the Philistines who repelled Hauptmann when he portrayed them in *Michael Kramer* or in *Peter Brauer*. Old Huhn is interesting as a lumbering, half-crazed unemployed worker; he is inadequate as a "furchtbarer Waldgott," as Michel terms him at the end of the second act, or as "die kosmische Macht der blind-zeugenden Urnatur."[3] And Michel himself, the embodiment of German youth in search of beauty, "das Symbol für das," according to Hauptmann, "was in der deutschen Volksseele schlummert,"[4] is an impertinent and presumptuous nuisance. Even a symbolic or mystical work, moreover, must have a coherence of its own kind, and critics with the best will in the world have been unable to make sense, on any level, of the details of Hauptmann's characters and action. The play ends as a riddle, as—to quote Schlenther—a sterile allegory, "eine duftlose Allegorie."[5] The dramatist himself indicated the source of its weakness when, in the course of trying to explain what it meant, he let slip the phrase, "Ja, was schwebte mir nicht alles vor."[6] Like *Griselda*

[3]R. Mühler, *Dichtung der Krise* (Vienna, 1951), p. 320.
[4]Quoted by Paul Schlenther, *Gerhart Hauptmann, Leben und Werke* (6th ed., Berlin, 1912), p. 219.　　　　　　　　　　　　　　　　　　　[5]*Ibid.*
[6]Quoted by Wilhelm Heise, *Gerhart Hauptmanns Dramen* (Leipzig, n.d.), II, p. 59.

and to an even greater extent like the earlier verse play *Die versunkene Glocke*, *Pippa* is a completely eclectic work; it contains everything from contemporary jargon to reflections from the worlds of fairy-tale and legend, of Maeterlinck and Boecklin, of Plato and Goethe's *Wilhelm Meister*. Some of these worlds Hauptmann was never able to represent with success. He has neither succeeded in mixing them here, nor in giving strong and moving expression to any.

But there is no need to dwell long on such mishaps. When we survey Hauptmann's post-war work, we may well regret the time he lost in repeated attempts to conquer fields not his own, to write symbolic verse epics or romantic comedies or visionary novels. But the majority of the prose plays written before 1914 are so excellent that occasional lapses are quickly forgotten. In the ten works which we have now to discuss he cultivated the ground that he had broken so successfully in *Einsame Menschen* and *Die Weber*, the ground of realistic depiction of the lives of his own contemporaries. Not all the plays are of the highest calibre, but they are all distinctive and impressive, and in some of them he penetrated and recorded deep and complex areas of human experience with a sureness and an insight which surpass the expectations roused by even the finest of his early works.

In *Vor Sonnenaufgang*, *Das Friedensfest*, and *Einsame Menschen* Hauptmann progressed from his first experimental attempt at realistic drama to mastery. *Die Weber* and *Florian Geyer* are related as historical plays depicting large numbers of characters. There are, to the best of my understanding, no similarly compelling reasons for grouping the remainder of the prose dramas in one way rather than another. The two comedies are closer to some of the tragedies than to one another. A great deal, to be sure, can be learned from chronology. The plays written before *Geyer*, as we noted at the end of the preceding chapter, are varied in nature and are not, on the whole, deeply pessimistic. It was followed by four tragedies—*Fuhrmann Henschel*, *Michael*

Kramer, *Rose Bernd*, and *Gabriel Schillings Flucht*—which may be regarded as the great prose masterpieces of Hauptmann's maturity, his equivalents of *Hamlet* and *Othello*, *Macbeth* and *Lear*. And the last two plays, *Peter Brauer* and *Die Ratten*, are bitter portrayals of a degenerate society. But, again, works like *Fuhrmann Henschel* and *Michael Kramer*, whose heroes belong to different spheres of society, are very unlike, for the subject-matter is always at least as important in setting the tone of a Hauptmann play as the date of its composition.

The most natural division, in the last analysis, seems that suggested by the themes. In six of the plays Hauptmann continued what he had begun in *Bahnwärter Thiel* and in *Die Weber*, portraying, in the main, figures he had known among the people in his father's hotel, on his uncle's farm, or in Berlin and its suburbs. The remaining four, which are discussed in the present chapter—*Kollege Crampton*, *Michael Kramer*, *Gabriel Schillings Flucht* and *Peter Brauer*—seem to belong together as successors of *Einsame Menschen*. They deal in general with the theme of artist or pseudo-artist in conflict with society, represented by the hero's own family and by the middle-class world from which Hauptmann himself sprang. At least three of them, incidentally, were inspired by people whom he had first learned to know during his study at the Art Academy in Breslau.

I

The comedy *Kollege Crampton* was written very quickly in the last weeks of 1891, while Hauptmann was still at work on *Die Weber*. Early in November of that year he saw a performance of Molière's *L'Avare*, and the French play seems to have inspired him with the desire to portray a similarly unusual and original figure, a professor whom he had known at the Academy, named James Marshall. He may also have been indulging himself in a brief respite from his scenes of despair and starvation. The play, as we might expect from the speed with which it was written and from these mixed motives, is not a masterpiece. But it has masterly things in it, and it deserves attention, partly on its own merits and partly as Hauptmann's first attempt at comedy.

The hero, like James Marshall, is a professor, and the first two acts play in his elaborately artistic studio in the Academy. The action begins at something after eight o'clock in the morning. The professor's first class is waiting in an adjoining room for a model. He himself is asleep on a divan. His clothes, like his surroundings, are picturesque, but shabby—an indication that the splendour of his establishment stems from the past, and that the present is not without difficulties. Statues of a drunken faun and of a Silenus offer a mute explanation. The first conversation, which takes place between Crampton, his factotum Löffler, and the *Pedell*—that powerful guardian of buildings and property who still dominates German educational institutions—confirms our suspicions: the professor drinks incessantly, neglects his students, is in debt to the fullest extent of what is clearly a very considerable capacity for borrowing, and has been afraid, for good reason and not for the first time, to return home the night before. But the first act also brings some promise of a brighter future. A young and wealthy student named Max Strähler, who has been expelled from the academy for some minor misdemeanour, seeks solace from Crampton whom he imagines to be, like himself, a misunderstood individualist. Crampton is in precisely the proper mood to give him all the sympathy he desires. And in addition he meets the artist's youngest daughter, Gertrud, the only member of his family whose affection for her father has surmounted all obstacles, who has come to assure herself that Papa is still safe after his night's absence. Moreover a note from the director announces the impending visit of a duke whom Crampton claims as his patron.

In the second act, to be sure, the situation in the school takes a sharp turn for the worse. The duke comes and goes, unaware, apparently, that Crampton exists. Instead the *Pedell* arrives, bringing notice of his dismissal. Finally Gertrud reports that, the bailiff having sealed their house, her mother has departed to live with her own relatives, taking the other children with her. Crampton asks Max to buy his daughter a railway ticket and to send her after her mother. He himself vanishes. But by now Max is deeply interested in the professor and his family, and he undertakes a rescue operation of considerable magnitude. First, since Gertrud is unwilling to leave, he shelters her in his own home with his elder brother and sister. Then he buys up Crampton's scattered furnishings and fits up two studios, one for the older man, and one for himself. Finally, through the mediation of the devoted and anxious Löffler, he finds the ex-professor in a small private room at the rear of a tavern, holding court for a circle of amused students who come to play cards and drink with him, subsidized by a respectfully adoring waitress, and tolerated by the owner, who is using him as a species of side-show for the benefit of his impressionable, lower-middle-class, but solvent customers. With the offer of a commission to paint his sister's portrait Max tempts the artist to the new studio, produces Gertrud as his fiancée, and suggests that henceforth they work side by side. And Crampton, overwhelmed, declares himself ready to begin life anew: "Jetzt müssen wir schuften, Max, wie zwei Kulis!"

Kollege Crampton is, like the French comedy which prompted it, and to an extent which is unusual for Hauptmann, a one-man play. And there is no doubt that the professor is one of his most vivid figures, an incredible egotist, an absent-minded mono-maniac, and a master of rhetoric. His sudden shifts of mood make him appear at times like a chameleon; he scolds or praises, laments or rejoices as the need arises and in order to maintain his illusions about himself and to remain master of any situation. We see him at his best at the very beginning of the play when, making a pretence of starting to work, he rummages petulantly among his disordered tools, nodding, at the same time, for Löffler's benefit, at a certain empty bottle in a corner of the room, until finally his longing overcomes him and he bursts out impatiently, "Sind Sie taub, Löffler!" Löffler's explanation that there is no money to be had anywhere wearies and disgusts his artistic sensibilities. "Ach Löffler," he whines, "Sie ennuyieren mich schrecklich. Sie langweilen mich. Ich will malen und Sie langweilen mich. Statt dass Sie mir die Pinsel gewaschen hätten, langweilen Sie mich. . . . Man vernachlässigt mich. Nichts ist in Ordnung. Ein Staub, fussdick, puh. Pfeu Deuwel!" By this time it has occurred to him that one of the carpets needs cleaning, and the understanding Löffler at once departs with it and the bottle, only just escaping the *Pedell*, who is of the opinion that the professor's furnishings now belong to his creditors and ought not to be pawned.

The play has many more such scenes. Crampton is in his element as he invites his colleagues to join him in bringing about a revolution within the Academy—the stuffy, airless nest—from which he is on the point of being dismissed. He is incomparable as he lords it over the impressionable circle in the tavern or, thinking that Max has fitted up the new studio for himself, proclaiming that the room is as dark as a potato cellar and that the lady whose portrait he has been invited to paint has an unpleasant, oily skin—"ein grauer, fettiger Ton." Moreover, Hauptmann has created excellent pawns for him in some of the minor figures, in the stolid, idolatrous Löffler, in the smitten waitress, and in the slightly befuddled house painters who visit him in the tavern and who beg him, in the name of their related professions and of their common humanity, to empty a bottle with them, at their expense.

If we take the play this far it seems clear that Hauptmann has been highly successful both in his characterization and in maintaining the appreciative objectivity and the sense of proportion which are necessary to good high comedy. He is, as Schlenther has observed,[7] more intent than Molière on the psychological as opposed to the moral problems suggested by his hero, and there is no hint in the play that Gertrud's marriage may be endangered by her father's actions or that the unseen Frau Crampton deserves a better husband. What interests and amuses

[7] *Gerhart Hauptmann*, p. 95.

us is the contrast between reality and Crampton's illusions: the way in which his sense of his own superiority enables him to ride triumphant over all circumstances and to appear master of any situation. There is, of course, as in the case of Harpagon or of Falstaff, a tragic as well as a comic aspect to his character and his fate. We could conceivably weep rather than laugh at this spectacle of human folly, of so much energy directed to such vain and pitiful ends. But Hauptmann does not stress this tragic under-current. We understand Crampton, we admire him; we remain, on the whole, amused.

Unfortunately the comedy has characters who are less striking than the hero and who are seen from a different perspective. The trouble begins with Gertrud and the Strählers. Crampton's daughter is a sister of Ida Buchner, a nice young girl, devoted to her father, and borne along by the joy of a first healthy, happy love. Max is an idealized portrait of the young Hauptmann himself; Adolf, the elder brother, an idealized version of Haupt-mann's brother Georg; and the sister an idealized young widow, benevolent and tranquilly resigned to her fate. It is true that the beginning of the last act, where Max and Gertrud chase one another about the studio and discover that first kisses are a breath-taking substitute for moving furniture, is a fresh and delightful scene. It is also true that Hauptmann tried to achieve some degree of humour and complexity in his portraits of the brothers, particularly of Max, who is both an idealistic late adolescent— he cannot bear his brother's teasing, and he sees Crampton through the rose-coloured glasses of his love for Crampton's daughter—and a slightly spoiled young hothead with a superb disregard for the money he has never had to earn. "Ach, die paar Sachen," he says impatiently of the expensive objects from Crampton's studio which he has been buying, "die kümmern mich gar nicht." But idealization predominates. What Haupt-mann presents, in the main, is an upper-middle-class family, without problems, whose members have the grace to tolerate one another's foibles and money enough to protect their idyllic-ally self-sufficient existence; and even if they were credible they are not very interesting. Pleasant and good-natured people are agreeable enough as casual acquaintances in real life. They do not make a comedy.

A conventional love story, however, need not in itself prove to be a serious defect. If the courtship of Max and Gertrud did no more than provide an irrelevant setting for the main character —as irrelevant, by way of comparison, as the match-making of Molière—we might pass over it lightly. But Gertrud, we remember, loves her father, seeing in him, like Max, an extraordinary man broken by a philistine world, and Crampton loves his daughter. And with this the balance of the play is lost. If the points had been lightly touched, all might still have been well. It is not out of keeping with the character of Crampton that he should suffer in some measure because his family scorns him and that he should cherish the one member who helps him to maintain his illusions about himself. And it is a fine perception on Hauptmann's part that he does not want Gertrud near him in his disgrace and that he tries to prevent Max from even mentioning her name in the tavern room where he seems otherwise so completely master of all he surveys. But Hauptmann goes too far; he begins to portray Crampton as Max and Gertrud see him. The man who has been, until now, a veritable master of rhetoric becomes speechless with emotion as he thinks of his daughter. And his words, once his throat has cleared, are bitter or sentimental. Only his child, he says, his little girl, truly loves him and understands that he is the victim of adverse circumstances and of a hostile world, where all men of genius are crucified— "Da heisst es nur immer: kreuzige!" The light has changed suddenly and it remains changed, on the whole, throughout the last act, leaving us with a Crampton who, overcome at the unexpected goodness of the world and laughing through his tears, resolves to redeem himself and to work like a coolie—an over-hopeful and sentimental conclusion which sends our eyes, somewhat ruefully, in the direction of the corner to see whether Max has not also succeeded in rescuing the wine bottle. A play which begins as a comedy of character has become a semi-serious study of a misunderstood artist with a happy ending. It is an interesting comment on the uncertainty of Hauptmann's handling of his material that it is impossible to decide, from the evidence given, whether Crampton has ever painted a really good picture or not.

Some of this uncertainty may well be attributed to the speed with which the play was written. Hauptmann was clearly under the sway of the character of his hero, but he did not give himself time to realize it more than imperfectly in an action or a milieu; and although action is often of secondary importance in his works, character and background are so closely related that he could not neglect the one without damaging the other. *Crampton* was also his first attempt at comedy, and *Vor Sonnenaufgang* had shown a like uncertainty. Yet the real root of the trouble lies elsewhere. Hauptmann did his best work, in both tragedy and comedy, in the portrayal of people and of the world which nourished them and gave them being. But he was surer of himself in tragedy. Comedy proved, all too often, not a channel through which he could express his deepest insight, but a relaxation. True, discussing *Die Weber* with Max Baginski, he claimed that he was by nature inclined to phantasy and to midsummer-night dreams, but that a hard inner pressure drove him to portray the distress of his fellow-man.[8] But if he did not write his tragedies easily, his comedies are lacking in conviction and in the wit, grace, and invention which can give even escapist art a certain validity. Once or twice, in *Der Biberpelz* or in parts of the novel *Die Insel der Grossen Mutter*, he succeeded in producing lighter works of high calibre. But *Kollege Crampton*, with its fine leading character resident in a rather banal world of wishful thinking, is indicative of what was to come, whether he was writing, as in *Die Jungfern vom Bischofsberg*, in prose and about his own day, or, as in *Ulrich von Lichtenstein*, in verse and about the past.

[8]Schlenther, *Gerhart Hauptmann*, p. 153.

II

Crampton was produced early in 1892. The fanciful verse play *Die versunkene Glocke*, which appeared in 1896, showed that Hauptmann had not forgotten the "problems" of artists. But not until 1900, in *Michael Kramer*, did he turn again to a direct portrayal in prose of the upper bourgeois world of the artist-intelligentsia. The play was written under the stress of death, for Hauptmann had lost his father in 1898 and in the following year both his oldest brother and his artist friend Hugo Ernst Schmidt, to whom it is dedicated. Not that he tried, at once, to record the fate of his friend, who died under tragic circumstances—he was not to do that until six years later, in *Gabriel Schillings Flucht*.[9] But Schmidt had been much maligned in the last years of his life, and Hauptmann portrayed a similarly misunderstood individual in the younger of the two heroes of *Kramer*. The prototypes for his main figures here were a Professor Bräuer, a worthy and industrious man under whom Schmidt had worked at the Academy, and a somewhat deformed student named Litt whom Hauptmann had met first in Breslau and later in Rome. Initially he disliked Litt intensely, he tells us in his autobiography, and with good reason; later he came to understand him better. In the play the two are father and son, Michael and Arnold Kramer, and the father too has misshapen shoulders.

Einsame Menschen is a fine and sensitive and deeply experienced work. But it is a long step even from the best of Hauptmann's early plays to *Michael Kramer*. For whereas the characters of the former are perhaps obviously tragic—though Hauptmann's treatment is not obvious—the figures of *Kramer* are not; indeed, other eyes might have seen in at least one of them only degeneration and perversion. Hauptmann does not mask or glorify degeneration, but he pierces it. Approaching his material carefully, he uses the experience and the comments and the interpretations of secondary characters to lead us through mean and grotesque incidents to moments of the purest human grief and of great

[9]Hans von Hülsen, however, in his *Gerhart Hauptmann* (Leipzig, 1927), p. 109, has suggested that Lachmann is a first study of Schmidt.

beauty. *Kramer* is a work in which a study of intense suffering
is succeeded by a deep sense of relief that the struggle is over
and that the misunderstandings and distortions of life have
been overcome by death. And the best way of appreciating
this is to follow in some detail the author's own line of explanation from act to act.

We see evidence of Hauptmann's slow and careful approach
to his central problems in the fact that the two main characters
do not appear until the action is well begun—the son at the end
of the first act, the father at the beginning of the second, a re-
tardation without parallel in the rest of his work. But the play
begins with a scene, an amazing miniature exposition, that
leads the spectator deep into the situation. Michaline, the daughter
of the house, unmarried, no longer young, and an art teacher,
sits reading beside the uncleared breakfast table on which the
lamp is still burning. Presently her mother comes in and is
established at once by her querulous interrogations as a nervous,
nagging woman, who is more than usually upset this morning.
"Bist du noch immer da, Michaline?" she demands, "Na, wenn
du nur nichts versäumst. . . . Denn wirklich, es bleibt so wie
so genug Sorge übrig. . . ." Then her anxiety crystallizes in
the question, "Hat Papa nicht noch etwas gesagt, als er fortging?"

MICHALINE: Nein!
FRAU KRAMER: Das ist immer das Schlimmste, wenn er nichts sagt.
MICHALINE: Ja, richtig! Das hätt' ich beinah vergessen. Arnold soll um
Punkt elf Uhr bei ihm im Atelier sein.
FRAU KRAMER: Ach je ja! Du mein Gott, du, du!

Arnold, it becomes evident, has come in very late the night before,
and for his mother the situation is desperate; whatever her
husband says or does not say, all hope is lost and all possibilities
are equally bad. Michaline's replies have been until now laconic,
but when the mother, with an animal-like devotion to her son,
complains about the father's severity, she defends him as strict
but not unjust. The argument is clearly one of the habitual
affairs already familiar from *Das Friedensfest* and from *Einsame
Menschen*. It reveals the basis of the conflict, for we learn in

the course of it that Arnold is a sickly, shiftless, and dissolute boy who has once gone so far as to forge his father's signature. But it does still more; it establishes the atmosphere of parental disagreement and of nagging and anxiety on the mother's side which cannot but have an injurious effect on the sick son. Even Michaline, who speaks at first with humour and self-control, is at last impelled to protest: "Ach, Mutter, wenn ich das alles so höre, da wird mir immer so eng! . . . So eng und beklommen. . . ."

Then come visitors, a former pupil of Kramer named Lachmann, who is now working in Berlin, and his wife. Through their visit Hauptmann accomplishes another of his indirect revelations. Lachmann is a man who can talk to Michaline on her own terms, as Anna and Johannes can talk, and who shares her admiration for her father and her feeling that Kramer's high seriousness is above petty bourgeois life. His wife is a younger, more vulgar Frau Kramer. We never see the parents of Arnold and Michaline together, but we have a vivid picture of the worst aspects of their relationship in the constant sparring between Lachman and his wife, until she finally departs to the more congenial atmosphere of a *Konditorei*. Yet even with all this by way of preparation, Arnold, who comes in just as Lachmann and Michaline are leaving for the studio, is hardly a figure who engages our sympathy. His first words are a mocking repetition of his sister's "Adieu, Mama, wir gehen jetzt fort." Then he shuffles to a mirror to examine his blotched skin. His mother questions him anxiously. He responds by staring at her, over his glasses, with his crooked shoulders raised, and asks, "Seh' ich nicht aus wie'n Marabu?" Inevitably she reproaches him and inevitably his answers appear to her still further flippant evasions. Only when she tries to find out whether he is involved with a woman—she thinks of a prostitute—does she provoke a small, weary flame of anger and despair. There is something wrong, he admits; he feels himself branded, he feels that the members of his family are strangers to him. But why make a fuss—"Soll ich deswegen etwa Alarm schlagen?" If he is driven too far, he will find a way out.

The second act plays in Kramer's studio and its beginning is in strongest contrast to the end of the first. The studio is a severe room with windows facing a stately avenue of high poplars which reminds Lachmann of a temple; and Kramer, scrupulously dressed, is preaching to his erstwhile student his creed of duty, hard work, and the seriousness of life and art. For the younger man, who has been reduced to doing hack writing in order to maintain his wife and son, has come to him in a dejected mood. Twice the sermon takes on a note of rapture: once when Kramer describes how, when Arnold was finally born after fourteen years of waiting, he had lifted the baby in his arms and offered him to God, praying that his son would be granted the genius denied him; and again when Lachmann asks him about the portrait of Christ on which he is known to be working, but which no one has seen. Their conversation is terminated by the arrival of a girl whom Kramer takes to be a model, and who seems naïvely offended at the suggestion without, at first, offering any alternative explanation. Then she lets fall the name Arnold, and from her we learn, for the first time, something of the boy's life away from home. The situation she describes is difficult and complicated rather than depraved. She is Liese Bänsch, the daughter of a restaurant owner, a foolish and affected girl, but troubled and not unkind. Arnold, it seems, embarrasses her by sitting night after night in her father's establishment, staring at her or drawing caricatures which puzzle and alarm her. Moreover, he has become the butt of a typical *Stammtisch*, a group of successful young men who jeer loudly at his infatuation, his appearance, and his lack of money. Once again there is an interruption. Arnold has come, as bidden. The girl is smuggled out. Kramer, though not unmoved by the tale, fails to see that the problems indicated are not of the kind that can be solved by a frank and manly confession. He attempts to be tolerant, he appeals to his son for honesty, he resolves to "do better" himself. And he crowns his platitudes with the bitterly ironical "Gesunder Körper, gesunder Geist; gesundes Leben, gesunde Kunst." Arnold takes refuge in fiction, in a tale so patently untrue that the father's assumed patience gives way to anger and rejection:

"Du bist nicht mein Sohn! Du kannst nicht mein Sohn sein!" The scene ends in utter frustration on both sides.

The third act takes us to the Bänsch restaurant. It is early in the evening and Arnold, alone with Liese, is wooing her in his fashion. He is pale, and still on the defensive, but he is less tense and cramped than with his parents, and we see for the first time through the twisted exterior into his heart, to his suffering and his desire for affection. His attempts to impress Liese by her own standards; his boasting of the money his pictures have brought him, for example, are so naïve that he appears a child. And to her alone he can make the simple confession that he suffers from his deformity: "Vielleicht bin ich auch wirklich lächerlich. Ich meine äusserlich, innerlich nicht. Denn wenn Sie mich innerlich könnten betrachten, da brenn' ich die Kerls von der Erde weg." Liese is touched, as she might be with a small boy who has bumped his knee, but uncomprehending. Her thoughts are mainly on the impending arrival of the "feucht-fröhliche Gesellschaft." And with this the nightly ordeal begins. We have just a glimpse of the gentlemen as they pass through on their way to their table in the adjoining room, whither Arnold follows them. Only one, who amuses himself by allowing Liese to call him her fiancé, remains for a moment to arrange with her for a type of rendezvous which is not quite orthodox bourgeois practice. The baiting takes place for the most part off stage. But we are kept constantly aware of it. And then the situation is made more complicated by the arrival of Michaline, who is followed after a short interval by Lachmann.

The two are preoccupied with one another, for, though they do not say so directly, they have been in love. But when Lachmann speaks of the spring he first came to Breslau, Michaline corrects him quietly, "Es war im Herbst." And in the last act, *en passant*, Hauptmann completes the story that has been told virtually without words. He, like Arnold, Lachmann confesses, had once desired such a girl as Liese, and his wish had unfortunately been granted: "und ich—dir brauch' ich's ja nicht zu verhehlen—war dadurch nachher viel schlimmer dran." Yet their talk is anything but irrelevant to the action proceeding in the room beyond. Lachmann is excited because he has been permitted, as a special favour, to see the Christ picture. And his attempts to describe what he has seen and to formulate his own difficulties are in the nature of an unconscious choric comment on the problems of the father and son. The power of illusion, he claims, thinking of his own fate, a man's faith in his own imagination, is lost if he is forced to live and breathe in the wrong air—"Ob du willst oder nicht, du musst sie einatmen . . ."— and he is struck by the contrast between the fog of beer and joviality now around him and Kramer's figure of Christ with its crown of thorns, "das feierlich-ruhige Christusbild! . . . mit seiner erhabenen Ruhe und Reinheit." And yet, though he does not manage to express his impressions clearly, he feels also that the perfect peace and purity for which Kramer is striving have not yet been attained. He values the picture no less because of that: "Das grosse Misslingen kann mehr bedeuten—am Allergrössten tritt es hervor—kann stärker ergreifen und höher hinaufführen, ins Ungeheure tiefer hinein, als je das beste Gelingen vermag." But he is puzzled. He does not yet know enough about the Kramers to realize how their difficulties are reflected in their painting. The spectator, however, who knows that Arnold is in the next room, and who has just learned, in addition, that the boy's tormented nights usually end in a brothel, is able to perceive the full meaning of Hauptmann's direct and natural symbols. Arnold sees the world as the world sees him— in caricature. And Kramer's picture will never become what he desires it to be until he understands his son, until he overcomes his disappointment that the boy has not become the simple and pious servant of God, the devout genius that he prayed for at his birth.

In the meantime the talk and the laughter in the next room have been growing louder and louder and Michaline, though she does not understand why, becomes increasingly apprehensive. Liese explains that the gentlemen are teasing a young man by making love to her before his eyes. Once two of them appear,

flushed and arrogant, to hasten a fresh supply of wine, and provoke Lachmann to the scathing "Und nähmst du Flügel der
Morgenröte, so entgehst du doch dieser Sorte nicht." Finally
Liese finds herself well advised to retreat once and for all from
the attentions of her drunken "fiancé." And a moment later
his voice is heard, teasing Arnold: "Geniert Sie das, wenn ich
meiner Braut einen Kuss gebe? . . . Kann ich nicht hier mein
Strumpfband zeigen? . . . Meinen Sie, dass ich das nicht darf?
Ich trage Damenstrumpfbänder, basta! Und wenn es nicht
meins ist . . . dann ist es am Ende gar Lieschens gewesen." Then
suddenly there are calls for the police and Arnold runs through
the room, with his tormentors in pursuit. He has, we gather,
drawn a revolver and placed it beside his plate. Michaline, for
all her uneasiness, has not expected this, and two or three minutes
pass before she realizes that the young man is her brother and
that she must follow him at once.

The final act, which plays two days later in Kramer's studio,
is in the nature of an epilogue. Michaline's search has failed. The
body of her brother lies in the background, dragged from the
Elbe. She herself appears only briefly, in the course of the dreary
round of errands which attend civilized burial of the dead.
Liese, tearful and more bewildered than ever, brings a wreath.
Lachmann arrives to watch with Kramer. But in the main the
act is elucidation and clarification. "Er gab sich wer weiss wie
alt und blasiert," Michaline realizes, "und war noch, wenn man
ihn kannte wie ich, im Grunde ganz unerfahren und kindisch."
Lachmann speaks of the letter that Arnold had written before
drowning himself, of his confession that life had become unendurable: "er ertrage das Leben nicht. Er sei dem Leben nun mal
nicht gewachsen." And Kramer, shaken and exalted, expresses
his understanding in a long series of virtual monologues. He
knows now that Arnold had struggled and that because of that
he can never be lost. He speaks of the sketches in the dead boy's
note-book which, in all their distortion, bear witness to his
gifts, and he speaks of the beauty that shines in his face now that
the need for distortion is over. He has been making drawings

of his son and in them, we may assume, he has achieved the vision of peace and purity hitherto denied his most serious and painful efforts. For the suffering that has killed Arnold now seems to him one with the suffering of Beethoven and of Christ. "Was jetzt auf seinem Gesichte liegt," he says, "das alles, Lachmann, hat in ihm gelegen. Das fühlt' ich, das wusst' ich, das kannt' ich in ihm und konnte ihn doch nicht heben, den Schatz." In the face of this revelation he is filled with a sense of the tenderness of death. "Die Liebe, sagt man, ist stark wie der Tod. Aber kehren Se getrost den Satz mal um: Der Tod ist auch mild wie die Liebe, Lachmann. . . . Der Tod ist die mildeste Form des Lebens: der ewigen Liebe Meisterstück." And although critics have sometimes been puzzled by the last speeches, it is not strange that Kramer's exaltation and his sense of the miracle just enacted sweep him, in the end, into a kind of choric ode on the wonder of existence and on the dauntless spirit of man. The play closes with a paean of praise to those who pursue through the streets the eternal ringing of unseen bells, to men, who tiny and isolated in an infinite universe, raise their voices like Beethoven in shouts of jubilation to the unknown, to the mystery which, transcending the explanations of church and of priest, is the essence of God.

In some ways *Kramer* is as simple and concentrated, in others as complex and refined a play as Hauptmann ever wrote. It is virtually plotless. There is not even an incident, an arrival, as in the earlier plays, to precipitate disaster. The coming of Lachmann has no direct bearing on Arnold's death, just as the presence of Michaline in the restaurant has nothing to do with plot. Liese, who might be expected to involve the play in some kind of a story, is the merest focus of Arnold's desire for life; it never occurs to us to ask whether she will listen to him or not. Nor are the life histories that seemed necessary to explain Wilhelm Scholz or Johannes Vockerat needed here. When we have seen Arnold with his parents and with the stridently successful men of the world we have seen all—the last stage, namely, of a situation that has always been fundamentally the same. And Hauptmann does not even give us his usual detailed and extensive recording of the milieu. His picture of the world is limited to Frau Kramer, understudied by Frau Lachmann, to Liese and to the gentlemen of the *Stammtisch*, whom he does not trouble to differentiate. This is not to say that what we see is insufficient or lacking in force. Even the patient Michaline is repulsed by her mother's mournful longing for a cheerful home—"einen gemütlichen Haushalt"—and all that appertains thereto; no youthful optimism softens the portraits of the men in the restaurant; and in none of the plays do we find a more striking enunciation of the difficulties of coping with such a world than Lachmann's, "Was leben will, braucht seine Atmosphäre. Das ist im Geistigen ebenso. Ich bin in die falsche hineingedrückt. Ob du willst oder nicht, du musst sie einatmen. Und siehst du, da wirst du selber erstickt." But the story and the environment are reduced to their essentials, and the same is true, in a sense, of the conflict. There is little enough that Hauptmann can portray directly. But the brief scenes between Kramer and Arnold and between Arnold and the Philistines are so sharp and telling that they could only be weakened by extension or repetition.

Yet the problems that Hauptmann had to portray are not simple, as his careful approach to his main characters indicates, and the time he devotes to comment and meditation and to presenting variations on his theme. The tragedy is concerned, in the first analysis, with the conflict between the gifted individual and the all too usual world, and then with the isolation of individual from individual. Indeed, if Hauptmann had not already called one play *Einsame Menschen* he might, appropriately, have used this title here, for the loneliness that marks the characters of the earlier work is heightened in *Kramer* and shown in its most varied aspects. Isolation and renunciation form the common lot of Kramer and Arnold, Lachmann and Michaline. Of the four it is Arnold who is the most rebellious and who suffers most acutely; he feels himself estranged from every living being except perhaps Liese, and in her presence he is treated as a clown.

Lachmann resembles him in his unwillingness to accept the situation in which he finds himself. But Lachmann's whole existence
is pitched at a lower key than that of the Kramers. He will
remain a fretful and gently frustrated man all his life, without
the courage to discard his wife or the heroism to accept and
ignore her. Kramer, on the other hand, has made a virtue of
necessity and glorifies his seclusion. The greatest works, he asserts,
are created when the artist is alone, through the hours and the
days and the years, "allein mit seinem Leiden und seinem Gott."
And Michaline, who has lost Lachmann, and who has desired
in vain the love Kramer has lavished on his son, has achieved
her father's resignation, but quietly and without exaltation;
and it is she who speaks some of the wisest words of the play,
asserting that one person must not interfere with another, even
when he is on a wrong path, because the deepest experiences
cannot be communicated: "Erfahrung ist eben nicht mitteilbar,
wenigstens nicht im tieferen Sinn." It is this common experience,
in all its individual variations, which makes the third act, with
its interplay of action and reflection, so complex and moving,
and which gives the play as a whole the shaded depth and the
resonance that mark Hauptmann's mature works.

The heart of the tragedy, however, lies in the relations between
the father and son, which form a special facet of the general
theme. Conflicts between generations and the realization of the
isolation of one generation from another are frequent both in
Hauptmann's plays and in those of his contemporaries. But the
perception here seems to be unique and Hauptmann has traced
the problem delicately and with great care. What he sees is that
the father has sublimated the suffering inflicted upon him by his
deformity, by his lack of genius, and finally by his disappointment
in his son, and made of it a cross which he tries, at long last with
success, to bear joyfully. But Arnold has inherited his misshapen
body from his father. He reacts, therefore, against his father's
method of coping with his difficulties and tries, not to rise above
the world, but to pit himself against it, to wrest recognition from

triumphantly invulnerable mediocrity until he can save his sense
of his own value only by death. Rilke has given us a fine analysis
of Arnold's position:

Endlich bettelt er sich zu dem Leben hin, indem er sich an die Kellnerin Liese
hält, von der er sich sagen lassen muss, dass er nichts ist, nichts hat, nichts
vorstellt, nichts wird. . . . Und doch irgendwo ist er noch etwas, irgendwo
ist etwas Stolzes, Stilles, das nie gebettelt hat, das, unberührt von aller Demüti-
gung, da ist, nicht wächst, sich nicht entwickelt, aber auch nicht verloren geht.
Aber es hat sich schon so weit zurückgezogen in sein Unbewusstes, dass
er nicht davon reden kann und dass er lügen und prahlen muss und das, was
er besitzt und was er nicht nennen kann, übersetzen muss in andere Besitze,
welche die Menschen begreifen würden.[10]

Arnold is tied to his father by blood, by lack of money, and by
the father's strong desire to shape him in his own image. But
the idealism which sustains the older Kramer, in a form that
verges at times on the platitudinous, repels the son and drives
him to conceal his suffering, first from his father and then from
the rest of the world. And as the father becomes more severe
in his grief, Arnold's struggles become ever more desperate and
uncontrolled until only death can untie the knot and effect a
reconciliation.

It comes as something of a shock to the reader, at the end
of the play, to recall that the starting-point for all these difficulties
is a simple physical deformity, a personal and restricted problem
in comparison with those that Hauptmann had dealt with in the
early plays. We should lose infinitely had he sought such private
themes as the basis of all his mature works; but it should be
stressed once again that, when such a problem did impress itself
upon him, he did not dwell upon its negative and esoteric aspects,
but on those which are positive and comprehensible to any
sensitive human being. An obvious point of comparison is
Thomas Mann's *Der kleine Herr Friedemann*, which appeared in
1897, three years before *Kramer*. Not for a moment do we find
Hauptmann regarding the problems besetting the deformed with
the ironic reserve of Mann. For the latter the passion of his hero
for the seductive red-blond Frau von Rinnlingen is at once

[10]*Briefe und Tagebücher aus der Frühzeit* (Leipzig, 1931), p. 414.

fascinating and ludicrous, and Herr Friedemann's fastidious dress
and refined artistic sensibilities are curious, at most pathetic, and
above all superfluous and extraneous to the main course of man's
existence. Hauptmann sees in the struggles of the Kramers basic
human love and dignity, and in their suffering and striving the
suffering and striving that make man man. *Friedemann* to be sure,
is one of Mann's earliest *Novellen*. But a juxtaposition of the
two works is only a fragment of the evidence that could be
gathered to show that Hauptmann's humanism, though it did
not put forth the brilliant intellectual blossoms that distinguish
the work of his North-German contemporary, has deeper roots.

There remains the question of the last act. There are critics
who are puzzled to find an apparently realistic play, in which
Hauptmann seems, as in earlier works, to be analysing human
life according to biology, pathology, and economics, ending in a
way which suggests that he has become, from one act to the next,
an irrationalist and a mystic; in consequence, they find the play
confused and unfinished and the ending undramatic and unsatis-
factory.[11] Others see in the last act an evidence of the author's
basic mysticism, of his "unbedingte Hingabe an das Mysterium,"
and value it all the more highly on this account.[12] Somewhere
between the two sets of opinions lies the truth. Few readers
would claim today that the first acts are mere expostulations of
scientific determinism. But it needs to be made equally clear that
the monologues of the last act are not synonymous with the
visionary idealism of *Till Eulenspiegel* or *Der grosse Traum*
because—and for Hauptmann this is a very important because—
they are psychologically based. The author is not trying to
speak directly, as he does in the later works, in the tones of a
seer or a prophet. He is absorbed in his characters, in the spectacle
of two men, both gifted, facing the same problems, reacting
differently and clashing bitterly in their different reactions. We
are prepared for the rhapsody of the last act by what we hear
and see of Kramer in the first three, and particularly by his

[11]F. Endres, *Gerhart Hauptmann* (Lübeck, 1932), p. 32, and E. Sulger-Gebing, *Gerhart Hauptmann* (Berlin, 1922), p. 72.
[12]C. F. W. Behl, *Wege zu Gerhart Hauptmann* (Goslar, 1948), p. 26.

conversation with Lachmann in the second. "Mysticism," if we wish to use the term for Kramer's outburst of thankfulness and wonder, is the natural reaction of such a man to what has just transpired, the heightening and intensification of an attitude that he has been developing all his life. The play does not simply jump from one plane to another; it associates the comprehensible and the incomprehensible, reality and a search for the meaning of reality, through the medium of its leading figure.

This is not to say that Hauptmann is working, in *Kramer*, on precisely the same level as in the early plays. The differences, as has already been argued, are great. Not only has his insight increased, and his ability to present delicate and difficult problems, but he has become more interested in portraying purely spiritual facets of human experience. Kramer's emotions are not, to be sure, more profound than those of a Thiel or a Käthe Vockerat, but they are more highly developed, more cultivated, and more articulate; and Hauptmann allows the last act of the play to become an elegiac monologue in order to give him an opportunity to express them. And the last act also—though it is not necessary to know this for a full appreciation of the play—bears the imprint of the author's immediate personal experience. In *Das Buch der Leidenschaft* he speaks of the lonely weeks spent in the Silesian village of Agnetendorf, during which *Kramer* was written. He was having a new house built, he writes, he stood on the threshold of a new life,[13] and the problems of the past and the future formed an incessant dialogue in his mind, which was quietened only by the reading of Plato. His own release became Kramer's; and Plato must have helped him to find the words through which Kramer tries to formulate his realization that the genius—the "ideal"—of his son has emerged clearly in death from the distortions of the flesh and of the world around him. All in all the tragedy marks a shift in stress in Hauptmann's works towards a type of experience which is less directly conditioned by environmental factors than in his early plays, and

[13]The house was intended for Margarete Marschalk, who later became his second wife, and for their child.

from analysis towards a more prolonged expression of emotional reactions. In these ways it approaches, like *Florian Geyer*, his poetic drama. But both *Kramer* and *Geyer* are extensions of the ground broken earlier. Both grow, to use Schlenther's term, from the "reallest reality"—"aus dem realsten Leben."[14]

III

Michael Kramer was dedicated to the memory of Hugo Ernst Schmidt. *Gabriel Schillings Flucht*, which was written in 1905 and 1906, depicts the actual fate of Hauptmann's friend, whose death continued to afflict him so that he would not allow the tragedy to be performed until 1912 and then only before a selected audience in the cultivated setting of the Goethe Theatre in Lauchstädt. The two plays, as we should expect, are closely related in many ways: they have the same refinement and intensity and the same poetic quality, their characters have similar interests and problems, and both contain a great deal of speculation about the meaning of life and about the presence of mysterious irrational forces in the universe. Above all, when we read Schilling's story, we understand the grief and anger that fire both plays, and the desire of the dramatist to vindicate men who have been slandered and tormented by a callous and unseeing world. "Wes Seele blind ist," he wrote much later, "den besucht das Glück—wes Seele auch nur blinzelt in die Welt, besucht das Schaudern!"[15]

Yet for all these general resemblances, *Kramer* and *Schilling* are as distinct from one another as, let us say, Shakespeare's *Twelfth Night* and *As You Like It* or Shaw's *Candida* and *The Devil's Disciple*, and must be discussed as separate entities to be appreciated. Nor does it give an adequate interpretation of *Schilling* to regard it, because both revolve around similarly constituted triangles, mainly as an intensification of *Einsame Menschen*. Such comparisons are valuable in establishing the

[14]*Gerhart Hauptmann*, p. 188.
[15]*Iphigenie in Aulis* (Berlin, 1944), Act II.

general field within which Hauptmann works, but aside from this, the main lesson that they have to teach is that his experience of individual lives triumphs over any similarity of plot or of problem or even of milieu, that with him, once again, every play is a new play. Its characters alone would make *Schilling* unique. But it is distinguished also by the mood and atmosphere which Hauptmann evokes by the out-of-door setting of three of its five acts. In some of his novels and *Novellen*—in *Thiel* or *Quint* or *Der Ketzer von Soana*—he has given us accounts of the relations between man and nature which are as moving and powerful as those that we find in the contemporary and in many ways related work of Thomas Hardy. *Schilling* is not the only Hauptmann play in which nature plays a role. But in none of his works does it make a more important contribution then here. It has been noted more than once that he was concerned to win for the drama aspects of life that had formerly been considered the province of the epic. There is no need to labour the point that, in linking man to the natural environment, he was again widening the bounds of the dramatic.

The story of Schilling, unlike that of Kramer, is presented in a straightforward and relatively orthodox way, and the action may be summarized briefly. The play takes place on the secluded Baltic island of Fischmeisters Oye—a pseudonym for Hiddensee[16] —in the early autumn days of a year "around 1900." Here the sculptor Ottfried Mäurer and his beloved, a young violinist named Lucie Heil, are enjoying their normal yearly recreation from the over-civilized concert and studio life of Berlin. They are joined, at Mäurer's invitation, by the painter Gabriel Schilling, who has wrenched himself free from the toils of a nagging wife and a nymphomaniacal mistress in a final attempt to regain his independence and, with it, the physical and moral strength to return to his long-neglected work. For a short time there seems to be some hope. There is, indeed, no visible improvement in

---

[16]A small island near Rügen to which Hauptmann was first taken by Hugo Ernst Schmidt. He went there again, for the first time after Schmidt's death, in 1906, and the island later became a permanent summer home. In 1946 he was buried there.

Schilling's health—he remains at a fever-pitch throughout. But the mood of reckless and abandoned despair in which he arrives gives way, after a few days on the island, to a kind of equally reckless defiance, a credulous-incredulous daring of the impossible. He agrees to spend the coming months with Mäurer and Lucie in Greece, and his friends believe that, if he is left alone with them, they may yet witness the regeneration they desire. But he is not to be left alone. By the end of the second act Hanna Elias, his mistress, has found him out. At the end of the third, again under her sway and exhausted by the struggle, he collapses. Then the doctor, an old friend whom Mäurer has summoned from Berlin, brings with him Schilling's wife, Eveline, and the two women, in their struggle for the possession of the sick man, give way to such degraded and envenomed jealousy that Schilling can endure life no longer. With a strength born of repugnance and despair he slips past his friends and seeks the cleansing obliteration of the stormy sea from which, in the last moments of the play, we see the fishermen bringing back his body.

Thus, in outline, the main action. Parallel to it and in contrast there runs a sub-plot involving Mäurer, Lucie, and Fräulein Majakin, an astonishingly precocious seventeen-year-old Russian girl who has come to the island with her countrywoman Hanna. The love between Mäurer and Lucie, though both prefer not to risk their personal independence by a formal marriage, is deep and of long standing. And there is some danger that Fräulein Majakin, who intrigues Mäurer, may cause a rift in this relationship. But here the good sense of the three persons concerned prevails, and the former balance, never very seriously threatened, is restored by the end of the play.

Hauptmann's main concern, then, is to portray the last stage in the struggle for Schilling's life, to show Mäurer and Lucie on the one side, trying to infuse into him something of their own healthy, creative energy, and Hanna and Eveline on the other, demanding, destroying, and undermining. The action has again the simple inevitability which is typical of Hauptmann at his mature best. There are no surprises, no chance encounters, no new factors; there is not even a new arrival with the exception of the minor figure of Fräulein Majakin. Yet the play moves without a moment's slackening or faltering through its five acts, carried, in the first instance, by a masterly portrayal of Schilling and of the two women in pursuit of him, then by the hopes and efforts of his friends, and, last but not least, by the island itself, by the landscape and the life of the people in all that they mean to Schilling in relation to his predicament. Only the sub-plot seems a little deliberate, at least as far as the temporary defection of Mäurer is concerned. But Fräulein Majakin provides interesting concrete evidence of the kind of world in which Hanna lives—although, at that, only of its rather better side—and it might have been difficult to keep her in the play in the role of a mere spectator. In any case the affair is not dwelt upon for long enough to distract our attention seriously from the main action.

To understand Schilling we must, as in the case of Johannes Vockerat, start from the beginning, and from the beginning he is, unlike Johannes, who is self-centred, unstable, and destructive, more sinned against than sinning. Schilling, according to Mäurer, was a quiet and simple man who fell into Eveline's clutches because he was indifferent to everything in the world except his painting, "weil er immer gegen die Äusserlichkeiten des Lebens gleichgültig war, wenn man ihn nur ungestört malen liess." And his own words speak to the same effect. He is a dreamer, he says, who has never been able to realize his dreams. Moreover, to fight the world on its own terms means inflicting pain on others, and of this he has a morbid fear. To cut himself off from the two women, to take his life again into his own hands, would be practical and realistic, but horrible, "recht grundgemein, schweinemässig praktisch." Painting had been for him self-evident and sufficient until Eveline tried to turn him into a decent provider and drove him into the more than Bohemian sphere of Hanna and her husband. In Hanna he thought at first that he had found his art again, only to discover, too late, that he had been used by the couple originally as a means of hastening their divorce, as a pawn in a "kaltblütig vorher abgekartete Trennungskomödie." But in the meantime Hanna has attached herself to him and his passion for her has grown into a disease that poisons his being, physical and moral. His friends have turned away from him because of a rumour that Hanna supports him on the money of her lovers. The rumour, we may be sure, is false; Schilling is not "practical" enough for that. But other and only too credible stories tell of the depth of his degradation. Hanna, in a curious but typical defence of their love, has a tale that would sicken any but this particular teller. "Er hat vor meiner Haustür gestanden," she says to Lucie, "als ich russische Herren zu Besuch in meiner Wohnung hatte, bei achtzehn Grad Kälte, stundenlang. Um elf Uhr ist er darnach fortgegangen, weil ich nicht bemerkt hatte, dass er da war, und ist nachts halb ein Uhr, wo alles still war, wiedergekehrt und hat mich mit Steinchen ans Fenster geweckt. . . . Er war halbtot, als er zu mir kam, und hat sich erst gegen Morgen erwärmt." To complete Schilling's enslavement, there is a sickly two-year-old son. He has done no painting worthy of the name for five years.

Such is the background of the man who arrives on Fischmeisters Oye to join his friends, having, he says, broken with Hanna once and for all. And for the first two acts his mood is one of exaggerated self-confidence and optimism. He responds to Mäurer's banter with an exuberance that verges on hysteria, swings a board on to the shoulder of the local coffin-maker with a great flourish, teases the innkeeper on all possible occasions, and swims in the cold clear water until he is blue and exhausted. The mood reaches its climax with his acceptance of Mäurer's invitation: "Sucht mich im Peloponnes, meine Herrschaften!"

But from the beginning there are moments when he relapses into anxiety, repugnance, and utter indifference. The news that Lucie's mother has recently died awakens in him a strange uneasiness and apprehension. When Mäurer first suggests Greece he answers that he no longer has the energy for such an undertaking: "Mein Junge, ich ziehe mir morgens die Kleider an und finde das manchmal schon zu umständlich. Ich ziehe sie abends wieder aus und habe etwas mehr Spass daran; damit habe ich mehr als genug zu tun." And once Hanna has arrived even his precariously maintained humour takes on a painful and distorted form, as he tries in vain to mask his weakness and his uncertainty. When he is alone with her he has moments of firmness, indeed of bitterness. But on the whole, knowing that she neither shares nor understands his desire for freedom, he is gentle and apologetic and begs her to be merciful. And the story is the same during his brief encounter with his wife. "Ja, woran liegt das alles?" he asks, "Ich habe nie bewusst nach dem Schlechten gestrebt! Ich hatte wirklich nie böse Absichten!" At the end of the third act, moreover, we have a vivid glimpse of the passion to which he has fallen prey, as he draws Hanna to him with the exclamation "Du Schwarze, du Schneekühle, du Braut von Korinth." The words are in themselves an expression of the eros of death, and of a dark, perverted death eros at that. There is for Schilling no "stirb und werde"—he feels himself both attracted and repelled by something menacing and unclean. And this impression is strengthened by the circumstances: the two are sitting beside a little cemetery, and only a moment before Schilling has been joking indecently about the dead who arrive on the island "mit etwas durchnässten Unterhosen." A moment later, as a crow caws hoarsely above, he feels an insatiable thirst and drinks from a green, stagnant pool. Then suddenly there comes to him a vision of the sea, and, overwhelmed by a feeling of his own degradation, he collapses.

It is this sense of repulsion, of being suffocated by something impure, that drives Schilling, in the end, to his death. From the beginning he has spoken with horror of the sticky air and the reeking sidewalks of Berlin and of the stupidity, meanness, and indecency which have blocked his path, in whatever direction he turned. Once, at the end of the second act, he makes a desperate attempt to shake himself free: "Die Erinnerung an . . . an . . . an den Gestank fängt an zu verblassen . . ." he says to Mäurer, "Warum lass' ich nicht alles mal sitzen und liegen und hocken und quetschen und stinken nach Herzenslust? Warum nicht? . . . Sie saugen sich an wie die Blutegel, sie binden einem Hände und Füsse delilahaft, sie knebeln einem das Maul mit Gemeinplätzen . . . und pauken einem . . . das letzte bisschen Ehrgefühl aus dem Tempel heraus. Sucht mich im Peloponnes, meine Herrschaften!" But the catharsis, though glorious, is brief. By the end of the fourth act he is begging the doctor to give him poison: "Der Ekel erwürgt mich. Gift! Gebt mir Gift! Ein starkes Gift, Rasmussen!" And in the fifth, he makes the decision anticipated early in the play—that he will die in freedom, but not be sucked down a sewer—and walks with uplifted hands into the sea. Johannes and Michaline experience something of this sense of disgust because of the sordidness of cramped, middle-class standards. In *Schilling*, as in *Geyer*, it is heightened and intensified to the point that it gives a distinguishing tone and colour to the whole play. And, as in *Geyer*, it finds its dramatic antithesis in a second prevailing mood, a mood established in this case by the sea and the island, which we shall have to discuss in greater detail in a moment.

The two women who are the agents of Schilling's destruction are probably equally responsible. Eveline is the most unsparingly delineated, unpleasant, and selfishly possessive *Hausfrau* in all of Hauptmann's works. She was a governess before her marriage, we learn, and she looks back with longing to the days when she was able to save her money and spend her vacations with a female friend in first-class hotels in Normandy. She has become a martyred, whining wife—"Eigentlich hab' ich sie, ehrlich gestanden," says Schilling, "nie wirklich bei guter Laune gesehen." Her one thought, in the presence of her sick husband, is that she has been deceived, that Hanna is with him and that the two are laughing at her behind her back. Hanna, Hauptmann's finest portrait of a seductress, is more complicated, though not less virulent, for whether she appears naïve or refined, clever or stupid, despicable or terrifying, we feel that her grip on Schilling is inexorable and that she is perversion incarnate—in reality and in the flesh. She neglects her child, but uses it to make an appeal to Schilling that is both sentimental and ill-timed.

Her tale of his long cold sojourn outside her window is intended to persuade Lucie of his great need of her, and in like vein she argues that she has sacrificed herself for him, has posed for him, naked in a cold studio, until she fell to the floor exhausted, failing to see in her "sacrifice" a morbid self-indulgence that cripples all it touches. She will, with all the flourishes of the persecuted refugee, threaten at one moment to return to face indescribable danger in Russia, and, at the next, with simple candour, tell him that she will always follow him because she cannot live without him—"Weil ich nicht ohne dich sein kann, Lieb." And she tries indeed to follow him to the end, into the water, a fact which softens Lucie's judgment of her, but not Mäurer's, for he understands clearly that Hanna is a diseased Aphrodite and that the more passionately she loves Schilling, the more surely she will destroy him.

But even apart from his concern for his friend, Mäurer loathes and fears Hanna; she seems to him inhuman and uncanny, she reminds him of a vampire—we remember Schilling's "du Braut von Korinth!"—or of a figure by Goya. "Diese blutleere Fratze," he storms to Lucie, "Diesen lemurischen Wechselbalg. Ich kriege das Grausen vor dieser Larve. Ich fürchte mich, wenn ich nachts unter einem Dache mit diesem Gespenste bin. Ich bin überzeugt, es springt ihr nachts eine weisse Maus oder was Ähnliches aus dem offenen Mund und saugt sich einem im Schlaf an die Pulsader." Mäurer's impressions are reinforced by the figure-head of a wrecked ship which lies on the beach, a woman carved in wood, with a pale face, long black hair, and the expression of one walking in her sleep, a figure of evil omen which has led the men who sailed behind it to their doom and which haunts the play from beginning to end. Lucie, when she first sees it, thinks of her dead mother, Mäurer and Schilling of Hanna. And as the rays from the lighthouse flash on it, in the last act, it draws Schilling in a trance from his bed, to retreat from it slowly and painfully, as he regains some measure of consciousness, until, with a final resolve, he tears himself free and turns towards the water. In the portrait of Hanna reality and unreality are blended in a way that may remind us of what Ibsen strove to achieve in *The Lady from the Sea*. But in such matters, Hauptmann is his superior.

Three such characters as Schilling, Eveline, and Hanna might easily have provided a dramatist, one would think, with all the tension requisite for one play. But *Schilling* is a work not only of depth but of contrast. The first, more obvious instance of this is the relationship between Lucie and Mäurer. For Schilling love has meant a bourgeois household in its worst aspects, or sin and degradation. For them it is a natural, essential part of existence, an element of their creative lives, and one that goes hand in hand with her music and his art, that unites them, physically and spiritually, without enslaving them. The contrast seems, at first sight, a little more mathematically conceived than is normal with Hauptmann, and Lucie and Mäurer themselves are shaped by some measure of idealization, above all by a concept of the naïve, pagan, and sinless nature of the Greeks to which he paid obeisance at times, though his direct, personal experience of Greece, which he visited the year after the completion of *Schilling*, was very different. Yet the association of Mäurer and Lucie with a land which symbolizes the hopes that Schilling will never see realized is natural and convincing, and in this as in other respects the two live as mature, sensitive, and highly developed individuals who hold our interest and sympathy from the first moment of the play, when we meet Lucie on the dunes, laughingly assuring the coffin-maker Kühn that she is Mäurer's grandmother, to the end, when, standing on the same spot and watching the fishermen bringing in Schilling's body, she speaks the dead man's epitaph, "Ich glaube nämlich . . . jetzt ist er für ewig geborgen," and Mäurer adds its "Gut. Amen."

But it is not only the love of Mäurer and Lucie that makes the life of Schilling stand out in all its tragic distortion. The island of Fischmeisters Oye itself, its people, its sand dunes, and the sea surrounding it, provide a similar contrast. Even Mäurer and Lucie appear as mere refugees from Berlin—Kühn associates them with migratory birds—in comparison with the simple, slow-moving, unperturbed natives. The professor must be a bit touched to want to buy the figure-head, "dat Wieb ohne Fiet," says one of them in the laconic *Plattdeutsch* which Hauptmann had clearly come to love as he did his native Silesian, and which gives the play unforgettable accents of quiet, humorous, practical, earth-bound life. With this group of men is associated, incidentally, the solid, scientifically minded Dr. Rasmussen, by birth a native of nearby Wollin, with whom Schilling had impatiently broken in Berlin. And associated with them also is the former Berliner Kühn who, when the city doctors gave him up, fled to the island and lived to make coffins for others. Still more powerful, as a contrast, are the natural surroundings, the sand and the air, and, above all, the sea. Clear and radiant, compelling and majestic, it shines through the play and triumphs in the end over the pavement, the sewers, and the night-cafés of the city. "Diese Klarheit!" exclaims Mäurer in the first act, "Dieses stumme und mächtige Strömen des Lichtes! Dazu die Freiheit im Wandern über die pfadlose Grastafel. Dazu der Salzgeschmack auf den Lippen. Das geradezu bis zu Tränen erschütternde Brausen der See. . . . Dieses satte, strahlende Maestoso, womit sie ihre Brandungen ausrollen lässt. Köstlich!" And it is impossible to stress too highly the importance of the water for Schilling. He bursts into tears as he watches the long, rolling lines of foam. The sound of the breakers summons him, in the third act, from the stagnant pool from which he has been drinking, and he cries out, as though in the face of a vision, "Oh!! . . . Das Element! Das Element!" And the rising waves cleanse and shelter him in the end. Of all the characters in the play only Eveline and the two Russians, significantly, are unaffected by their surroundings. The realm of Hanna is, at best, the café; that of Schilling's wife an apartment, *zweiter Stock*, and, in the summer holidays, the table d'hôte of a fashionable hotel. The precocious Fräulein Majakin sees here, at most, a cold and frightening beauty which has neither attraction for her, nor meaning. "Ich kann in die tote Natur," she says to Mäurer, "keinen Sinn bringen."

Berlin and Fischmeisters Oye then, the atmosphere of corruption and that of purity, clean sand and shining water, are opposed to one another and help to form the dramatic tension of the play. But this does not mean that the island stands for life, simply, in contrast to the death of the city—the manner of Schilling's suicide would not make sense if it did. And thoughts of death and of a world beyond the present are associated with the island from the beginning. The cuckoos which dash themselves to death against the lighthouse, the cemetery, and even the fact that Schilling's first and last words are spoken to the coffinmaker Kühn are incidental examples of this. More important is the sensitivity of the characters, particularly of Schilling and Lucie, to the air and the water, which, in their stainless clarity, seem to be transparent media of another world, of some intangible sphere not normally accessible to the human senses. Dreams and visions form one element of this strange experience: Lucie speaks of dreaming so vividly that the pictures of the night remain with her in the bright sunshine of the day; and Schilling, as he talks to Kühn in the last act, sees his own funeral procession pass soundlessly before him in a rain that has not yet come. But the awareness of a space and time beyond is even more direct than that transmitted by dream or vision, more elusive and more difficult to formulate. "Es ist ungefähr so," says Lucie, "als wenn jemand durch eine Tür in unbekannte Räumlichkeiten gegangen ist, und während die Tür sich öffnet und schliesst, folgt man ihm mit dem Blick und der Seele ein Stück ins Unbekannte hinein." Both speak, on another occasion, of a feeling that all is in transition, and yet immortal. Schilling remembers that he has read somewhere the lines, "Gott löscht nicht aus im dunklen Grabesschoss, was er entzündet hat im dunklen Mutterschoss"; and Lucie declares that she believes that even the singing of the birds and the sound of the waves will, some day, take on new form. "Ich weiss nicht, ich glaube nicht, dass das alles: das Rauschen, das Licht, das Lerchengetriller, endgültig ist." Even the stage directions indicate that Hauptmann expected help from that quarter in the intensification of such impressions.

At the end of the last act, to take only one example, as the men carrying Schilling move silently past, we read, as we have read at an earlier point, "Etwas Lautloses, Unwirkliches liegt in dem Vorgang." Clearly death is as ubiquitous on the island as it is in Berlin.

Death on the island, however, means passing into a world that is strange and unknown, but not fearful or repulsive. When Mäurer warns Lucie that the contact with the dead that she is experiencing is dangerous, she protests that she is in no way depressed or upset: "Es ist mir heiter, es ist mir nicht aufwühlend." And Schilling speaks similar words: "In Freiheit zugrunde gehn, meinethalb—nur nicht vergurgeln in einem Abraumkanale," and "Keine Automobilomnibusse, keine Strassenbahnwagen. . . . Frischer, gesunder, nasser Sturm! Der schöne Salut des Meeres überm Grabhügel!" Death here means that he, like Arnold Kramer, has rescued beyond the reach of all perversion a part of his original wholeness and purity. The last act, accordingly, like the last act of *Kramer*, brings with it a measure of triumph and reconciliation. Hugo Ernst Schmidt died, in reality, in Berlin, under ugly and sordid circumstances. In the two plays associated with his friend Hauptmann endeavoured to clarify his fate and to indicate to the world that the features he loved, though sullied and distorted, remained recognizable to the end. He accomplished this in *Schilling*, in part, by transferring the action to Fischmeisters Oye.

I spoke, at the beginning of the analysis, of a certain refinement and concentration that *Schilling* has in common with *Kramer*, and of a similar interest in irrational forces. The world in which Schilling moves and thinks, it is true, is larger and is painted in greater detail than that of the earlier play. But we know less of his early life than we do of Johannes Vockerat's, and less of Eveline's than of Käthe's. And whereas complex and quite specific circumstances tend to make the love of Anna Mahr a disruptive rather than a constructive force, Hanna represents something much more radical and absolute, an eroticism so virulent and destructive that it seems to defy any attempt to account for it in natural, human terms. Moreover, our impression of the irrationality and incomprehensibility of man and the cosmos is heightened by the experience of Lucie and Schilling in relation to Fischmeisters Oye. Hauptmann is painting with sharper, crueller strokes than in the early plays; he is, at the same time, placing a greater stress on emotional states *per se*, and on atmosphere.

Yet here again, as in the case of *Kramer*, we must not forget in our preoccupation with new developments the basis on which Hauptmann's works are built. *Schilling* is, by comparison with other works, both early and late, a relatively private play, in the sense that it is less exclusively related than they to specific social, scientific, or economic problems. But Hauptmann is not ceasing to portray life as he saw it in his own day. Hanna would play her role admirably in the first *Walpurgisnacht*. But she is also a member of a somewhat less mythological world, a refugee, a product of a disintegrating society and a piece of an international flotsam severed from any vital *raison d'être*. Schilling, for his part, becomes entangled in this driftwood because he too has been ejected from a world whose inhabitants live by standards so artificial as to be hostile to life. Eveline, Mäurer points out, was formerly energetic and independent and might well have helped to support herself, even after her marriage. But—carrying the argument a little beyond Mäurer's actual words—it would not have befitted her status as a married, middle-class woman to do so. She goes hungry instead, she laments, and she attempts to force Schilling, against his nature, into the socially acceptable role of provider. The picture of Mäurer and Lucie supplements, of course, this condemnation of bourgeois *mariage à la mode*. Berlin, finally, as the most radically new type of *Lebensraum* that had emerged on German soil during the last third of the nineteenth century, is represented as the breeding ground of all that is perverse in the play, and Fischmeisters Oye, without fallacy or sentimentality, as its opposite, a place where a sound life is still biologically possible.

For all his stress on the irrational, moreover, which both gives the play tension and deepens its perspective, Hauptmann is still working on an inductive, psychological plane. We know that

Lucie's experience is connected with the shock of the recent death of her mother. And the doctor offers us a strictly rational, physiological explanation of all that has happened and happens to Schilling. "Das Leiden," he explains to Mäurer—Schmidt died of diabetes—"hat in schleichender Form wahrscheinlich seit einem Jahrzehnt in ihm gesteckt. Seine moralische Schlappheit wird dadurch erklärlich. Sonst hätte er wahrscheinlich den Weibern und allen korrumpierenden Einflüssen, seiner Natur nach, mehr Energie entgegengesetzt." Mäurer, to be sure, upholds the vampire theory. "Als er oben am Kirchhof zusammengebrochen war und wir kamen dazu und sahen diese Hanna über ihm, da kam es mir vor, als müsste irgend welcher höllische Hakelbärend zu dieser vollendeten Hatz Halali blasen." And Mäurer's voice determines, to a far greater extent than that of Dr. Rasmussen, the mood of the tragedy, the emotional response that it evokes. But Mäurer himself has no wish to dwell on such aspects of life. He grants Lucie that the island extends men's awareness of another world, but he warns her that the cultivation of such sensations is dangerous to healthy, rational life. "Mit offenen Augen soll man nicht träumen; an hellichten Tage träumt man nicht. Ich habe selbst die Erfahrung gemacht, dass alle diese Gespenster Blut trinken. . . . Und [der Mensch] schaudert vor dem Anblick von Todesfällen und den damit verknüpften aufwühlenden Folgezuständen ganz vernünftigerweise zurück." Not only is the play concerned, that is, with the emotional, psychological state of its characters rather than with the evocation of the irrational for its own sake, but it is not without voices which, in the midst of death, direct us back to life.

IV

In the spring of 1908, two years after the completion of *Schilling*, Hauptmann began to write the fourth and last of his artist plays, which he called *Peter Brauer*, with the notation, *Tragikomödie*. This time his hero was drawn after a painter named Glitschmann, whom he met in his parents' house when he himself was first considering studying art—a stout and somewhat irresponsible little man, according to the autobiography, with a serious young wife.[17] It seems possible also that the figure of Professor James Marshall, the original of Crampton, was still on the poet's mind and giving him no rest, either because he felt that his earlier work was not consistent in its presentation of the hero, or because his understanding of such situations changed with the years. Indications are that he did not find the solution he sought easily or quickly. He had made sketches for the new play long before he set to work on it in earnest in 1908, yet it was not completed until the spring of 1910, only a few weeks before its tragic counterpart, *Die Ratten*, and not published until 1921. But the long period during which Hauptmann was feeling his way towards the appropriate light in which to present his hero, and during which character, incidents, and milieu were slowly growing together to form a whole, bore excellent fruit. *Peter Brauer* is a sharper, more subtle, and more unified piece of work than its predecessor. It is also a work which deserves more attention than it has received.[18]

The situation and problems of Brauer are, in outline, like those of Crampton. He is an artist who does not paint, whose wife and daughter treat him with contempt, and whose son alone has retained for him something midway between tolerance and affection. Like Crampton also, he is deeply in debt. Some months ago, by dint of cleaning old paintings, he has managed to make a down-payment on some new furniture for his normally unappreciative household. In the interval most of the pieces have found their way to a pawnshop, and the legal owner is threatening to prosecute. But, like Crampton again, Brauer is given a chance—this time at the beginning of the play rather than at the end. He claims that he has a commission to paint murals in a garden pavilion, begs fifteen marks from his wife and son for railway fare, and flees from domestic hostility and impending

[17]He also saw Glitschmann in later years in Berlin. For details see F. A. Voigt, *Hauptmann-Studien* (Breslau, 1936), p. 59.

[18]Joseph Gregor, for example (*Gerhart Hauptmann*, Vienna, 1951), devotes one paragraph to *Peter Brauer* and *Der rote Hahn* together, dismissing both as worthless.

legal action to a small provincial town. Here he takes up quarters in the prosperous *Wirtshaus zum Goldenen Lamm*, makes a pretence of sketching the sights of the district, and hob-nobs with the inn's regular patrons, above all with the local veterinarian and a retired major. Just as the innkeeper is wondering how he can get rid of this non-paying guest without resorting to force, Brauer is introduced by his new friends to the aristocratic industrialist Freiherr von Behaimb. Von Behaimb has inherited money, he has twice married it, and he understands how to invest it very well indeed. In matters of art he is ingenuous. He has just bought a nearby estate as a pleasant trifle for his young second wife, on which, by a strange coincidence, there is a small pavilion, a jewel of a building in a classical style, which is in need of restoration. Casually, he invites Brauer to paint murals on the inside. Before Brauer can catch his breath there is, to be sure, an interruption. An itinerant photographer appears who has known Brauer of old, and involves him in an unpleasant and highly personal discussion of art. Brauer, he claims, cannot paint. Fortunately he confuses the issue by arguing that in any case photography will soon replace such old-fashioned methods as drawing and painting and von Behaimb, missing the first point, rises to the defence of the real artist.

We find Brauer, accordingly, at the beginning of the third and final act, sitting before the pavilion, happily engaged with newspapers and a punch of sour wine flavoured with fresh *Waldmeister*, a pleasant herb which the children of the neighbourhood bring him in large bunches in return for pennies. He has undertaken to make a painter out of Hellmut, the innkeeper's son, who is busy at an easel beside him, he has a long list of commissions, he has a drawing account at the local bank, and he has sent money home. He needs only one thing in the world to make him supremely happy, a visit from his family, so that they may see him in his triumph. And he does not hope in vain. They are suspicious, but they come. The photographer turns up and takes a family picture. But the idyll is of short duration. Just as the picture is being taken von Behaimb turns up too, with his wife, his son, and a visiting Scotch painter, all fresh from a brilliant exhibition in Munich and anxious to view their local project. Brauer leads the way, somewhat reluctantly, into the pavilion. Hellmut, full of admiration, describes to Brauer's family what the master has so far accomplished. He has been painting gnomes and dwarfs, not many, for he has asthma, and can work only for short periods. But Hellmut finds them "wunder-wunderschön" with their red peaked caps and little aprons. The daughter groans; the German fairy-tale figures seem to be a specialty of her father's which she has seen too often before. The visitors emerge and depart. But in a moment von Behaimb the younger returns, amused and apologetic. His father, he says, has nothing against dwarfs, and he himself finds them quite agreeable, but his step-mother is unhappy. Would Brauer be good enough to return the pavilion keys to his father's lawyer and to present his account. Without waiting to hear what has been said Frau Brauer and her daughter leave for the station. The son escorts them promising to return. Brauer sits alone, staring at the ground.

Any analysis of *Peter Brauer* must begin with praise of the sensitivity and precision with which Hauptmann has handled his difficult material. The play is not a great masterpiece; its theme is slight and its characters, in many cases, are only sketched. But it has depth and reality and, unlike its predecessor, it balances between comedy and tragedy, between the farcical and the pathetic, between the trivial and the universally valid with complete certainty and without a false note or a wrong perspective. We do not know, for example, at the end of *Crampton*, how much of the hero's trouble is to be ascribed to himself, and how much to his environment. But from the beginning of *Brauer* to the end, from the moment when we first see him in his tiny fourth-floor studio with its meagre furnishings and its inferior copies of popular portraits of the royal family, to the moment when he sends his son after his departing wife, it is clear that nature has destined him for failure. Frau Brauer is perfectly right when she says, "Aber Peter kann doch nichts."

And yet we feel for Brauer; whether he deserves it or not, we wish him a better fate.

But to speak in more general terms: plot, character, and milieu alike serve to establish the balance of the play and to maintain it. The story is casual, the outcome of an accidental meeting, an unfortunate incident in an unfortunate life. From the point of view of Peter's fate and character it is even irrelevant; he will be unsuccessful whether circumstances are with him or against him; the fact that they seem to be with him here only serves to illustrate the extent of his inadequacy. But as a parable, as a means of imparting Hauptmann's attitude towards his hero, the incidents have a significance which should not be disregarded. The way in which Brauer, in his blind retreat from home, is picked up on the roadside by fortune's chariot and, having settled down to a happy snooze instead of seizing the reins, is tossed out again with as little ceremony, is a vivid illustration of the negligent way in which life handles her problem children, and a spectacle which arouses in us an indefinable blend of amusement and compassion. A story of one kind or another is usually more important in Hauptmann's comedies than in his tragedies. *Crampton* has its plot, devised by Max. *Der Biberpelz* is a maze of intrigue and counter-intrigue. And *Brauer* is no exception. The action, which is amusing in the first act, astonishing in the second, and only too inevitable in the last, is an important factor in setting the tone of the play.

Yet the main weight of the play lies, as is usual with Hauptmann, on the environment and on the characters, above all on the hero himself, who is on stage almost without interruption from beginning to end. We have noted that Brauer, unlike Crampton, cannot paint. But even aside from this he is a sorrier and more wretched figure than his predecessor. He makes some attempt to speak about matters of art in an authoritative manner, particularly to the provincials, but he is without Crampton's eloquent tongue and he has no worshippers among the lower classes. He too, moreover, has dreams and illusions in plenty, dreams of the freedom and greatness of the artist and illusions of having been misunderstood by all men from his schooldays on. But he has little success in convincing anyone, even himself, of their reality, for the world is shrewd and harsh and he is a timid man. When his wife approaches, he grows pale. When his daughter speaks rudely to him, he endures it with only the feeblest of protests. When the photographer Schmolcke attacks him, he replies with such fear and embarrassment that anyone but an industrial magnate and a retired major—in mourning for a pet dog who was, he says, more intelligent than most men—would sense the truth. As the play proceeds, we realize that Brauer, though he is a good-for-nothing, is also the most helpless and hapless of mortals. He is dazed when von Behaimb first suggests that he help with the pavilion, and his heart beats so violently that he cannot speak. He is, moreover, unpretentious. He has nothing to give the world, but he demands little, and he suffers, as the doctor said of Hoffmann, "so viel er überhaupt leiden kann." We grant him gladly the simple and transient joys of a cool punch and of a family photograph before the pavilion, even though we suspect that he has done no work, and we fear for him when the moment of discovery comes. It is no longer necessary for Hauptmann to make any claims for his hero or to portray him as more than the little man that he is in order to engage our sympathy. The comedy of *Brauer* is much gentler than Chaplin's *Modern Times*, but the two are not unrelated.

A glance at Brauer's family and at his environment will confirm the impression made upon us by the artist himself. For if Hauptmann has no illusions about his hero, he has none whatsoever about the world with which the poor man has to contend. The attitude of Erwin, the son, corresponds roughly, it is true, to that of Gertrud in *Crampton*, but only roughly. Erwin has none of Gertrud's crusading spirit, he is merely a pleasant lad who would gladly help his father if he could. In *Crampton*, moreover, we only hear about a scolding wife and about other children who support her, but we see Frau Brauer and her daughter Klara. And Frau Brauer is at once better and worse than we might expect—not a carping *Hausfrau*, but a fine and delicate lady with a sweet mouth which sometimes utters sweet words, but not always and not to her husband, for she is also embittered and suspicious and coldly resolved never again to become enveloped in the mists of sentiment which once betrayed her into marrying Brauer. And her gentle mouth quietly refers to her husband as a lazy beast and a useless lump of fat—"ein träges Pferd" and "ein unnützes Fettgewicht." It is quite comprehensible that Brauer's asthmatic breathing grows more difficult still when he has to contemplate asking her for even the smallest sum of money. The daughter, for her part, is a hard, unattractive girl, in severely plain clothes, who is studying to become a teacher. She feels a sentimental pity for her mother and she despises her father. The light on the picture is dry, the strokes are sharp and precise. The women are right, but they have no basic humanity. Brauer is useless and a burden to his family, but if Frau Brauer cared less for appearances and if Klara were pretty, life would be happier for him without being any the worse for anyone else.

The picture is the same if we look from Brauer's family to the society in which he is expected to make a living. "Und heut schneidet man Häcksel für diese Gesellschaft," says Lachmann, as the successful professional men of *Kramer* withdraw to the next room with their champagne. Brauer, such as he is, finds himself in the middle of the modern world of business. His employer in Berlin, when he has one, is Carlowitz, a manufacturer of "antique" furniture, for whom he makes the portraits of the royal family that we see in his studio in the first act. The pictures of course are bad, but then Carlowitz pays very little for them, only a small fraction of the cost of the gilt frames which will shine in the contemporary bourgeois parlour. For Brauer's romantic gnomes there is presumably no market at all. It is with some satisfaction that we leave Carlowitz to dispute with the pawnbroker about the ownership of the furniture which Brauer has obtained on credit from the manufacturer's wife, the lady having been ill at the time and less efficient than she ought to have been. Nor is the scene lacking in another feature of modern economic life, that of forced and embittered competition. The aggressive photographer Schmolcke reveals himself, in the end, as the tool of circumstances. A lawsuit has stripped him of every possession except his camera. "Das sagen Sie so: bescheidener auftreten," he says to Brauer, "wenn einem das Messer an der Kehle sitzt, das Wasser bis hierher steht und das Feuer unter dem Fracke brennt. Da geht man los, und da nimmt man, was man zu packen kriegt."

In the provinces, moreover, Brauer meets a veritable cross-section of the population, from the servants of the inn up to the local nobility, landed and industrial, and the picture, on the whole, has an unpleasant tinge. The innkeeper and his wife are decent and not unkindly. But the servants and the young girls, daughters of the innkeeper and of the major, are pert. The gentlemen who gather about the *Stammtisch*, while they are portrayed much more lightly than their counterparts in *Kramer*, are vacuous and inane and very sure of their own importance. On the estate bought by von Behaimb Brauer meets the last surviving member of the family which had held it for generations, a twenty-five-year-old idiot who plays with a toy pistol. "Das liegt im Blut mit dem Schiessgewehr," says the theology student who looks after him, "Wenn ich ihm diese Kinderei lege, verfällt er mir aber auf schlimmere Dinge. Ich habe schon alle schiessbaren Sachen eingeschlossen und fortgehängt. . . . Übrigens geht er von seinem Stammsitz und merkt es nicht." And the stuttering son of von Behaimb, "Gardehusar Rittmeister von Behaimb," does not presage a brilliant future for the new ruling family. The aristocratic group, finally, which comes to inspect Brauer's work, does not engage our sympathy by discussing the "provincial" artist, in his presence, in English. The whole picture, it should be stressed once again, is lightly painted. Brauer is not the victim of his environment. He is, as he himself says, a "Pechvogel"—an unlucky bird—the world's fool, not its tragic antagonist. But it is not too much to say that Hauptmann's portrait of a world which has no charity for the fowls of the air and the lilies of the field underlines Brauer's role as a harmless unfortunate who tries, not very successfully, to dream for his life, and who harms no one except himself.

Hauptmann's comedy, like his tragedy, is at its best when it is inspired by direct observation of the world. *Brauer* is a better play than *Crampton* because it has none of the tendency to escapism that mars the earlier work. Indeed Hauptmann moves here in the opposite direction and interprets in the light of comedy a scene that might well have inspired a tragedy, which is presumably what he meant to indicate by giving the play its subtitle *Tragikomödie*. This change both from the relative optimism of his early work and from the sharp, unmitigated tragedy of plays like *Geyer* and *Rose Bernd* seems to represent a new mood, a new phase in the author's reactions to the world. For the qualities that distinguish *Brauer* are to be found in a still more pronounced form in *Die Ratten*, which was written at the same time and which Hauptmann also called a tragicomedy. The two plays have the same apparent casualness of plot and the same varied and often unimpressive world, and Hauptmann approaches the characters with the same blend of coolness and deep sympathy. In *Brauer*, in the second act, the tension grows too much for the buttons on the hero's one poor shirt, and as they fall to the floor, to the amusement of von Behaimb and the other gentlemen, Brauer makes weak jokes about the traditional negligence of artists in matters of personal appearance. Yet his last words to his son, his "Geh, geh! Keine Angst um mich, guter Junge," are simple and moving. Only in *Die Ratten* does Hauptmann move us in a like manner from one facet of experience to another, from the pathetic to the ridiculous and from the grotesque to the tragic. The two works together suggest that he was looking at the pre-war world with a half bitter and half detached pessimism which precluded the pure tragedy of earlier years and gave birth instead to problem plays, in the sense that we use the word to describe Shakespeare's *Measure for Measure*, to plays whose comedy is intended to leave us with a slightly unpleasant aftertaste and whose tragedy—as in *Die Ratten*—is in danger of being demeaned by association with the criminal and the debased.

V

The works just discussed reflect a change in Hauptmann's attitude extending over some twenty years, a change which is equally marked in the plays he wrote about the common people. Nor is this the only resemblance between the two groups, for in both Hauptmann is depicting men of his own day and in both he gives us broad pictures of society. But the present plays are distinguished to some extent from their fellows by their heightened tone—artists being men given to the cultivation of their emotions—and by their concentration on the middle-class background from which, in each case, their heroes come. They give us a fairly uniform picture of what Hauptmann considered the problems and shortcomings of the German *Bürger* around the turn of the century, namely the difficulty of any real expression of individualism, a growing narrowness and complacency, a tendency to accept the status quo, and a loss of any standards other than those established by social convention and economic success. Speaking very generally, we feel, when we compare these plays with those about the lower classes, that the industrial revolution and the economic boom which changed the life of the proletariat radically during these years left the middle classes in a state of degeneration and stagnation.

The rigidity and callousness of bourgeois society are underlined by the fact that the heroes of all four plays are artists. Not that Hauptmann—to turn for a moment to a question that has been vexing writers and critics for a century and a half—sees artists as radically different from other men or as facing problems peculiar to their calling alone. But he does postulate that the nervous and emotional development of the artist is higher than that of the routine member of the bourgeois world and that he is endowed with the precious and sometimes dangerous gift which Lachmann defines as the power of illusion and faith in imagination. His main concern, furthermore, is to free himself from all influences that may prevent him from expressing his vision, from writing or painting or composing, as the case may be. He is therefore particularly endangered when, in a world of time-clocks and regular office hours, he has to provide a wife and family with an adequate and regular income. Eveline married Schilling, says Mäurer, "und da war er mit einemmal ihr Ernährer." There is also the subtler peril entailed by living with those whose ideals are limited to the maintenance of the happy domestic life which they conceive as the fitting reward for the discharge of a respectable public office. "Jetzt plagst du dich," Frau Kramer reproaches Michaline, "wie Pape sich plagt, und es kommt nichts heraus als Missmut und Sorge." Indeed, even where there is no economic problem, as in the case of Mäurer, there is fear of this less tangible bond. Tradition and custom have so limited the roles of husband and wife that, although he thinks of his association with Lucie as permanent, he fears the loss of his independence as a self-determining, creative individual if he marries her. In a week or so, he tells Rasmussen, he will pack her up and be off to Florence. When the doctor asks, "Warum heirat'st du denn das Mädel nicht?" he answers, "Weil das für un-sereinen immer die Klippe ist." And behind the ideals of family life that have become so fixed as to be intolerable, the artist encounters the philistinism of the business and professional world, which may have its own peculiar standards of beauty or which may ignore all such questions completely. "Verflucht geschmackvolle Kneipe das," says the architect Ziehn in *Kramer*, as his eyes rove appreciatively over the "altdeutsches Lokal" that he himself has designed. "Wieder scheene Bilder jemalt?" asks Carlowitz, looking at Brauer's easel. But when Brauer answers hopefully, "Was, da läuft Ihnen wohl das Wasser im Munde zusammen, Carlowitz?" the manufacturer cuts him short with a dry "Nich janz," and proceeds at once to business.

Yet Kramer has his position in the Academy and Mäurer is an artist of international renown who has just completed an important and well-paid work for the city of Bremen. And artists are not the only people in Hauptmann's plays who face economic difficulties or who find the world lacking in charity. The social and economic problems of the artist are the social and economic problems of modern man, heightened by his sensibility and by the fact that he comes from a class which, though it has its *entrepreneurs*, has become static and conventional. It is interesting to note also that, if orthodox society is often hostile to the artist, he will not solve his problems, according to Hauptmann, by an escape into Bohemianism. Crampton does not paint in his tavern, or Schilling in Hanna's apartment. An artist needs freedom to work, inwardly and outwardly. But a completely uprooted existence, however one may laud it in the name of experience, exposes him, individualist and dreamer that he is, to the peril of losing himself in some form of intoxication. His need is not merely to defy convention and not—though he may wish to be alone while he is working—to withdraw into himself entirely; his need is, like that of other men, love and understanding—and a better society.

At first glance such perceptions may not appear very unusual or exciting. They become so when, bearing in mind Hauptmann's accomplishments, we compare his conception of the difficulties of the artist with that of his contemporaries. For then we realize that for him, to a degree which is quite exceptional in the modern world, art is in no way problematic. About religion he is not always sure. He is at least aware, as we perceive above all in *Quint*, that psychologists may interpret man's religious aspirations as mere sublimations of doubtful validity. He must have known that art had been questioned in the same way. He remained unimpressed. There is some probing of the way in which an artist's work reflects his individual nature. Crampton has painted a Mephistopheles. Arnold Kramer draws caricatures. Brauer has his wistful predilection for brightly coloured gnomes. This is the same kind of psychological insight that marks his presentation of all his characters.

There is, in *Schilling*, one brief conversation that looks as though it might lead to an investigation of some complex and paradoxical relation between the artist's life and work. "Ich habe gedacht an eine lange, bleiche Gestalt," says Fräulein Majakin, who has seen some of Mäurer's engravings, "mit kohlschwarze Augen und dünne Lippen, an einen Mensch, der vor die viele grosse und furchtbare Visionen wie von eine Fieber ausgehöhlt und gefoltert ist. Und nun sehe ich eine gesunde Gelehrten." But Mäurer shrugs his shoulders and laughs and that is the end of it. We can find an explanation for her remarks if we look into the background of the play. Hauptmann visited Max Klinger in 1905, and Klinger's spectacles, his red beard, his devotion to solitary work, and his reputation as a highly nervous, brooding, and pessimistic artist left their mark on Mäurer. But even here the dramatist went no further than to note what he had observed.

In general, Hauptmann simply accepts the dreams and illusions of the artist as part of creative life. He does not puzzle about the nature of the vision, he does not even, after *Einsame Menschen*, question the justification of art in its relation to society. And above all he does not try, in the manner of a Thomas Mann, to separate art from life. If an artist finds the world inadequate, that is one thing. But there is no suggestion that he cannot enter fully into experience as other men do or that art is a compensation for the inability to live. If there is one Hauptmann figure who retreats into art from life it is Brauer, and Brauer cannot paint. Arnold begs for experience in a way that has attracted the sympathy of both Mann and Rilke. But he begs because he is a cripple. Neither his hunched shoulders nor his begging have anything to do with the fact that he paints. He paints, as his father does, and as Schilling and Crampton and Mäurer do, because he wants to paint, because he has the desire and the talent. And in this Hauptmann's artists resemble Hauptmann himself, who wrote plays because he had a genius for writing plays, and who was too powerful, too naïve, and too spontaneous a creator to question the origin or the validity of his own activity.

V. Plays of the Common People

THE PLAYS that Hauptmann wrote during these same years about the common people, the proletariat of country, village, and city, are six in number: two comedies—*Der Biberpelz* and *Der rote Hahn*—and four tragedies—*Hanneles Himmelfahrt, Fuhrmann Henschel, Rose Bernd,* and *Die Ratten.* A word of explanation is perhaps necessary about the inclusion of *Hannele,* for it has verse passages which might suggest that it be dealt with separately as a bridge between the prose drama and the poetic. But some of the plays which contain no formal verse, *Florian Geyer* or *Michael Kramer,* for example, with their heightened prose, their intensification of emotional effect, and their stress on irrationalism, are equally important as bridges. And the basis of *Hannele,* like that of the other works discussed in the present chapter, is a realistic account of the contemporary world. As in the case of the middle-class plays, not all of the plays about the people are masterpieces. *Hannele,* like *Crampton,* is marred by sentimentality. *Der rote Hahn,* interesting both intrinsically and as a prefiguration of *Peter Brauer* and *Die Ratten,* is a collection of sketches, some of them successful and some of them not. But, all in all, Hauptmann portrayed the figures from the lower classes whom he had met in Berlin and Silesia, sometimes as a boy and sometimes just before he wrote the play in question, with a sureness and an insight which he sometimes equalled in other works but never surpassed. The present group of plays, especially if we add to it *Die Weber,* forms the most impressive single unit of his work and is his greatest contribution to modern drama. Others—Ibsen or Shaw or Chekhov—have matched him in their handling of the middle classes. In the simple and profoundly humane presentation of characters from the people he has no peer.

I

Der Biberpelz and *Hanneles Himmelfahrt* were written in quick succession—the former in the summer and fall of 1892 and the latter in the first months of the following year—to the astonishment of Hauptmann's audiences, who found it difficult to understand how such a tender tragedy and such a robust comedy could spring from the same pen within such a short period of time. We cannot always tell why Hauptmann wrote a particular work when he did, but it seems certain that much of the responsibility here, at least for the order in which the two plays appeared, lies in the hands of the Berlin police. The dramatist had seen the red-headed girl who was the model for Hannele while he was in Silesia collecting material for *Die Weber*, and the two plays are so closely related that the one might have followed directly on the other if the police had not made their decision in March 1892 to forbid the performance of *Die Weber*. Hauptmann had had some highly unpleasant experiences with the Prussian bureaucracy during the Erkner years. The banning of his play apparently brought things to a head and diverted his attention not only from *Hannele* but from *Geyer*, on which he had already begun to work. He made it quite clear in *Der Biberpelz* what he thought of witch-hunting and of the intelligence of the average official. And then he turned at once to *Hannele*. *Der Biberpelz* itself, ironically, was not forbidden because the censor who read it considered it "ein ödes Machwerk," a play so dull and uninspired that it could not but fail on the stage.[1]

"Ich lebte damals," Hauptmann once said to Behl, speaking of his years in Erkner, "in einer durch die Nähe Berlins mitbedingten tragischen grossen Phantasmagorie. Trat ich des Abends vor das Haus, so sah ich im Westen bei klarer Luft den Widerschein der Riesin Berlin blutrot am Himmel." And he added that he had met all the characters of *Der Biberpelz* at that

[1] C. F. W. Behl, *Wege zu Gerhart Hauptmann* (Goslar, 1948), p. 148.

time.[2] Specific details about some of these figures are to be found
in the autobiography and they are interesting evidence both of
the realism of Hauptmann's portrayal of the suburban settlement
which is the scene of the play, and of the creative power with
which he shaped and inspired his material. The model for the
Rentier Krüger was Hauptmann's own landlord, a craftsman
who had somehow come into money. *Amtsvorsteher* von
Wehrhahn was fashioned after an arrogant chief of police who
had rejected in an offhand way the poet's attempts to be helpful
in tracking down some of the thieves who infested the area.
And the adventurer Motes was inspired by a forester who had
come to grief in his profession and who irritated Hauptmann
intensely by his inquisitiveness in political matters and by his
habit of blowing a horn in the forest in compensation for the
shooting now denied him by law, a habit, incidentally, that
accounts for one of the casual bits of conversation in the play
which, while we may not always understand their full reference,
give it the impression of being saturated with life. "Lass du doch
den dämlichen Motes blasen," says the heroine, the washerwoman Frau Wolff, to her anxious husband—the two being
engaged at the time in counting ill-gotten gains—"Der is im
Walde und denkt an nischt."

Hauptmann's experiences in Erkner had already been reflected
in *Bahnwärter Thiel* and, to some extent, in *Einsame Menschen*.
But Thiel's life is untouched by modern industrial civilization;
the trains which speed past his guard's hut belong, in his thoughts,
to a remote world in which he has no interest; and in *Einsame
Menschen* the light is concentrated on the domestic and intellectual
difficulties of the Vockerats. In *Der Biberpelz* Hauptmann gives
us a cross-section of the life of the settlement and traces in detail
the changes being wrought by the new era and above all by
the rapid growth of Berlin. For all the ease of his presentation
the picture is a complex one and justifies the "phantasmagoria"
of his words to Behl. But it is not, or, to phrase it more carefully,

[2]*Ibid.*, p. 98.

not yet, "tragic." Certainly the struggle that is taking place within the little community is not a delicate one: its inhabitants are caught in the *Strebertum*—the desire to climb far and fast—characteristic of boom years, and they are pestered by the reactionary policy of the government. A few years more and the scene will be as tragic as that of *Vor Sonnenaufgang*; Hauptmann painted it, a decade later, in *Der rote Hahn*. But in *Der Biberpelz* the changes are just beginning. And without falsifying the picture in any way, he allowed his delight in his shrewd and vigorous heroine, Frau Wolff, to set the tone of the play, and depicted her untiring and efficient manipulation of her world with evident enjoyment. What he did not like he ridiculed. *Der Biberpelz* is a comedy in which character, satire, and situation all play a part.

The scene is a small community on the Spree, in the first and third acts the kitchen of the washerwoman Mutter Wolff, in the second and fourth the local police office. The action is based on two interlocking but to some degree independent stories, the first of which begins when Leontine Wolff, the elder daughter of the heroine, refuses one winter evening to carry a load of wood from the garden into the house of the retired carpenter, Krüger, for whom she works, and runs home. Her mother, coming in later, and dragging a poached deer, finds her asleep in the kitchen. From here on Mutter Wolff takes charge, with energy enough to propel a dozen plays. She has chores for all, for her younger daughter Adelheid, for her husband Julius, and even for the weary Leontine. She sells the deer to a boatman, Wulkow. She fights a round with Motes, an unemployed forester, who, strolling with his wife through the woods in the winter night, has found snares near the house, and comes in to do a little blackmailing. Then, with the assistance of the slow-witted constable Mitteldorf, who has just remembered that she is to wash the next day at the house of von Wehrhahn, the hamlet's new magistrate, she helps her reluctant husband to make ready their sleigh.

On the following morning Krüger's wood is gone. The old

man comes to von Wehrhahn to demand that the police help him to recover his stolen property and his runaway servant. Frau Wolff, summoned from her washing, is adamant: even if it means that Krüger will no longer employ her as a washer-woman, she will keep her daughter at home. Nothing—and here the second story begins—could interest von Wehrhahn less than petty theft. His mind, such as it is, is concentrated on the ferreting out of disloyal, democratic elements in the community, and Motes has just given him a most gratifying report on the activities of a young Dr. Fleischer, a man of letters who lives in Krüger's villa, where Motes had also lived until he failed, once too often, to pay his rent. The magistrate gets rid of Krüger as quickly as possible, dismisses the theft from his mind, and con-centrates on the *affaire* Fleischer. But he is to have no peace. Wulkow, who has rheumatism, has suggested to Frau Wolff that he would pay a good sum for a beaver coat such as Frau Krüger recently gave her husband. A short time later the coat has gone, and Frau Wolff is in possession of a considerable amount of money. Krüger dismisses his second washerwoman, apologizes to his first, and appears again before von Wehrhahn.

This time the situation is more complicated. Frau Wolff and Adelheid have brought a bundle containing a vest belonging to Krüger and a key, which the girl has "found." Wulkow, his boat caught in the freezing Spree, comes to register the birth of a daughter. And Fleischer, rowing on the river the day before, has seen a boatman wearing an expensive-looking fur coat. The magistrate, bewildered by this varied clientèle, and expecting Motes again, tries repeatedly to send them all away. But Krüger insists that he examine the evidence. Von Wehrhahn turns to the boatman present. Wulkow assures him that boatmen often have fur coats, in fact he has one himself. The magistrate considers the matter settled. Fleischer at once proceeds to settle another. Following a hint given him by Frau Wolff, he has obtained from Motes's new landlady a written statement to the effect that Motes has tried to persuade her to give false evidence against him. For a moment, while Wulkow and Frau Wolff look silently on, accused and accuser and police and plaintiff fill the air with their shouts. Then there is a superb anti-climax. Von Wehrhahn becomes interested in the stolen coat. He maintains that it has been taken to Berlin. The washerwoman, on the best of terms with all present, supports Krüger in his belief that it is still in the neighbourhood. When the others have departed she even defends Fleischer to von Wehrhahn as a fine young gentleman. The magistrate assures her in a fatherly manner that not everyone is as guileless and innocent as she. And she confirms his confusion by stating the truth. "Da weess ich nu nich," she says, shaking her head, "I'm not so sure."

An outline of *Der Biberpelz* can give, at best, only a faint idea of its comic qualities. But even when it is read it may seem—particularly to a modern, English-speaking public accustomed to consider comedy almost synonymous with the stylized characters, the brilliant dialogue, and the deliberately provocative, intellectual paradoxes of a Shaw, an Oscar Wilde, or, more recently, a Christopher Fry—almost too realistic to be good comedy. There are parts of the third act, especially, in which Fleischer brings his small son to visit Frau Wolff, which may appear to us as no more than a naturalistic slice of life which happens, for once, to be pleasant rather than tragic or depressing. This impression vanishes when the play is seen on the stage. There seems so little chance that any of Hauptmann's works will be acted, in the immediate future, before English-speaking audiences that virtually no mention has been made of their effectiveness in the theatre. But it should be stressed that *Der Biberpelz*, even more than the tragedies or the "higher" comedies, needs to be seen to be appreciated, and that it gains far more than the plays of Shaw or Wilde in comic effect as well as in other respects when it is acted rather than read.

This does not mean that there is no humour in Hauptmann's dialogue or that he relies on broad and farcical effects to make us laugh. But Shaw's dialogue, for example, often has its own life,

apart from that of his characters—it would frequently be just
as effective in a preface—and even when he is intent on portraying
a person or on developing a situation, he seems to dictate the
role or the scene, so that we can picture them in a reasonably
sufficient way. Hauptmann's language, in his comedy as in his
tragedy, belongs, in the main, to his people, and it is suggestive
and evocative rather than peremptory. We may, if we are fortunate, see *Pygmalion* realized on the stage; we see *Der Biberpelz*
grow. And the humour, based on a combination of character
and situation not easily visualized in reading, becomes brilliantly
evident in the theatre. There is a good instance of such a scene
at the end of the first act, when the constable Mitteldorf arrives,
even more than usually befuddled by beer and domestic affliction.
If he goes home, he says, his wife scolds, and if he goes to the
tavern, she scolds even more—"det soll man nu ooch nich.
Ja nischt soll man!" Frau Wolff is sympathetic, but she is on
the point of setting out to steal Krüger's wood, and her sympathy
does not interrupt her preparations for one second. Moreover,
in her presence Mitteldorf, like everyone else, has to work, and,
still lamenting and being comforted, he reaches laboriously
for the sleigh harness and holds a lantern to light the pair on their
way. We recall the incident with twofold joy when, in the
second act, von Wehrhahn asks whether Mitteldorf has seen
anything suspicious on the previous evening, and the constable,
after profound meditation, answers that he has not. But the finest
example comes at the climax of the fourth act when von
Wehrhahn, with both malefactors in his presence and the evidence needed to convict them lying in a chain before his very
nose, severs the chain by smashing one link against another—
accepting Wulkow's confession as a proof that Fleischer is a
fool and that the investigation of crime should be left to the
police. Only the stage can give us the timing and the movements necessary to bring out the effectiveness of such a scene,
can convey a full sense of the varied and conflicting emotions
of the characters, and only the stage can make us see Frau Wolff,

who stands in the background, interested and sympathetic, but too polite to intervene in matters beyond her understanding, and uttering never a word.

Hauptmann's comedy, then, will hold its own in the theatre with the more sophisticated works of his own or other nations. It must be admitted that even German critics, who can see it on the stage and who know the peasant comedies of Kleist and Anzengruber which are its literary progenitors, have sometimes argued that it would be a better comedy and a better play if Hauptmann had paid more attention to traditional dramatic form. The first audiences, it is said, sat waiting for a fifth act like that of Kleist's *Der zerbrochene Krug*, where a dishonest judge is unmasked and flees the scene of his transgressions, and found Hauptmann's ending, in consequence, somewhat flat. And Schlenther confessed that he would have been happier if Hauptmann, again like Kleist, had limited himself to one main action; he found his attention divided between the Wolff household and the court with all that each represented.[3] Yet *Der Biberpelz* is no more unorganized than Hauptmann's early tragedies. It is shaped, it is true, within the limits of a realistic portrayal of a specific social scene, but it is shaped; and its comedy is not less effective because it springs from the situation as Hauptmann saw it rather than from an attempt to emulate something that had been done before. The first and the third acts, as Heise has pointed out, in which we see Frau Wolff in her kitchen, set the stage for the second and the fourth, and as the first theft is followed by a second, which is more serious, so the first futile investigation is followed by one which is futility itself. And every thread of the play is gathered into the moments of the fourth act which form its climax. True, there is no single knot and there is no resolution: Frau Wolff is not caught and von Wehrhahn is not dismissed. To say that Kleist was able to finish his play so neatly because he had a greater faith in the wisdom of the authorities than Hauptmann would perhaps be incorrect. But Hauptmann was at once more realistic and more satirical.

[3]*Gerhart Hauptmann, Leben und Werke* (6th ed., Berlin, 1912), pp. 104-5.

What he saw was a comedy of cross-purposes, of an aristocratic and reactionary bureaucracy fighting in the dark and oblivious of the forces which quietly, behind its back, are digging its grave. Von Wehrhahn, by virtue of his ancestry and of his office, ought to be Frau Wolff's chief opponent; but no one is less aware of her ambition and of the full scope of her activities than he. A more conventional ending would not only have been "unnaturalistic," it would have spoiled the joke.

The remarkable virtue of *Der Biberpelz*, in fact, is that it is at the same time so real and so amusing. The thieving and witch-hunting by which Hauptmann achieved his—incidentally often quite traditional—comic effects, are the natural outcome of the social situation. And the humorous aspects of the characters, above all of the heroine, are grounded in their lives and in the problems of their day. Frau Wolff is a newcomer in the district, Hauptmann once pointed out—"Zugewanderte Schlesierin"[4]— who has a settler's energy, and who has picked up as well a facility in the use of her tongue characteristic of more than one of the world's great cities and no less characteristic of Berlin than of London or New York. Resolute, shrewd, and indefatig-able, she surveys the changing scene, eager to take advantage of every opportunity to get ahead and bending her not very promising family to her will. When the muttering of her stolid husband—"Det hätte ick man sollen früher jewusst hebben," for example—warns her that she is moving a little too quickly for him, she puts a few nails in his hands and directs his attention to a loose board, or, if that fails, packs him off for a day's relaxa-tion in the tavern. Leontine, she insists, must stay with the Krügers until she has learned how people of higher classes behave, and whining will do her no good; if she feels so sorry for herself that she would really rather jump in the river than return, her mother will give her such a shove that she won't miss—"dasste ooch ja und fliegst nich daneben." She is not even daunted by the precocious and all-too-knowing Adelheid: the young lady, eyeing the stolen wood, may insinuate as clearly

[4] Behl, *Wege zu Gerhart Hauptmann*, p. 98.

as she pleases that she will hold her tongue if her mother will allow her to go skating—she is sent back to her room in no uncertain manner to learn her Bible verses for tomorrow's confirmation class. And she manages the members of the community with equal skill. Mitteldorf is tied to her apron strings. She allows Motes to blackmail her and knows that she is losing less than she gains. She bargains with Wulkow like a market-woman and sets Krüger and von Wehrhahn against one another with the innocent candour of a diplomat. Yet with all this she remains a good washerwoman, a hard-working wife, a fond mother—and a woman of the people, whose knowledge of the world, for all her shrewdness and for all her ambition, has its limitations. Money, she knows, is important. But culture, she thinks, is important too, and she has brought up her daughters "gebild't." The local doctor has once made the mistake of calling Leontine a beauty and from that moment her mother has destined her for the stage. And Adelheid, even now, could recite poetry to Fleischer's Berlin guests: "Die is Ihn treiste, die legt glei los. Se deklamiert Ihn zu wunderscheene." Frau Wolff is without doubt in the *avant-garde* of her day, but, realist as she is, she has her illusions about her daughters, and her notions of the world towards which she is climbing are as naïve as those of a girl in her early teens.

The problems connected with a rapid change from a rural to an urban society are reflected also in the figures surrounding Frau Wolff, some of whom belong, like herself, to the new world, some to the old. Even within her own family the differences are clearly marked. The ideals of Julius are traditional in the strictest sense: slow and steady work, and a little poaching or illegal wood-cutting on the side; and his life with his wife is dominated by the fear that every new venture will end in a term in prison. "Wat hab ick davon," he says more than once, "wenn ick sitzen muss!" Leontine is a younger and softer version of her father who would, indeed, follow the lure of the Berlin sewing-machine shops if her mother would allow her, but who will remain at the bottom of the ladder whatever she does. Adelheid, on the other hand, takes after her mother, and will, in a sense, outstrip her, for she has Frau Wolff's wit and boldness without her decency and warmth. Mitteldorf, to turn to the other inhabitants of the hamlet, is a hangover from an older, easier régime, and utterly bewildered by the new. Life may be difficult for him at home; but the tongue of his wife cannot be sharper than that of von Wehrhahn, who regards him as the living image of the inefficiency of the old ways and takes advantage of every opportunity to tell him so. Krüger is a former small craftsman, with the craftsman's virtues of independence, exactness and thrift, who has become, under the stress of age and of the new era, an irritable and parsimonious old man with a somewhat exaggerated sense of his own importance. The new, liberal intelligentsia is represented by the figure of Fleischer. And Motes is an opportunist who tries to take advantage of the intensification of the social struggle by working with or against both sides, a scavenger and a parasite, like Frau Wolff an adventurer, but without her ability, her energy, or her scruples. All of these figures are realistically portrayed. But Hauptmann's attitude towards them varies a little from person to person. The strokes that paint Julius and Mitteldorf are clear and vigorous, but not harsh. The pictures of Adelheid and Motes are sharper and more severe. And this difference in attitude is still more strongly marked in regard to the figure of von Wehrhahn, a blend of the old era and the new. He too is drawn from real life, but through the medium, not of humour, but of satire.

There is a real sting in this portrait of the Prussian Junker in office, with his monocle, his high boots, and his shrill commanding voice, the "Unteroffizierston" that Hauptmann had learned to hate as a schoolboy. His dislike of the type, with its traditional arrogance and class prejudice, was not ameliorated by his subsequent experience in Erkner and with the censorship in Berlin. He had also serious misgivings about recent attempts of the Prussian government ro reinforce its authoritarian and militaristic principles by prolonging army grants and by antisocialist legislation. In 1887 he himself had been summoned before a court in Breslau to give evidence about a student club with which he had been associated and which dreamed of establishing an equalitarian settlement in the backwoods of America. All of this is reflected in von Wehrhahn— Hauptmann dislikes him personally, he dislikes the tradition he represents, and he dislikes his new and radically reactionary tendencies. The *Amtsvorsteher* is pompous and condescending to those whom he trusts and favours, and so arrogant to those whom he does not that even the gentle Fleischer has difficulty in controlling his anger in his presence. He feeds his sense of his own superiority by directing his sarcasm at the wretched Mitteldorf. His narrowness and prejudice are revealed in a masterly way by his routine and patterned interrogation of Motes: he asks precisely what Motes expects him to ask and Motes tells him exactly what he expects to be told—that there are meetings in Fleischer's rooms, that books and newspapers arrive, some of which are sure to be subversive, and that there has been a disrespectful word about a person of high rank. But von Wehrhahn also has dreams of greatness which indicate that the traditional hierarchy, in its attempts to remain rigid, is crumbling from within; and he has more than a touch of fanaticism. "Ich stehe hier ja nicht zu meinem Vergnügen," he says to Motes, "Zum Spass hat man mich nicht hierher gesetzt. . . . Die Herren freilich, die mich ernannt haben, die wissen genau, mit wem sie's zu tun haben. Die kennen den ganzen Ernst meiner Auffassung. Ich erfasse mein Amt als heiljen Beruf."

It is true that when we abstract and list these characteristics we make von Wehrhahn appear more sinister and dangerous— and perhaps especially to a mid-twentieth-century audience— than he is. For his actions are both ineffectual and ridiculous. He jumps at people like the game-cock which his name suggests and he darts from one piece of business to another without ever accomplishing anything. Frau Wolff deceives him. Krüger defies him. Fleischer comes out unscathed in the end. The only person, in fact, who is really shaken by his jurisdiction is Mitteldorf, and even the poor constable has his moment of unwitting triumph. At the beginning of the fourth act Hauptmann allows him to explain the new order to Frau Wolff, and there follows a beautiful *reductio ad absurdum* of the aims and ideals of his superiors: "Et kracht, und wenn et kracht, Mutter Wolffen, denn—hat et jekracht. . . . Et muss wat jeschehn. Det jeht nich so weiter. Der janze Ort muss jesäubert wern. . . . Ick könnte Ihn'n all noch ville erzähln. Ick hab man nich Zeit. . . . Et kracht, Mutter Wolffen, det können Se mir jlooben." Yet there remains in the portrait a note of disgust and of aversion. The intellectual understanding of a Shaw would have disposed of the magistrate and all his kith and kin with sovereign ease. Hauptmann, with his primarily emotional approach, cannot dismiss him so lightly. And there is no question at all of his accepting him with the tolerant humour which, on the whole, he displays towards his other characters. Readers of the comedy have sometimes been disturbed by this mixture of satire and humour within one and the same work maintaining that it endangers the aesthetic unity of the play. But Heise has risen to Hauptmann's defence, pointing out that the dislocation was not devised intentionally and that Hauptmann was painting von Wehrhahn as he saw him.[5] If some tenuous conception of unity is imperilled thereby, the circumstances are entirely to the dramatist's credit.

Basically, *Der Biberpelz* is built upon the portrayal of limited, often lumbering, sly, and yet naïve people and upon the ludicrous and complicated situations which are typical of peasant comedy, whether the peasants are those of a Shakespeare or a Synge, of a Gryphius or an Anzengruber. But most peasant comedies portray a relatively static and timeless world. Hauptmann's play, with the wind blowing from Berlin, is a significant drama of its own day and of a period of rapid change. His people will not remain as they are or continue to live as they do. Mitteldorf, Krüger, and Julius already belong to a bygone age. There will be more visitors from Berlin—Frau Wolff looks forward to enlarging her house so that she can take in "summer guests"—and the children of the community will, in their turn, leave to work in the city. Even the present is not without its darker aspects, and what we can see of the future points to a heightened struggle,

[5]Wilhelm Heise, *Gerhart Hauptmanns Dramen* (Leipzig, n.d.), IV, p. 30.

and to degeneration. It would be surprising, for example, if Adelheid survived the indoctrination in double standards, to which she is being subjected by her mother, with any integrity at all. This does not mean that such considerations are uppermost in our minds when the curtain falls on Frau Wolff's beautiful affirmation of her own dishonesty—far from it. But we may suspect that Hauptmann lowered it just in time to keep *Der Biberpelz*, as it is, a humane and realistic version of a traditional comic genre, spiced by some vigorous criticism of important social and political trends.

II

Der Biberpelz was written in 1891. In 1901, in *Der rote Hahn*, Hauptmann returned to the same theme to portray the fate of the Spree community and of the Wolff family ten years later. He called the new play, like *Peter Brauer* and *Die Ratten*, a tragi-comedy, and its atmosphere is very different from that of its predecessor. The settlement in the meantime has grown by leaps and bounds and belongs to what we should now call the metropolitan area. The forest has retreated, apartment buildings are replacing the villas and cottages, the population has increased and changed in character, and organizations and meetings are the order of the day. But it is not the encroachment of the city alone that is responsible for the difference. *Der Biberpelz* was written during the brief liberal regime under the Chancellorship of Caprivi, which followed the dismissal of Bismarck. But after Caprivi's fall in 1894 the forces of reaction, with Junker and industrialist now firmly united, moved ahead at accelerated speed. In all respects, in the tragicomedy, the worst has come to pass, and its theme is degeneration—"Verwilderung," to quote von Wehrhahn, "auf der janzen Linie."

Der rote Hahn, like most continuations, is not entirely successful, and there is no need to give more than a brief indication of its action and of its characters, old and new. Julius is dead and Frau Wolff has remarried, a shoemaker named Fielitz whom she has described of old as "der lausige Fielitzschuster" and as a procurer, a spy, and an informer. Leontine, who has persuaded her mother after all to let her work in Berlin, is now a seamstress with an illegitimate child and a dubious future: she is pursued, in the course of the play, by two married men, the present constable Schulze and a blacksmith named Langheinrich whose wife is extremely ill and who, Frau Wolff hopes, will soon be a widower. Adelheid, with the help of a certain fatherly pressure from the church, has secured as her husband a master builder named Schmarowski, an upstart and a speculator, who is on his way to great wealth and power. Other new figures are Ede, Langheinrich's assistant; Boxer, a native of the community who has just returned home after a long semi-voluntary political exile as a ship's doctor; and a former constable named Rauchhaupt, a widower with a large number of children, one of whom, Gustav, is an imbecile. Von Wehrhahn is still in command, but growing old. The real new master of the scene is Schmarowski. The action centres about the last of Frau Wolff's exploits: she manages, with the help of a candle concealed in a box, to have house and shop go up in flames while she and her husband are absent in the city. The property is heavily insured. There is an investigation, conducted as in the past by von Wehrhahn, and the responsibility for the fire is attributed to Gustav, who had had an errand at the house in the course of the morning. The play concludes with the death of Frau Wolff, who suffers a heart attack on the very day that the weather-vane is being erected on the apartment house built by Schmarowski with the proceeds of the fire.[6]

To portray such characters and such an action in any light but that of unmitigated satire would be very difficult and it is small wonder that Hauptmann did not entirely succeed in achieving

[6]According to Walter Requardt ("Erkner im Leben und Werk Gerhart Hauptmanns," dissertation, Hamburg, 1951) Hauptmann, who moved to Silesia in 1889, visited Erkner several times before the turn of the century and saw the growing industrialization there. He heard the arson story, however, in the nearby village of Kragel, from its inhabitants and from his friend Moritz Heimann who, together with a young Erkner doctor, Georg Anselm, inspired the figure of Dr. Boxer.

the blend of comedy and tragedy for which he was striving. The play is marred, in the first place, by an attempt to carry something of the humour of *Der Biberpelz* into its very different and highly unpleasant situations. We enjoy ourselves thoroughly when Krüger, brandishing a stick of his own wood in his hand, swears to Frau Wolff that he will catch the thief yet, if it should cost him a thousand dollars. But when we watch Frau Fielitz, during the trial of the innocent Gustav, kissing von Wehrhahn's hand and weeping crocodile tears about the destruction of her property, we feel that the spectacle is mean and distasteful rather than amusing; and we are outraged when she goes on to insinuate that the damage has been done deliberately by someone whom her husband has reported to the police and that they are, accordingly, suffering for their services to the nation.

The last act, which brings the play to the verge of tragedy, is more convincing. Rauchhaupt, unable to face the thought that he, a former servant of the Prussian state, has a son in prison, has attempted to hang himself. And Frau Wolff, as she feels her own death approaching, is not without a sense of guilt. She makes no open confession of her sins, but she explains to him at length and in a semi-repentant vein that her life has been a long and incessant struggle which has left her, today, a broken and unhappy woman. "Was sein mir: Sie, ich und mir alle zusamm?" she asks, "Mir han uns musst schinden und schuften durchs Leben, eener so gutt wie der andere dahier. . . . Wer ni mitmacht, is faul, wer de mitmacht, is schlecht. . . . Unsereens muss jeden Dreck doch anfassen! Da heesst's immer: gutt sein. Wie fängt ma's ock an? . . . Uffbegehrt ha ich, das is wahr. Nu ganz natierlich ooch! . . . Ma langt . . . Ma langt immer so . . . Ma langt nach was." Her words are, in part, true and affecting. But, while Platonic longing may well be an element in the struggles of every human being, its formulation here is a little too deliberate and ethereal for the lips of Frau Wolff.[7] Nor is it easy to believe that she has become merely the gullible

[7]This can perhaps be explained, though not excused, by the fact that *Der rote Hahn* was written in the same year as *Michael Kramer*.

victim of her ambitious son-in-law and sacrificed her insurance money to further his plans. Her *volte-face*, like that of Crampton, is too sudden to be credible and the tragedy—perhaps in an attempt to compensate for the humourless humour—is on the whole over-stated and sentimentalized.[8]

Yet there is much in the play to evoke our interest and admiration. Hauptmann was able to depict his new characters more freely than those who had already appeared in *Der Biberpelz* and, while they are only sketched and do not hold our interest to the same extent as the similarly varied group in *Die Ratten*, the sketches are lively and reflect the changes that have taken place during the past years in a way that speaks well for the breadth and acuteness of Hauptmann's observation. His amazingly detailed recording of the most urgent social problems of the day gives the play a significance that makes up in some measure for his relative lack of success with his major character and his main action.[9]

The general impression of the scene is, we have noted, degeneration. Its landmarks are chauvinism, anti-Semitism, a close association between religion and the government, a perversion of labour movements, and the cynicism and self-interest that flourish in all quarters after a few years of economic prosperity combined with social and political regression. Some of this Hauptmann attempts to take lightly, merely noting with a satirical touch that the words "Preussen" and "Deutschland" are on the lips of all, that Rauchhaupt, who is proud of having fought for emperor and country, has painted the word "Jott" on Julius' tombstone in Prussian blue, and that von Wehrhahn, still busy defending the nation, is now an ardent advocate of a

[8]In the fall of 1956, however, the Heidelberg Städtische Bühne presented the rarely acted play in a special performance, in which its inherent satirical and tragic possibilities were brilliantly vindicated by Heinz Menzel's adaptation and by the acting of Lola Mebius who managed to interpret Frau Wolff from the third act on as a tormented and harassed being.

[9]Hugh Garten, in his *Gerhart Hauptmann* (Cambridge, 1954), though he does not go into details, agrees that *Der rote Hahn* has "an interest of its own." Among earlier critics a positive appraisal, such as that of Julius Bab in *Gerhart Hauptmann und seine besten Bühnenwerke* (Berlin, 1922), is the exception rather than the rule.

strong navy. But he is seriously concerned that both the Junker and Schmarowski are important members of the great new church. Hauptmann was never favourably impressed by the orthodox ministry. When he heard Christianity invoked in support of militarism or of the existing social order he became furious, and his depiction of characters who think in such terms verges on the grotesque. We never see von Wehrhahn in a worse light than when he is admonishing the imbecile Gustav that all the disorders of the day are a result of neglect of religion. "Der janze moralische Niederjang," he explains, "die Verwilderung auf der janzen Linie ist Folge des Mangels an Religion! . . . Nächstenliebe! Christlicher Geist! Hosen stramm und den Hintern versohlt! Prügel! Ohrfeigen! Christliche Zucht! Und keine Jefühlsduseleien." Gustav, who is clever at imitating animals, responds, perhaps rather obviously, with a loud bray. But it is a finer touch that he, like von Wehrhahn, is an admirer of the church and sits for hours in a nearby ditch gaping at the bells. Von Wehrhahn and Schmarowski are also united in their anti-Semitism. The *Amtsvorsteher* does not yet admit his hostility openly. But he reports that Boxer's mother recently came to him to complain of stones thrown through her windows, and dismisses the matter with the obviously appreciative, "Übermütige Bengels jewesen." The builder is already a member of a consciously anti-Jewish movement. "Es ist mit uns nich jut Kirschen essen," he snaps at Boxer, who has done nothing whatsoever to provoke him, "Wir lassen nich mit uns spassen, jawoll. Und von die Rasse, zu der Sie jehören. . . ." It is possible that Hauptmann thought of Fleischer as Jewish; he pictured him as a man with very black hair, gentle manners, and a gentle voice. But he saw no need to stress the matter, one way or another. Ten years later he felt that he had to make a definite answer to the von Wehrhahns and the Schmarowskis. Boxer is the most humane and likeable character in the play, and his dead father has held the Iron Cross.

The picture is equally forbidding if we turn from questions of nationalism and religion to those of social and economic rela-

tionships. The story here is centred about Schmarowski, Langheinrich, and Ede. The blacksmith and his helper are both in
many ways good-natured and decent men. Langheinrich sends
the builder packing for his attack on Boxer though he knows
that it may mean a loss of work. They are also Hauptmann's
first socially conscious proletarians. The Frau Wolff of *Der
Biberpelz* is completely unaware that she is taking part in a
revolutionary class struggle, and even ten years later, when she
talks of the universal fight for life, she thinks of herself merely
as belonging to the poor who are condemned to make their way
by any and every means. Langheinrich and Ede on the other
hand give the impression of being conscious of their position
on the economic front and of the movements, the means, and
the devices by which men seek for power in a modern industrial
world. The blacksmith speaks bitterly of those who flay their
employees and then sit piously in the new church with their
ears hanging like melancholy rabbits. And both, as members
of the local fire brigade, answer von Wehrhahn's questions man
to man, with a frank and jovial *insouciance*. "Sie haben wohl
tüchtig jeholfen, was?" asks the *Amtsvorsteher*.

EDE: Derbe! Sonst macht et ja keenen Spass.
VON WEHRHAHN: Ich meine, janz besonders beim Biertrinken?
EDE: Det ha ick ooch richtig verstanden. Jawoll.

But neither their personal characteristics nor their understanding of the mechanics of society get them very far. Ede, who has
already been in prison for taking part in a riot, has still some
hope that common action on the part of the workers will lead
to a better world; but Langheinrich has become cynical and
decided that he will work for no one in a world where no one
will work for him. "Ick mir vor andere abschinden?" he protests,
"Ei, wo! Jott bewahre! . . . Mir jibt woll ooch keener wat."
And both in the end succumb to Schmarowski, Langheinrich because the builder, after all, can provide him with enough work to
keep four assistants busy and Ede because he is deluded. Schmarowski has shrewdly decided that it is good business to become the
people's man. "Soziale Sache," he explains privately, "Riesen-

jeschäft. Natürlich bin ich bei mittenmang." He announces his change of heart at a public meeting and, as the people cheer their new leader, Ede explains to Boxer that he too has been impressed. "Ick ha dem Kerlchen nich riechen jemocht. Aber nu . . . nee . . . wo er vernünftig is un so for jesunde Ideen tut instehn: keene Willkür und Polizeijewalt, denn . . . denn . . . nu lass ick ihm ooch mit hochleben all!" English workers felt that the rebels in *Die Weber* were so naïve in their ideas that the play was politically outdated when it appeared. There is much in the present work that is not outdated today.

"Ich habe dem Politiker in mir jeden Tag mit einem Hammer den Schädel einschlagen müssen, um zu leben: es wäre verkauftes Menschentum, wenn ich es in meinem besonderen Falle nicht getan hätte," Hauptmann once wrote, and the sentence has been widely quoted as an indication of his resolve, after the early plays, to redirect his sights towards so-called eternal problems and values. *Der rote Hahn* is one piece of evidence among others that, if he suppressed his longing to enter the lists as an active reformer, at least his desire to record the problems of the contemporary social scene was not nearly as dormant as is sometimes supposed. True, it is not easy to judge to what extent and how deeply his thoughts were preoccupied, around the turn of the century, with the conditions described in the play. His personal affairs were in a highly critical state. Among other things he needed money, and he may have hoped to repeat the success of *Der Biberpelz*, which had been very popular, by writing another play about the same scene and the same main characters. But the wish to make money can hardly have prompted him to paint a picture as unpleasant as any to be found in the novels of a Heinrich Mann. The satire of *Der Biberpelz*, moreover, was not unprovoked by personal experience. There are, as far as I know, no such incidents to account for *Der rote Hahn*. It may well be that, until the material in the Hauptmann archives is reassembled and examined, the attitude of Dr. Boxer provides us with the best key that we can discover to the dramatist's own position. Boxer, we remember, has felt himself obliged to take a three-year respite from affairs in contemporary Germany, and he denies that he is seriously concerned by what he sees when he returns. "Ich leugne ja nicht, dass die Chosen mir Spass machen," he says, and he accepts Ede's capitulation to Schmarowski with no more than, "Na, Ede! Aber natürlich! Gewiss." But he thinks, in the end, that he will return to sea again. It was just three years after the failure of *Florian Geyer*, by which he had hoped to awaken the conscience of the nation, that Hauptmann began to write *Der rote Hahn*, returned, that is to say, like Boxer, to the public scene. If the parallel is valid we may take it that he found the spectacle unbearable. Yet he did not himself put out to sea, at least not permanently. The first general outline of the novel *Emanuel Quint*, which deals at length with some of the problems touched on in the tragicomedy, was written down in the following year, though he did not begin to work on it steadily until 1907. And when it was finished, in 1910, he turned again, in *Peter Brauer* and more especially in *Die Ratten*, to depict the same type of heterogeneous and sharply decadent society that he had sketched, as yet somewhat uncertainly, in *Der rote Hahn*.

Hauptmann never attempted, in the manner of Balzac, to portray the world he saw about him, section by section, in a series of works. He described those scenes which, within his own experience, had impressed him most deeply, and in view of what he accomplished it would be folly to wish that he had done otherwise. But we might perhaps wish that he had written the present play a little later or a little less quickly; we might then have had, in *Der Biberpelz, Der rote Hahn,* and *Die Ratten*, a trilogy without parallel about the advance of a modern metropolis and its effect on the lives of those who are caught in its toils.

III

In pursuing the fate of the Wolff family across a decade we have departed from the chronological order otherwise observed within these chapters and have now to retrace our steps. As soon as he had completed *Der Biberpelz* Hauptmann began a two-act play which he called a "Traumdichtung" and to which he gave the title *Hanneles Himmelfahrt*.[10] It occupied him during the spring and summer of 1893 and was acted for the first time in November of the same year, a few weeks after the première of *Der Biberpelz* and before *Die Weber* had seen the lights of a public theatre.

Hannele plays in a village poor-house on a cold, stormy winter night. It opens with a glimpse of the various inhabitants, and then a worker named Seidel comes in, and with him the school-master Gottwald, carrying in his arms a girl of fourteen whose long red hair hangs over his shoulder. They have just dragged her from a pond in which she has attempted to drown herself; they place her on a cot and try to warm her. They are followed by the chief of police, Berger, by a doctor, and by Schwester Martha, a deaconess. As Hannele revives, Gottwald urges her to speak, but she will say only that she is cold, hungry, and afraid, and that Christ has called her to join him and her mother in heaven. Seidel, however, can give further details: the girl's mother has recently died and her drunken step-father maltreats her. And the doctor discovers marks of severe beatings on the emaciated body and fears that she may not recover from the shock of the freezing water. Berger leaves in order to have Mattern, the step-father, arrested, although Seidel remarks that he will not do so, that he is himself Hannele's father, and that he will not dare touch the man who has brought her up.

Alone with Martha, Hannele talks more freely. It is her father she fears, she says, and she fears also that she has committed an unforgivable sin. But as Martha sings her a lullaby, her mind begins to wander. She confuses the deaconess and her mother. She speaks of the heavenly bridegroom and gives him the name of Gottwald. She begins to see visions, which appear on the stage, first Mattern, threatening her, and then her mother, followed by

---

[10]The play had originally a third, entirely poetic act, but Hauptmann, feeling that it was superfluous, refused to have it printed, even in the 1942 edition. For details see F. A. Voigt, "Zu 'Hanneles Himmelfahrt'," in *Hauptmann-Studien* (Breslau, 1936).

a chorus of angels, telling her of the joys of paradise, and promising her that she will soon be recompensed for all that she has suffered. Once, briefly, she opens her eyes and shows Martha the yellow primrose, the "Himmelsschlüssel," which, she thinks, her mother has given her. Then she sinks still more deeply into delirium and experiences her own funeral and resurrection. The angel of death appears, pale, stern, and beautiful. A village tailor dresses her in white silk and slippers of glass, and she lies in a glass coffin. Gottwald brings her schoolmates to sing on the way to the grave, and the old women of the village gather, as usual, to admire the body, and exclaim that angels have been seen in the street and that the dead girl is a saint. Mattern comes again to threaten her, but he is checked by a pale stranger with the features of Gottwald who calls him to account for his cruelty to God's child, and, when a radiant green-gold flower appears in Hannele's hands, the step-father flees, howling that he will hang himself. The stranger's cloak falls to the ground, revealing gleaming white robes, and Christ-Gottwald bids Hannele rise. Angels again fill the room, singing to her, in rhymed couplets, of the joys that will soon be hers, and, in the end, taking up the lullaby with which the visions began. Then the stage darkens, and by the sole remaining light of the deaconess' lamp we see the doctor bending over the bed and nodding his head as he speaks the word, "tot."

The audiences who first saw *Hannele*, knowing Hauptmann only as the author of *Vor Sonnenaufgang*, *Einsame Menschen*, and *Der Biberpelz*, and having decided that he was a thorough-going naturalist, were astonished—as they were to be astonished more than once in the coming years—both by its poetry and by its dreams. The interest in human illusions and aspirations was not, of course, as foreign to Hauptmann's work as it appeared in 1893. Dreams at their best, as we have noted, were for him a part of man's creative life, and, even at their worst, a support in circumstances which might be otherwise unendurable. Yet even to those who know many of the later works *Hannele* may come as something of a surprise, for it is Hauptmann's most direct attempt to make his plays fulfil the task he had set himself at an early age. The soul of the poet, he proclaimed in the first poem of *Das bunte Buch*, must be like a harp in the wind,

> Und ewig müssen
> die Saiten schwingen
> im Atem des Weltwehs;
> denn das Weltweh
> ist die Wurzel
> der Himmelssehnsucht.
>
> Also steht deiner Lieder
> Wurzel begründet
> im Weh der Erde;
> doch ihren Scheitel krönet
> Himmelslicht.

The conviction that a poet must place equal stress on the sorrows of the earth and on the longing for heaven is reflected, in *Hannele*, in the extent to which Hauptmann develops his heroine's dreams and visions, crowning his work by contributing from his own imagination to the heavenly light that the poem demands.

The sources of the play, which are quite different in nature, further accentuated the juxtaposition of the real and the imagined. The action seems to be based on a local Silesian legend which Hauptmann used first in *Das bunte Buch*, in a ballad called *Die Mondbraut*. The poem tells the story of a child driven forth by a cruel guardian into the snow and the night to collect wood and, lured by the moon, climbing a tall fir tree in an attempt to reach heaven and her parents, only to fall to her death at its foot. His interest in the tale must have been awakened again by a young girl whom he met during his trip to the Silesian weaving villages in 1892. "In dieser Behausung," writes Max Baginski, "traf Hauptmann eine Witwe mit einer etwa dreizehnjährigen Tochter. Das Mädchen fiel ihm auf, es hatte schönes, weiches, goldgelbes Haar, tiefe Augen, einen zartblassen Teint. Ich erfuhr später ... dass Hauptmann dem Kinde hin und wieder ein Geschenk sandte, und als ich später *Hannele* las, wollte es mir nicht aus dem Sinn, dass der Dichter an dieses Reichenbacher Kind gedacht haben müsse, als er seine Dichtung schuf."[11] The figure of the girl in the familiar environment of the Silesian village seems to have inspired the attempt to give new, more detailed, and more realistic life to the theme briefly and conventionally formulated in the ballad. The result is a play which has its full measure of the living environment, the sensitive penetration, and the love and understanding that are characteristic of Hauptmann at his best, but which is strongly marked also by the mood of the legend and by a conscious effort to portray man's longing for a better world. If the two aspects of the work are not always in complete accord with one another, the quality of the play as a whole is such that it is the duty of the critic to enunciate its virtues before proclaiming its flaws.

The village and the inhabitants, in the small space that Hauptmann has at his disposal, are only sketched, but they are sketched with the sure hand of one who is completely at home in the world he is depicting. When the characters talk of their surroundings, of the upper and lower village, the school and the churchyard, the apothecary's shop and the blacksmith's, and the deep pond with the spot that never freezes, we feel that they are talking of places they have known all their lives. And each of the characters has his own being which, however briefly glimpsed, is not soon forgotten: the stuttering, kind-hearted old Pleschke gravely playing the part of "Bräutigam," of the fiancé of the aged woman who lives with him in the poor-house; Berger, a former army captain and something of a man of the world, who is out of his sphere in this remote Silesian nest; Schwester Martha, with a kindness that is professional and yet genuine; the garrulous Seidel; and the serious and correct young schoolmaster. But our strongest impressions are of the poor-house—a vivid representation of the kind of life Hannele has led—and of the girl herself, with her dreams in the midst of her wretchedness and misery.

[11]"Gerhart Hauptmann unter den schlesischen Webern," *Sozialistische Monatshefte,* I (1905), pp. 186-7.

All that makes Hannele what she is is finely perceived and finely marked. She is an adolescent and, as an illegitimate child, an outcast. Continually abused at home and at school, where the other children call her Cinderella, she has become timid, passive, and withdrawn to the extent that she seems stubborn in her silence. Her quiescence and her sense of guilt have been strengthened by the teachings of the church. "Man soll nicht klagen," says her dream image of Schwester Martha, "Still geduldig muss man sein." And she sees in her mother a woman who, having sinned in conceiving her, cannot enter fully into divine bliss. But she responds gratefully to the slightest touch of warmth and affection, and church and fairy-tale have comforted her with promises of happiness ever after. She has a sweet sense of triumph in a death that confounds her tormentors and makes of her a princess and a saint; sweeter still is the forgiveness she accords her penitent classmates; and sweetest of all is the moment when religious teachings and the stirrings of adolescence, which have given additional tension to all her emotions, combine to evoke the vision of the divine bridegroom, and the eroticism of the flesh and of the spirit become one. In the face of her suffering her dreams seem, to us as to her, deeply moving and almost incredible in their beauty.

The structure is as satisfying as the characterization. The play moves, as a whole, from reality into dream, and the transition is skilfully and carefully done. At first Hannele is only partly distracted: she thinks, for example, because of the pain that racks her body, that someone is tormenting her, but she recognizes Gottwald and Martha. A little later she suffers the first, brief hallucination of her father from which she is partly roused by the returning deaconess, only to begin almost at once to confuse Martha with her mother and Gottwald with Christ. And as the play progresses she sinks deeper and deeper into delirium until, except for one or two half-waking moments, her dreams take over the stage and carry the action through the details of the funeral to the end.

Within the visions themselves, moreover, there is a sense of progression, of heightening and intensification throughout the whole course of the play. The elements of Hannele's dreams are grounded in her experience, and Hauptmann's juxtaposition of the near and the remote, his blending of the real world and the world of fantasy and longing, his interweaving of the conscious and sub-conscious, reflect dream states that are familiar to us all. Hannele has been in Gottwald's arms in reality before he raises her, as Christ, to eternal life; she has experienced Martha's kindness before she begins to confuse her with her mother; fairy-tale and Bible suggest the vision of her step-father as half ogre and half Judas, and provide as well the basis of all the glory and ecstasy of which she dreams. Her mother speaks briefly, in the first vision, of fruit and wine, of the beauty of angels and of wide meadows sheltered from the storm, and lilies of the valley growing from her mouth give an impression of the rare and intense joy which fills Hannele at her appearance, and which is a foretaste of the joys to come in the later visions.

But, for all the dramatist's faithfulness in the portrayal of the sub-conscious and the imagined, the continuity and order of the dialogue and the rising sequence of events in the second act give the whole a shape and coherence and a steadily mounting tension which betray his own ordering hand. And, particularly at the end of each act, Hauptmann has himself taken over, elaborated the pictures that a child might reasonably see, and given poetic embodiment to the joy that possesses her. The song of the angels in the first act is perhaps the most beautiful lyric that he ever wrote, suffused with the sense of a rich, tender, and sustaining nature and illuminated by the anticipation of paradise:

> Auf jenen Hügeln die Sonne,
> sie hat dir ihr Gold nicht gegeben;
> das wehende Grün in den Tälern,
> es hat sich für dich nicht gebreitet.
>
> Das goldene Brot auf den Äckern,
> dir wollt' es den Hunger nicht stillen;
> die Milch der weidenden Rinder,
> dir schäumte sie nicht in den Krug. . . .

> Wir bringen ein erstes Grüssen
> durch Finsternisse getragen.
> wir haben auf unsern Federn
> ein erstes Hauchen von Glück. . . .

Then, at the end of the second act, from hints in the Bible and religious song, Hauptmann builds in verse a radiantly sensuous vision of the eternal city. It would be tempting to look for equivalents of his impressionistic reproduction of scent, sound, and touch, and above all of light and colour in the contemporary lyric of a Holz or a Dauthendey, but the manner is so much Hauptmann's own, and so closely allied to his genius for noting the tones and movements of men, that there is no need to search for influences. There is some sign of his gifts in the early poems—a golden butterfly flutters through the winter snow, the morning lifts a horn of rubies, and the pine trees clench red fists in the lead-heavy descending darkness—although there such details are lost in abstract and conventional diction. But in *Thiel* the changing light gives the heavy landscape an ominous glow or invests it with a delicately luminous beauty in a way that anticipates the verses here:

> Maigrün sind die Zinnen, vom Frühlicht beglänzt,
> von Faltern umtaumelt, mit Rosen bekränzt. . . .
> Das weite weite Meer füllt rot roter Wein,
> sie tauchen mit strahlenden Leibern hinein.
> Sie tauchen hinein in den Schaum und den Glanz,
> der klare Purpur verschüttet sie ganz. . . .

And continuing in this vein, the dramatist, so to speak, compensates Hannele for her suffering by pouring over her all the bliss of soul and body that his poetic imagination can conceive; he gives her visions of white swans ruffling their wings in an air filled with blossoms and music, he promises her soft linen to caress her sick and fever-shaken flesh, and warm, fragrant fruit to freshen and delight her tired body. The verse is not part of the dialogue, and it has no narrative or argumentative function. It points, therefore, only in a restricted way to the later poetic dramas. But the desire to attain heightened emotional expression by the use of verse is in itself a significant extension of Hauptmann's early goals, and his verse drama uses the same vividly sensuous images and impressions to represent psychic and emotional states that we find in *Hannele*.

It is not easy, in the face of all this, to define why and to what extent *Hannele* fails to measure up to the best that we expect from Hauptmann. The setting and the characters are alive and convincing, the dream is psychologically legitimate, and we can hardly quarrel with the author for giving his heroine a beautiful death unless, on the same principle, we are willing to set about cutting *Richard III* and *Hamlet*. The theme of the death of an abused child is not, it is true, a subject to inspire a great tragedy; but Hauptmann has not tried to pretend that it is. And if we feel that the flaw in the play lies in sentimentality, in an excess of pity, we have to proceed carefully. There was much talk of Hauptmann, in the early days, as the poet of pity, "der Dichter des Mitleids," as though, having realized that men are helpless in the grip of the natural and social forces surrounding them, he considered that the only function of the poet was to sob over the mutilated corpses. Hauptmann's compassion was rarely so gentle or all embracing, even in his first plays; he showed little disposition to forgive Dreissiger or von Wehrhahn or those who betray the cause of national unity in *Florian Geyer*. He has, to be sure, a genius for "Einfühlung," for identifying himself emotionally with his characters, above all with their suffering, and the compassion that springs from this participation is such a basic source of his judgments and of his desire for justice that we can hardly overstress its importance. But his pity does not distort or evade, it goes hand in hand with his interpretation of the whole situation.

Hannele, however, does much to account for the earlier exaggeration. For the impulse that moved Hauptmann to reward the girl for her trials by shining dreams is not by itself an adequate response to the situation he portrays, but rather, like his assumption of a benevolent, upper-bourgeois *deus ex machina* in *Crampton*, an escape. The scene he paints is a harsh one: a man begets a child and ignores her existence; another beats her and drives her from the house in a drunken fury; and yet a third simply bundles her up in dry clothes after she has tried to drown herself and carries her to the unsavoury atmosphere of a poor-house. Something in the nature of anger would seem to be in order also. But the dramatist was too intent on evoking a sweet sorrow to have time for more than a brief expression of shocked disapproval. And in his one-sided preoccupation he blurred and confused his picture; for the cruel world, which has certainly known of Hannele's plight and has done nothing to alleviate it, becomes improbably gentle at the end, and Gottwald strokes her hair in pity, Martha comforts her and sings to her, and the doctor assures her that she is with good people—"bei guten Menschen."

It is difficult, finally, to accept without reservations the child-like wistfulness of Hannele herself. True, adolescent girls tend to be sentimental, but Hauptmann lingers with such obvious satisfaction on Hannele's dreams of fairy-tale glass slippers and of a heaven without medicine that the play is lacking in the tension necessary to reconcile us to the fact that this child is also the girl who longs for the oblivion of a bridegroom's embrace, and we are left with some sense of discomfort. Wedekind managed better in *Frühlings Erwachen*, and Hauptmann himself, in *Quint* and in *Der arme Heinrich*, portrayed adolescents with a profound understanding of the difficult and often drastic nature of their problems. Around *Hannele* there still lingers, like a legacy from the ballad or from Hans Christian Andersen's *The Little Match Girl*, an aura of sweet pity which detracts from its basic realism and from the moving and genuine beauty of many of its visions and of much of its language. Its power remains, but it would have been greater if Hauptmann had been more exclusively concerned with his heroine and her environment and less with the expression of emotions that belong, if they belong anywhere, to a gentler and less realistic portrayal of the world.

IV

It was 1897, four years after the completion of *Hannele*, before Hauptmann turned again, in *Fuhrmann Henschel*, to a play of his own day and his own province. And *Geyer*, with its bitter pictures, separates *Hannele* and *Henschel* as it separates *Crampton* and *Kramer*. There is no tendency to sentimentality in *Henschel*. It is the first of the great dramas of Hauptmann's maturity, a work with all the vigour of *Der Biberpelz*, with a deep insight into a nature and a struggle not easily seen or comprehended, and a work of intense and sombre tragedy. But, in part because its subject-matter is drawn from Hauptmann's earliest days in his father's hotel, it portrays the dissolution of a world whose outlines can still be seen clearly rather than, as in *Die Ratten*, a conglomeration of shipwrecked existences. The mood in *Henschel*, like that in *Kramer* and *Schilling*, is unbroken by the sense of futility and hopelessness that we find in the later works.

What prompted Hauptmann to write a play about the Preussische Krone at this time, we do not know. Schlenther has suggested that the work was in the nature of a flight home from Palestine, the remote realm of *Das Hirtenlied*—and, we might add, from the equally far-off realms of *Elga* and of *Der arme Heinrich*—in which he had been dwelling during the months just past.[12] But if we cannot tell why the fruition came when it did, we know something, again from *Das Abenteuer meiner Jugend*, about the genesis. In the basement of the Preussische Krone lived a coachman named Krause, who transported the guests of the hotel, and Hauptmann writes of the simple meal he once ate in the man's apartment with his family and his old helper, each person in turn, decently and without haste, dipping his fork into the earthenware pot of sauerkraut and dumplings that stood in the middle of the table and conveying the skilfully

---

[12]*Gerhart Hauptmann*, p. 78. Hauptmann noted in his diary in May 1898 that he had been deeply moved, some months before, by Moritz Heimann's account of Hermann Stehr's Silesian story *Der Graveur*. He had begun the first version of *Henschel* in November of the preceding year. See Behl, *Wege zu Gerhart Hauptmann*, p. 107. The two works have affinities in theme and in characterization.

wound mass to his mouth with such care that not a drop fell on the clean, scrubbed wood. The life of these lower rooms, the strength and simple, patriarchal dignity of the carter and the propriety and order of his household—all of which, incidentally, was in striking contrast to the luxury, the ostentation, and the more complicated social pattern of above stairs—impressed themselves so indelibly on Hauptmann's mind that he could record them, a score of years later, with a sureness and a vividness not surpassed in any other play.[13] For although he was writing about the home to which he had been so deeply attached and which his family had had to leave, and although Henschel's tragedy is based in part on the fact that his way of life is passing, there is little of mere nostalgia in the play and little fruitless longing for the better days of old. Its scenes are as fully and immediately alive, as much "volle Gegenwart"[14] as those of *Der Biberpelz* or *Einsame Menschen*, which grew out of recent experience.

Four of the five acts of the tragedy play in the basement apartment of the carter, Henschel, in the hotel Zum Grauen Schwan of a small Silesian resort. Henschel is a man of forty-five. Six months before the opening of the play his wife, who is herself nearing forty, has given birth to their first child. The baby is sickly and she is still ill. Depressed by forebodings of death and morbidly jealous of the maid, Hanne, she asks her husband to promise that, if she should die, he will never marry the maid; and this Henschel does readily, even lightly, since nothing is further from his mind. But when his wife dies and Hanne threatens to leave his service because of gossip, he does not know how to carry on. He is also faced with other changes. Railways are being built and are carrying the hotel's wealthy and distinguished patrons to more remote and fashionable resorts. Siebenhaar, the owner, is in financial difficulties. And in any case the railways mean the end of Henschel's work as a carter. He has planned to buy a small inn, and then a wife will be more indispensable than ever.

[13]For further details see Behl, *Wege zu Gerhart Hauptmann* pp. 105-8.
[14]According to the *Ausblicke*, a requisite of good drama.

Hanne seems to him resolute and intelligent, and, after discussing the matter with Siebenhaar, he marries her.

But she is lustful, ruthless and avaricious, and she destroys his life. Mother of a neglected, illegitimate child, she has dismissed a current lover until she is sure of Henschel, but soon after her marriage she finds another in the person of an impertinent Saxon waiter, George. She persuades Henschel to dismiss his lifelong helper, Hauffe, urging that the man is too old. She alienates her husband's earlier associates, Siebenhaar, Wermelskirch, a broken-down actor who leases the hotel's *Schenkstube*, and Walther, the brother of his first wife. She is furious when, after the baby too has died, Henschel brings home her own daughter, Bertha. Matters come to a crisis when the hotel has to be sold, and there is a rumour that the Henschels plan to take over the tap-room driving out the actor and his wife and daughter. Coming in one morning for a glass of beer, Henschel finds himself the centre of a hostile group—George, Hauffe, Walther, Frau Wermelskirch, and Fabig, a pedlar who knows how cruelly Hanne has treated her child. Their taunts and accusations culminate in the charges that Frau Henschel and her baby have not died from natural causes, and that Hanne is unfaithful. Henschel, despondent since the death of his first wife, isolated, and wounded by Hanne's continual harshness, has been brooding increasingly on his misfortunes. This is the final blow. A few nights later, sleepless and wracked by doubts, he commits suicide.

The story of Henschel is thus, in outline, the story of an unhappy second marriage. But the tragedy is not to be explained simply, or on one level. The relation between private and social spheres is not as close here as in *Der Biberpelz*, and the carter's life is not as rigidly and specifically conditioned by his environment as, let us say, the lives of the weavers. But the hotel is more than a background. We have to attempt to understand Henschel's fate first through the medium of this, his society, and then through the details of characterization and plot.

Henschel has worked in the hotel and among its inhabitants

for years, has worked for Siebenhaar's father as he now works for Siebenhaar. His combined kitchen and living-room, whose windows face the court, is a centre not only of his family life, but of the life of the whole house. Strangers stop here to ask their way, and the owner and members of the staff drop in for advice or for a chat. And the Grey Swan, with which he is so closely connected, is both a reality and a symbol, a world where life is decent and generous and ordered, and where there is room for all classes, from the labourer Hauffe to the aristocratic guests, and even for the *déclassés*, for the former actor and his somewhat picturesque wife and daughter. The relations between these various people, for all the inevitable small rubs and pricks, are regulated and stable. The keystone of the harmony is Siebenhaar himself, the gentleman of the upper bourgeoisie, humane, just, courteous, and tolerant, and equally at home in the great drawing-rooms, in the carter's apartment, or in the tap-room, drinking his morning wine with Wermelskirch. Hauffe has worked for Henschel's father as Henschel has worked for Siebenhaar's. Wermelskirch is, by comparison, a new arrival, but he too, in his plebeian fashion, is a decent man with respect for himself and others. Frau Henschel, when we see her, is distracted by her illness, but we have the impression that she has managed her own affairs and not interfered with others. Even Wermelskirch's daughter Franziska, the most volatile element of this ordered microcosm, light of limb, of tongue, and of thought, and cherishing a somewhat more than childish infatuation for Siebenhaar, has a heart as harmless as the kitten with which she plays, and her most serious offence is to stand in the balcony, when Siebenhaar dances in the ball-room, eating prunes to console herself for her role as spectator, and pelting his partners with the pits.

It should be stressed again that there is no sentimentality in this portrait. Hauptmann knows that such a world, because of the very ease of its relations, is bound to be shaken by the advent of a new era; and there are no invectives against the railways. What is important to understand is that this is the world which has formed Henschel, which is the source both of his strength and of his weakness, the world which has given him the good nature, the assurance, and the tolerance so evident in him at the beginning of the play, and which has made him, at the same time, accommodating, co-operative, indeed guileless and passive, rather than egotistical and aggressive. When new and hostile forces enter his life he is, accordingly, open to destruction. He has kept his first wife in her place; when Hanne is inhospitable to Walther, he accepts the insolence of his former maid, and lets his brother-in-law go with a mere "Leb gesund." But his unhappy second marriage and the shaking of the familiar, sheltering structure by the coming of the railways do not merely run parallel, they interlock. Hanne, if we do not try to push the analogy too far, is, like Frau Wolff, a newcomer on a changing scene and a forerunner of restless and ambitious elements in the fourth estate. She has counterparts in the tourists who are beginning to occupy the hotel's guest rooms, demanding all they can get for their money, and in the waiter George who likes to address his employer as "du." The changes in the hotel encourage her inveterate ambition, her desire to rise quickly in the world, and she plays havoc, not only with her husband's personal and domestic existence, but with his social and business relations. It is highly significant that the climax plays in the publicity of the tap-room, with all the carter's associates directly involved. Henschel's whole being, his habits, his thoughts, and his emotions are bound up with the old order; when this order is invaded, he falls.

Once the relationship between the individual and the environment has been established, we may turn to consider other aspects of the play, those factors, namely, which make it a unique and particular tragedy as well as the tragedy of a man in his day. For life in the provinces in the sixties is not moving as quickly as in Frau Wolff's Berlin suburb some twenty years later, and there is room, within this relatively relaxed society, for permutations and combinations within a given set of conditions, and allowance for a variety of individual existences and events. Indeed the difference is so marked that the action of the play is based, not on Hauptmann's usual analysis of a ripe situation, but on a plot, in which the nature and coincidence of events seem, in part at least, accidental. It is inevitable, by way of comparison, that Johannes, whose whole life is based on search and compromise, should marry a girl like Käthe, find her insufficient, and be attracted to someone like Anna. It is significant, but not inevitable, that Henschel's wife should die and that the woman who seems the obvious person to help him in his difficulties should be a woman of the disposition of Hanne.

Hauptmann uses this coincidence, in the first place, as a basis for placing the same emphasis on Henschel's inner life, on the conflict in his mind and emotions, that we find among his more cultivated brothers in *Schilling* or *Kramer*. The carter, in a way that Silesian writers, Jakob Böhme or Hermann Stehr or Hauptmann himself, have taught us to believe characteristic of his countrymen, is puzzled by what has happened, and searches his soul for its moral and transcendental significance. As early as the beginning of the second act we find him, on his dead wife's birthday, at her grave, asking for a sign to guide him and receiving none. In the third, sick at heart at Hanne's rejection of Bertha, he bursts out that his wife has taken his own child with her: "Gustel ist tot. . . . Die hat sich de Mutter auch noch geholt." And his mind is wracked, in the end, by problems of guilt and innocence, of free will and necessity. He has broken his promise to his wife, he thinks, and therefore he is guilty. Everywhere and at all times, when he is feeding the horses, when he enters the bedroom, he sees her accusing figure, he hears her hand at the window, he feels her touch at his breast. But his misfortunes began before his second marriage: his animals became ill or were injured, and his wife herself died. Moreover, her request was the request of a sick woman, and he knew no other way out of his predicament but the one he had taken. Therefore neither he nor Hanne can be entirely responsible for what has happened. Like Schilling, who wonders "Ja, woran liegt das alles? . . . Ich habe nie bewusst nach dem Schlechten gestrebt?" he concludes, towards the end, that a snare must have been set for him which he could not escape and which has involved him in guilt: "Ich hab's woll gemerkt in mein'n Gedanken, dass das und war uf mich abgesehen. . . . ane Schlinge ward mir gelegt, und in die Schlinge da trat ich halt nein. . . . Schlecht bin ich geworn, bloss ich kann nischt dafier." Yet even then he continues to brood: "Meinswegen kann ich auch schuld sein. Wer weess's!? Ich hätte ja besser kenn'n Obacht geben. Der Teifel is eben gewitzter wie ich." And with the knot unresolved, he takes his life.

But it is not only Henschel who puzzles about the meaning of what has happened; to a certain extent the reader too, as he looks back, will ask the same questions and share the same doubts. Some things, certainly, he will understand which the carter does not; that the stability of life in the hotel, for example, has not adapted Henschel to control the aggressive force of Hanne. And he may also be inclined to affirm with Siebenhaar —who, like Mäurer, sets the tone of the play—that Henschel has no cause to think in terms of sin and punishment: "Von Sünde und Schuld ist da gar nicht die Rede." But with Siebenhaar too he may have no final explanation for what has happened other than the resigned, "Das Leben ist keine Spielerei. . . . Gewisse Schicksale treffen den Menschen. Da hat man zu tragen." Or, with Alfred Kerr, he may call the play a modern parallel to the book of Job or a modern tragedy of fate—fate, that is to say, in the sense of events beyond our comprehension.[15] It is, it should be stressed, a *modern* parallel. In writing it Hauptmann was not rejecting the insight into nature and human nature gained by the sciences in the nineteenth century. But men in themselves, as we have already had occasion to note, had always been for him something of a revelation and a wonder. "Man muss [die Menschen] sehen," he wrote in the *Ausblicke*, "als wüsste man gar nichts von ihnen, und erführe alles zum erstenmal. Dieses vollkommen Fremde muss dem Beschauer in seiner kleinsten Funktion das ganze Mysterium, in seiner vollen Wunderbarkeit und Unbegreiflichkeit ausdrücken." In his good plays our impression of the living reality of his people always

[15]*Das neue Drama* (Berlin, 1905), p. 42.

outdistances our ability to account for this vitality by rational or intellectual means. And in *Henschel* Hauptmann went a step further: he relaxed the punctilious motivation of his early plays and stressed his hero's doubts and qualms in order to indicate, as he indicated in *Schilling* though in a different way, that behind the known is still an unknown, and in order to deepen our sense of the incomprehensibility and the imponderability of events and of human life.

There are, however, some critics of *Henschel* who seek to explain the tragedy in another way; who, whether they call their interpretation moral or psychological, seek a deeper basis for Henschel's sense of transgression than the breaking of a promise exacted under duress by a sick woman. Frau Henschel was not wrong, they say, at least not completely, for subconsciously at least her husband desired his maid: in spite of his own troubles he remembered an apron she asked him to bring from town; he thought of marrying her before he confessed his intentions to Siebenhaar; and he was tolerant in the matter of the child because he himself was attracted by the warmth of her blood. And only such a desire can explain a sense of guilt strong enough to break a man like Henschel.[16] To attempt to read the play in this way is to read what is not there. No one would argue that Henschel is an ascetic—on the contrary, if we do not dwell on the implications of the one, frail child born to him after many years of marriage, he seems a hearty and vigorous man. But not even in all the discussion in the last act is there a hint that desire, however subconscious, has played any role in his decisions. And Hauptmann could and would have indicated any such undercurrent had it been present; he was highly skilled and sensitive in such matters, as is evident, to take only one instance, in his fine presentation of the subtlest erotic ramifications in *Rose Bernd*. Henschel remembers Hanne's apron and pardons her child because he is kind, because he is not a Philistine, and because he is secure enough in his world to be able to ignore its narrower aspects.

[16]Emil Glass, *Psychologie und Weltanschauung in Gerhart Hauptmanns "Fuhrmann Henschel"* (Erlangen, 1933), p. 34.

The danger of such Freudian interpretations is that, like Wermelskirch's advice to the Henschels to settle their differences by filling the cradle, they are well meant but so insufficient as to be bitterly ironical. In the early *Bahnwärter Thiel* Hauptmann had written the story of a man who, like Henschel, took as his second wife a coarse, domineering woman and who then found his spiritual life destroyed by his passion for her. But *Henschel* is almost as far removed from *Thiel* as it is, let us say, from Eugene O'Neill's *Desire under the Elms*. The carter's breakdown is a result of his feeling of the incongruity between his actions and their result; he has intended, by his new marriage, to restore the order menaced by the death of his wife and has witnessed instead the destruction of his whole formerly harmonious relationship with the world around him. His sense of justice and morality, of freedom and self-determination, is wounded to the death. Hauptmann's triumph lies in his vision of a man of the lower classes who is in a full sense a human being and—his Silesian heritage and the hotel have seen to that—emotionally and socially, if not intellectually, highly developed. And for all the preoccupation of the modern drama with the proletariat, there are too few characters who can be placed beside him in this respect—Hebbel's mid-century Meister Anton, perhaps, or Gorki's Antipa Zykov—for us to misinterpret one when we find him. Hauptmann does not relegate man's instincts to some lower and inferior level of his existence; but to search for them when they are not there and, in this search, to neglect other elements in his work, is to pervert and dehumanize it, just as we pervert and dehumanize the figure of Rose Bernd, important as eroticism is in her life, if we consider her nothing more than a peasant seductress.

Hauptmann's skill in evolving a man like Henschel from such a rich and detailed background and in depicting his heart and soul are not the only qualities that mark the tragedy as a work of his maturity. It is distinguished also by the deeper and more drastic sense of conflict and of suffering which is characteristic of his plays from *Florian Geyer* on. In reaction perhaps from the brutal harshness of his portraits of peasants in *Vor Sonnenaufgang*, he had placed great stress, in *Die Weber*, on the gentle humility of the oppressed. True, the humility is justified on biological grounds; but the weavers are swept unconsciously to their doom and the last act resembles nothing so much as the slaughter of the innocents. Henschel on the other hand, though he is not aggressive, has within his limits a very real strength; he has self-control and endurance, and he struggles to maintain these qualities till the end. There are signs in the third act that his acquiescence in Hanne's shrewishness stems not only from weakness, but from an effort to be patient, and that he will not endure her ways forever. "Ich denk immer, 's werd amal andersch wern," he bursts out in answer to her charge that he has brought the child home only in order to shame her in the eyes of the neighbours, "aber 's wird bloss immer schlimmer. . . . Wenn das nich bald a Ende nimmt. . . ." And the fourth act has a strong tension and a crushing force without parallel in the early work.

It begins on a harmless level, with Wermelskirch trying his rusty voice at the piano and George, in smart new spring clothes, listening with approval. But old Hauffe, who has been drinking heavily since he was cast off, is crouched at a table. And when Fabig wanders in, followed by Walther—it is the hour of the *Morgenschoppen*—gossip begins, and the atmosphere becomes increasingly tense. By now the sale of the hotel is imminent, and Frau Wermelskirch, a pitiful old wench of a woman, laments that the Henschels mean to take their place. Not only Hanne's ruthlessness, however, but Frau Henschel's jealousy have born fruit. The others join in accusations, and the burden of their song is that Frau Henschel and the baby had to make way for the maid. At the height of it the carter comes in with a blacksmith whom he has been helping and with Bertha. He and the child are clearly unwanted at home, and he faces a long ordeal of unfriendliness, insinuation, and attempted provocation here. For a time he seems unperturbed. George greets him: he ignores him; Walther suggests that he is about to become the new host: he quietly denies it; Hauffe, in a surly manner, refuses an offer of work: he accepts the refusal mildly. Even when the old man remarks bitterly that he had better look after his own affairs, that his own house is filthy enough, he merely grasps him calmly by the collar and puts him out. But then Walther carries on in the same vein: "Wenn du bloss und wärscht noch der alte wie frieher; aber wer weess, was in dich gefahren is. . . . Frieher, da hatt'st du bloss Freinde, heute, da kommt kee Mensch mehr zu dir, und wenn se und wollten auch zu dir kommen, da bleiben se wegen dem Weibe weg. . . . wenn eener kommt und sagt d'r de Wahrheit, der fliegt an de Wand. Aber so a Kerl, so a windiges Luder wie der Schorsch, der kann dich beliigen, Tag und Nacht. Dei Weib und der um die Wette dahier. . . . Die betriegen dich ja am lichten Tage!" And now Henschel has had enough. As Walther, somewhat embarrassed at his own out-burst, rises with a half apologetic, "Hadje, nischt fir ungut," the carter takes his wrist in an iron grip and orders him to wait until Franziska has fetched Hanne. There is a panic of retraction, but Henschel remains firm, and, unable to free himself, Walther is goaded to the final charge—that Frau Henschel and the baby have not died from natural causes. Hanne comes. Her peasant cunning is not equal to the threat of public disgrace. With a cry of "Lügen verdammte!" and with her apron over her face, she flees. Henschel crumples like a felled ox, his head on the table and a rattle in his throat like that of a dying man. We feel more than pity at his destruction, we feel something of the terror that accompanies the fall of the mighty.

The same sense of a harsher and more radical conflict is inspired by the figure of Hanne, the hard, grasping, calculating, and prejudiced woman of the people. She has, it is true, her limits. It is hardly credible that she is deliberately responsible for the death of Gustel; at most we may suppose that her rough energy would not make a suitable nurse for a sickly baby. She is cowed by the public accusations in the fourth act, and, like Lady Macbeth unaware that she is using in her husband a tool too fine for her purposes, she is cowed in the end by the spiritual power manifest in the carter. But she has none of the illusions, the veiling of

convention, in which even an Eveline Schilling attempts to
mask her egotism, both from herself and from the world. Once,
and once only, when Franziska—whom she hates and despises
—accuses her of avarice, she denies the charge with the words,
"ich halt's bloss zusammen." Otherwise she goes her way frankly
and ruthlessly, almost naïvely, greedy for money and greedy
for sensual pleasure, with no attempt to justify herself in her own
eyes or in those of anyone else. And she dominates the action
from the death of Frau Henschel to the moment when the carter's
friends close in to attack him, discarding her current lover,
denying her child, taking advantage of Henschel's predicament
to force an offer of marriage, deceiving him with George, inter-
fering with his business, and driving away his friends. Her energy
gives the play a central, driving force and a clearly marked
action which balance the increasing bewilderment of Henschel,
until, at the end of the fourth act, he makes the stand which she
has not anticipated and pits himself against her, to accomplish
her destruction—for she is broken and intimidated at the end—
and to complete his own. Like her namesake Hanne Elias she
approaches an absolute, and she gives to *Henschel* the same sense
of a sharp and merciless struggle that we owe to the Philistines
and to the two women in *Kramer* and *Schilling*.

Henschel has Hauptmann's insight into character and environment, his ability to give depth and tension to the most everyday
scenes, and his skill in recording the living language, at their best.
It is written with a sure and quiet mastery and with a slight
detachment which is perhaps an indication that it was evoked
purely by the weight of memories and not, as in the case of *Die
Weber* or *Kramer* or *Rose Bernd*, as a reaction to some unhappy
incident in the present. Not that the dramatist was not deeply
immersed in his scenes and his characters or that he shows any
lack of sympathy for his hero. But he accepts the tragedy with a
calm and a resignation that are rarely evident in his work. It is
not merely that there are no specific accusations in *Henschel*,
there is not even the feeling that the world which he is depicting
could stand improvement. And the play accordingly has not a
hint of a social message, unless it is the general one implied by

the fact that a man who, a generation before, would have appeared on the stage only to announce that the carriage was ready has now become the hero. Six years later, in *Rose Bernd*, Hauptmann followed it with a work of equal importance and force.

V

In April 1903 Hauptmann served as a juryman during the trial of a peasant girl charged with perjury and infanticide. In October of the same year *Rose Bernd* was acted for the first time, in the Deutsches Theater. It is the story of an unmarried girl who strangles her newly born child, and it is set in the Silesian country-side and among people whom Hauptmann had known from his youth, as he had known the scene and the people of *Henschel*.[17] Its theme was not, to be sure, as novel as that of its predecessor. Unmarried mothers, along with free thinkers and young lovers bent on disregarding class differences, had appeared on the German stage with the first crop of bourgeois tragedies in the middle of the eighteenth century, and had agitated dramatists ever since, the most powerful and moving of the formulations being Goethe's Gretchen tragedy. But John Middleton Murry, who once wondered whether the power of Shakespeare's tragedy is not so great that it has inhibited all subsequent would-be English tragedians—numbed or frozen them—might find an answer to his question here.[18] If such inhibitions had any notable force the Gretchen tragedy would surely have frustrated any later dramatist writing on the same theme. And Hauptmann's play, in direct antithesis to the fourth-rate imitations of the foregoing genera-tion, is in no way slighter or less original or less moving because it is not the first to deal with its particular topic. His direct experience was strong and vital, and his knowledge of Goethe's work seems not to have interfered with his understanding but

---

[17]In Lohnig. For details of the originals of some of the characters see C. F. W. Behl, *Zwiesprache mit Gerhart Hauptmann* (Munich, 1948), p. 100. The figure of the heroine seems to have been inspired not only by the peasant girl, but by Anna Grundmann, whom Hauptmann met during later visits to his uncle's farm, although it is difficult to tell to what extent. The little verse epic *Anna* which deals with her story is so confused and badly written that her features cannot be seen distinctly.

[18]*Shakespeare* (London, 1936), p. 11.

to have enriched it, to have made him doubly sensitive and receptive to the related theme. The fact is, apparently, if we are to argue from a specific case to general truths, that literature, in its process of exploration and formulation, deepens and widens the field of human experience, but never exhausts one aspect of it or expresses one facet conclusively and with finality. Any genre or any theme would seem to be as infinitely extensible as life itself.

Rose Bernd begins at the heart of the matter, with a meeting between the young peasant girl and her lover, the middle-aged landowner Christoph Flamm, one warm Sunday morning in May, on a tree-shaded field near a small village. It has been a joyous rendezvous, for their love, although unsanctioned by society, since Flamm is married, is warm and tender. But according to Rose it must be their last meeting. Her mother is long since dead, and her father has been urging her for some time to ensure his future and that of the younger children by marrying August Keil, an ailing but hard working and pious suitor who is about to open a shop for religious literature. The time has come when she must comply. A far deeper shadow falls, however, when, after Flamm has left, Rose is accosted—and not for the first time —by a threshing-machine operator named Streckmann, a man with a well-founded reputation as a woman hunter. He indicates unmistakably that he has seen her with Flamm and that he intends to take advantage of it; and he continues to threaten her, in a veiled manner, after they have been joined by August and her father.

The dangerous interference reaches its climax in the two following acts. In the second Rose comes with her father and her fiancé to the house of Flamm, who is the local registrar, to set the date for her marriage, but in the courtyard she is detained by Streckmann and, deeply disturbed, again postpones it. In the third, as Bernd and August eat their vesper meal near a spring, they are joined by Streckmann and a group of harvesters, who taunt the sickly August, now soon to be a bridegroom, and encourage Streckmann to hint that he has some power over

Rose. There follows a bitter dispute between the girl and the machinist: she has gone to him, we learn, hoping to bribe him into silence, and has been virtually raped. The sound of her angry voice brings August to the scene, and he flies at Streckmann's throat, only to be hurled to the ground so violently that he loses an eye.

Rose in the meantime has confessed to Flamm's shrewd and kind-hearted invalid wife that she is pregnant and, although insisting that she cannot accept it, she has seemed comforted by the older woman's offer of help. She has also said a final good-bye to Flamm, and it appears that the break between them will be clean and in good faith. But her self-righteous father starts a court action against Streckmann for defaming his daughter's good name and the frightened girl, as she confesses to Frau Flamm, simply denies all accusations. Flamm, listening, realizes at length that Streckmann has sworn that she has been his mistress, and the machinist, he knows, is not the man to commit perjury. He bursts into the room and drives her out with bitter and loathing words. A few hours later an old labourer helps her into the kitchen of her home, ill and exhausted. And now August too, having talked with the penitent Streckmann, realizes some measure of the truth and urges Bernd to withdraw his suit. The old man responds by cursing his daughter. But the catastrophe is already in the past. Under a willow tree, shortly before, Rose has given birth to her baby and strangled it. At the sight of her suffering August's shy love flowers in all its compelling gentleness, but it is too late. A gendarme who has come with a document hears her confession and takes her away. And whatever the law may do, her life, in any real sense, is at an end.

The warmth of the earth fills *Rose Bernd* as the sea dominates *Gabriel Schillings Flucht*. The characters do not, it is true, talk about nature—they would not be peasants if they did. Only Flamm, who has had some experience of town life and disliked it, proclaims that he is happiest when he is free to roam the country, directing his workers or catching butterflies, which hang, with antlers, guns, and a photograph of his dead son, on the

walls of his living-room But the land is present in the people
and their work, in the warm spring and full summer, in pear
tree and cherry, well and field, and above all in Rose herself,
and in the love between her and Flamm. Indeed it seems to be
present in the basic texture of the play, giving it, for all its pictures
of agony and perversion, a steadiness of perspective and a sense
of values comparable to those we find in *Henschel*. And within
this simple and powerful atmosphere stand characters and scenes
so surely and steadily drawn and so valid and representative that
we feel them as classical. The whole Silesian countryside seems
concentrated in the play: the labourers, with their hopes of
wedding feasts and their admiration for a man who can run a
machine; Streckmann, the country braggart and dandy, blinded
by his rapidly rising lust and jealousy, and broken, in the end,
by the unforeseen consequences of his own desire; the hypo-
critical and domineering Bernd; August, the orphan of the
community, shy and sickly and genuinely humble; the somewhat
easy-going country squire Flamm; his wife, with her conviction
that there are two basic necessities in the world, to keep order
in one's house and to cherish life; and finally Rose herself, the
strong and self-reliant young peasant girl who, if she wastes no
words on those whom she dislikes, is warm and unselfish towards
those whom she loves. The story and, in part, the characters,
become complex, for the play is modern and a work of Hauptmann's maturity. But we never lose sight of the simple fundamental human problems and ties from which it springs. In the
third act Flamm, who has been waiting until Rose was alone,
joins her at the spring. She has been avoiding him, he charges,
and he forces her, in penance, to fetch him water in a jug and to
hold it until, on his knees and with his hands clasped over hers,
he has drunk his fill. The scene is as sound and fresh as the water
itself, and it will stand as a prototype of its kind beside the pictures
of Jacob and Rachel and of Goethe's Hermann and Dorothea.

As in *Henschel* two forces or sets of circumstances bring about
the catastrophe, the connection between Rose and the Flamms on
the one hand, and the interference of Bernd and of Streckmann

on the other. And here again the two interlock, so that Rose, like the carter, feels that snares have been set for her and that she has stumbled from one to the other, until she has lost all consciousness of what she is doing. "Hernach bin ich von Schlinge zu Schlinge getreten," she says to August in the last act, "dass ich gar ni bin mehr zur Besinnung gekomm."

The love between Rose and Flamm is, in itself, an old and complicated story. The Flamms had had one child, Kurt, a boy of her own age with whom she had often played. Then the boy died and her own mother died, and the Flamms were glad to have the motherless girl in their quiet house. Rose and Frau Flamm, moreover, make a cult of their memories of the dead boy; Frau Flamm talks of him before she invites the girl's confidence in the first part of the play; and Rose, faced by the misunderstanding of husband and wife towards the end, reveals how cruelly she has been wounded when she stammers the name of Kurt: "Wie hab ich ock das um Ihn verdient! Wenn das bloss mei Kurtel, mei liebes Kind. . . ." Yet at what point, if at all, we can separate her love for the father from her love for the son is difficult to say. Frau Flamm speaks once of the dolls with which the two children had played, Rose, as the mother, washing and dressing and feeding them, and on one occasion, she adds, unaware of the significance of her words, when Flamm happened to be watching, "da hast d'r se gar an de Brust gelegt." Flamm, for his part, admits to an early love for Rose, which he cannot dissociate from his love for his son. "Kann sein, meine Begriffe verwirren sich. Ich hatte das Mädel aufwachsen sehn, es hing was von der Liebe zu Kurtel daran." The chain, then, has been long in the forging, and the final links are added by Frau Flamm's illness and by Bernd's insistence that his daughter marry the apparently so unsuitable August. "Erstlich wollt' ich sie nur von dem Unglück zurickhalten . . . ," says Flamm, "und schliesslich . . . da sind eben alle Dämme gebrochen." But between Rose and Frau Flamm also there is a deep and sympathetic understanding and affection which, to a remarkable extent, survives the very difficult circumstances with which it is faced. And the tragedy of the play, from this aspect, is the tragedy that we first glimpsed in *Einsame Menschen*: it is love itself, the love between parent and child and the love between man and woman, that involves the characters in their dilemma and makes it insoluble. The Flamms have drawn Rose close to them with the best of intentions. The love of Rose for Flamm is sound and vital and tender. But it brings her into Streckmann's power and holds her there, for she cannot defy the machinist without betraying her lover. And her affection for Frau Flamm makes it impossible for her to name the father of her child to the one woman who could and, under any other circumstances, would help her. Yet her silence only confuses the situation further, as is evident above all in the fourth act, which must be traced in some detail if we are to understand the full extent of the catastrophe.

Frau Flamm, who has not seen Rose for some time, has sent for her. Moreover, she has found her husband of late restless and depressed, and she thinks that the time has come to tell him of a cherished project. She suggests cautiously that they adopt a baby, and, knowing that men sometimes have unaccountable prejudices, she is even more careful about naming the baby's mother. Before the stunned Flamm has time to recover August arrives to say that Rose is in court but will be here soon. Flamm flees before him. His wife tries now to enlighten August, to the extent of urging him to desist from his charges. Ironically, it is not August who is enlightened, but she herself. Bernd is implacable, August answers, he would not even heed a similar plea from Flamm when the latter was called to court. Frau Flamm had not known of the summons; she now understands her husband's unhappiness. She does not rail at him when he returns, but she recalls that Rose was entrusted to them by her dying mother, and she is hurt and confused. Yet as Rose is announced she pulls herself together and resolves to do her best, not for his sake—"sondern weil's richtig is"—but because it is right that she should. What she cannot anticipate, for even now she does not know the whole story, is that Rose is no longer the girl to whom she talked a few months ago, but a seemingly defiant creature, decked out in all the finery she can muster, whose features are sunken and debased, and who addresses her in tones of shrill politeness, ignoring all references to her former confession, and merely insisting, stubbornly and angrily, that Streckmann's charges are false. It is at this point that Flamm rushes in to reject her. And it is because he and his wife have been so deeply shaken by all that they have just learned that neither is in a state to heed the girl's broken appeal to the memory of their son or her protests that she has been hunted and persecuted and to connect them with her repeated, " I was ashamed." The act is a miraculous portrayal of wounded and perverted love and, as Rose leaves, we look deep into the past and feel that this crippling misunderstanding between people who have known and loved one another for years is as deeply tragic as the destruction of Gretchen, whose purest impulses lead her through madness and prison to the block.

If the relations between these three are in themselves a sufficient cause of tragedy, the catastrophe is also brought about and given a particular bitterness by the actions of Bernd and Streckmann, the accusing parental spirit with its *dies irae* and the Mephisto of the late nineteenth-century pastoral world. Bernd, to be sure, is by no means a simple and straightforward man. He seems pious and obsequious; he is, and always has been, hard and vain and self-righteous. Once the overseer on a large estate, he held a whip, so Streckmann charges, over all who worked under him; and the charge is confirmed by the cry of "Leuteschinder" which he hears across the fields, not for the first time, on the day of the catastrophe. Then, dismissed with the coming of old age, he has heightened the severity of his manners and beliefs in an attempt to reassert his lost prestige. He wants August as a husband for Rose because the young man is highly regarded by the leaders of the religious sect to which they belong, ignoring the fact that, physically weak and ailing, he seems hardly a suitable husband for a healthy young girl whose blood is, to use her mother's words, "a wing gar zu heess." He interprets her resistance as a

sign of pride and vanity, castigating in her the qualities he refuses
to recognize in himself; and he insists that any deviation on her
part from rigidly conventional standards would banish her
from his house: "Da lägst du längst uff d'r Strasse draussen!
Aso ane Tochter hätt ich nich." His rigour reaches its climax in
the last act: he covers his ears with his hands, as Rose comes in,
bends his eyes on the Bible, and laments that her conduct will
force him to resign his proud trusteeship of the church missionary
box. He has perverted the Christian concept of spiritual love
into an instrument for the maintenance of his own authority, and
forced his daughter into an engagement foreign to her nature;
he now thinks only of the public shame she has brought upon
him.

Streckmann, the inevitable opposite of Bernd, whose stress on
licence is the reverse of Bernd's ideal of the rejection of the flesh
—Hauptmann makes this clear in the first meeting between the
two, when they immediately exchange thrusts, the one parading
his piety, the other proclaiming his worldliness—completes the
work of destruction. In itself her love for Flamm brings Rose no
sense of sin, at most she is anxious not to be caught with him.
But the scenes between her and Flamm, on the fields and by the
spring, are each followed by the ugly glosses of Streckmann,
just as the sound of his threshing machine drowns her shy attempt
to tell Flamm about the baby. For to Streckmann she is merely a
woman having her fling like any other and, as a challenge to
prudish convention—so he notes in the first act—under a wayside
cross at that. From the beginning Rose feels in his presence,
like Gretchen in that of Mephisto, a deep sense of shame and
repulsion. At the end of the first act, when he forces all to drink
from a flask to the coming wedding, she does so in tears and
with great repulsion, sensing perhaps that she will marry only
on his terms. "Auswendig is a geschniegelt," she exclaims later,
"inwendig is a von Mad'n zerfress'n: d'r Ekel kommt een zum
Halse raus." The actual rape is only the most vivid symbol of this
desecration of her love. And like Gretchen too, she wanders

in a *Walpurgisnacht* where all is foul and obscene,[19] where even
Flamm seems to have abused and soiled her, beaten her and wiped
his shoes on her defiled body. To August, in the last act, she
speaks of herself as a hunted animal. "August, se han sich an
mich wie de Klett'n gehang'n!—ich konnte nee ieber de Strasse
laufen! Alle Männer war'n hinter mir her! Ich hab' mich ver-
steckt. Ich hab' mich gefircht! . . . 's half nischt, 's ward
immer schlimmer dahier!"

But Rose is, if not stronger than Gretchen, for strength can
manifest itself in many ways, harder and of tougher fibre. She
does not swoon, but retreats into stubborn and bitter defiance,
trying to protect the core of her love by refusing to admit to
others or to herself what has happened and the injury that has
been inflicted upon her. For a long time, in the third act, she
will not recognize Streckmann, but flings at him the scornful,
"Wer sein Sie? . . . Wer sein Sie denn ieberhaupt? . . . Wo hätt
ich Ihn denn schonn gesehn?" She pretends to be ignorant of her
former conversation with Frau Flamm, responding to the latter's
"fer dei Kind wird gesorgt sein," with the cold, "Ich weess halt
ni, was Sie meenen, Madam." She sets her word, in court,
against the word of the men, though the changes in her body—
we must assume that the birth of the baby is very premature—
already belie her oath. The catastrophe is the last stage in this
blind and desperate attempt to shut out what has hurt her, and
it is a retreat, this time, which means the rejection of life itself—
not, indeed, for her own sake alone, but also for the child's.
" 's sullde ni laba!" she says, and her voice has a savage and terrifying coldness, "Ich wullte 's ni!! 's sullde ni meine Martern
derleida! 's sullde durt bleib'n, wo's hiegeheert." We have seen
suicide in Hauptmann's earlier plays, death in war and death in
rebellion, and death in war is not, to him, heroic, but a slaughter.
But *Rose Bernd* is the first tragedy, with the exception of the
melodramatic *Elga*, in which he portrays a murder. And if
the long connection with the Flamms weaves the first snare in

[19]See Barker Fairley, *Goethe's Faust* (Oxford, 1953).

which Rose is caught, it is the actions of Bernd and of Streckmann which drive her to the point of breaking the most basic human tie that the world knows, and taking the life of her child.

In some respects *Rose Bernd*, compared with a number of its eighteenth-century predecessors, is a private tragedy. The question of the difference in rank between Rose and Flamm, for example, is of relatively slight importance. At most we might surmise that he would not have taken possession of her so readily or she submitted so easily had he not been master and she maid. But Bernd's conventional austerity and Streckmann's equally conventional licence are so typical of the world in which they live that the play becomes also a condemnation of society, of a society whose ways have grown so rigid and perverted as to be hostile to life. There is no learned enunciation of women's rights. But Rose, in comparison with, let us say, Gretchen, or with Klara, the heroine of Hebbel's mid-nineteenth-century *Maria Magdalene*, has developed as a woman and as a human being in a way that makes *raisonnement* superfluous. And both she and Frau Flamm, on the basis of their own experience, have something to say about the position of women in the world. Gretchen is, so to speak, pure being, who grows—as she does, in her way— almost entirely through the completeness of her surrender and the intensity of her suffering, and her comprehension of her fate goes very little beyond the wondering, "Doch—alles, was dazu mich trieb, Gott! war so gut! ach war so lieb." For Klara the situation is more complicated, both psychologically and intellectually. But the moment of confusion which Hebbel allows her on the night of her seduction, when she gives herself to her fiancé because she has felt an old love for another coming to life within her, is only a premonition of Hauptmann's portrayal of the power of sex—at long last, one is tempted to say, although he had been anticipated in the novel by Keller and Fontane—in a heroine who is neither a *Machtweib* nor a free-thinker nor a *prima donna* nor a courtesan. Klara's subsequent hatred of her seducer and her suicide only anticipate the change in Rose from a warm and sound young woman into an apparently defiant and degraded creature and then again into a woman ripened and broken by the dreadful wisdom acquired in suffering.

Hebbel was convinced that a girl of the middle class could not, in his day, oversee and judge her world. Klara, in consequence, can protest only that she is suffering for reasons she does not understand, for "ich weiss nicht, was." Rose too, though to a lesser degree, shares the prejudices that help to destroy her. But she becomes conscious of a complication of events and forces which widen her horizon, and she stands in the end as the prosecutor of her environment, condemning those who, in their limitations, would condemn her. "Voater! Ich lebe!" she cries in the last act, "Ich sitze hier! Das iss was, . . . dass ich hier sitze! . . . O Jees, ei een kleen Kämmerla lebt ihr mitnander! Ihr wisst nischt, was aussern der Kammer geschieht! Ich wiss! Ei Krämpfen hab' ich's gelernt! Da is . . . ich weess ni . . . all's von mir gewichen . . . als wie Mauer um Mauer immerzu— und da stand ich drauss'n, im ganz'n Gewitter . . . da seid ihr de reenst'n kleen Kinder dagegen." And when her father reminds her of her own earlier attitude—"Du hast frieher de strengste Meinung gehabt"—she retorts bitterly, "Itze weess ich Bescheid." Frau Flamm, for her part, mourning still for the dead Kurt, urges that children are a woman's care and a woman's business: "Mir sein ieberhaupt de Väter ganz gleichgiltig: ob's a Landrat oder a Landstreicher is. Mir miss'n de Kinder doch selber zur Welt bring'n. . . . 's doch a Glick, was du hast! Fer a Weib gibt's kee greesseres! Halt du's feste." Few would take her words as an expression of a desire to abolish marriage and the family unit. But she and Rose begin to speak for themselves; and they stand beside their more enlightened urban or professional sisters—Hauptmann's own Anna or Michaline, Ibsen's Nora or Shaw's Candida—as women claiming to make their own judgments about the world around them, judgments which are not subservient to those of their male contemporaries and not necessarily the same. If women, Hauptmann wrote in a paragraph of the *Ausblicke*, were fully conscious of their value as the mothers of all human beings, their pride would raise them from their present unworthy position in society; society justly forbids a woman to kill her child but robs her of the freedom, "wodurch sie wahrhaft lebendig macht," which is necessary to give life in the fullest and truest sense.

There remains the question of the scale of values which emerges in *Rose Bernd*, as in all Hauptmann's plays, but nowhere more clearly than here. For the professional self-righteousness of Bernd and for the society which the old man represents he has, of course, no sympathy at all, and he has not much more for the bravado of Streckmann, though the latter is forgiven in the end. He values the vitality and the tenderness of the love between Rose and Flamm. But that love has its limits, on his side, if not on hers, and they are evident in his bitter and jealous rejection of her at the end of the fourth act: "Wenn ich noch an'n Finger riehr' in der Sache, da such' ich mir selber an'n Strick dahier und hau' m'r den um meine Eselsohren, bis ich de Hand vor a Augen ni seh'!" Even Frau Flamm, whose love has grown from suffering, from illness, from the death of her son, from the long years of watching in silence the somewhat wayward course of a husband younger than herself, cannot in the end sustain Rose in her plight. This challenge is met by August alone. When Rose, in her final agony, cries out that people are too much alone in the world, he, whose whole life has been based on renunciation, turns to her with a love which is Christ-like in its absolute purity and compassion, and which promises her help and support: "Rosla, steh uff, ich verluss dich ni! . . . Mag kumma, was will, ich halte zu dir! . . . Mir wern mitnander a Auskumma hoan! Ei jeder Beziehung aso und aso. Itze sein mer vielleicht erst reif dazu." And it is he who, with the deeply significant, "Wer weess, welche Liebe stärker is: ob nu de glickliche oder de unglickliche," goes with her to the court for judgment.

There are times when Hauptmann depicts the love of the spirit as hostile to the love of the flesh and glorifies a pagan *eros* which, in the tradition of Schiller and Heine, he proclaims as characteristic of Greek civilization. We have already seen some reflection of this belief in the love between Lucie and Mäurer in *Gabriel Schillings Flucht*. But for the most part he succeeded in giving it convincing formulation only in an idyllic setting, in retreat from the world. *Rose Bernd*, in its complexity, is a more valid expression of his deepest persuasions, and its evidence is definite and clear. Hauptmann values the natural, physical love between man and woman and would reject any doctrine that brands it as sinful. He values more highly yet the love which, nourished on renunciation and pain, and inspired by the figure of Christ, shelters and supports the lives of others without seeking the furtherance of its own. But there is need for both, and unless they are perverted they do not conflict.

VI

Die Ratten, begun in the spring of 1909 and completed in the following summer, is the last of Hauptmann's great prose plays about the life of his own day. It is based on experiences which go back to the winter of 1884–5 when he was in Berlin studying to become an actor. Its main theme, that of a childless woman who tries to satisfy her maternal instincts by means not strictly within the law, is not unrelated to that of *Rose Bernd*. But its tone and atmosphere are very different. It is a play about an inorganic metropolitan world, the tragic counterpart, we have noted, to *Peter Brauer*, and in a sense the continuation of *Der rote Hahn*. And it is marked by an ironic contrast between suffering and pleasure, between innocent young love and sordid crime, and between play-acting and reality.

The action takes place in two rooms of a former barracks, now a tenement house, in a slum section of Berlin, partly in the top-floor studio of Harro Hassenreuter, a former theatre director who now lives by renting costumes, and partly in the combined living-room and kitchen of Frau John, the wife of a mason who works in Altona. Each room has its own story, but Frau John is Hassenreuter's cleaning woman, and the groups associated with the two are in constant contact.[20] The first act, for example, which takes place in the studio, introduces us to most of the characters and gives us the basis of both actions. On a Sunday afternoon, when the room is normally deserted, Frau John has brought here a Polish servant girl named Pipercarcka, who is soon to bear an illegitimate child. The older woman, whose only son has died three years ago, is begging for possession of the unwanted baby. Her brother Bruno, an uncanny looking individual, is setting mousetraps in the adjoining rooms. But the conversation is interrupted and Pipercarcka has to retreat to the loft when Hassenreuter's daughter Walburga arrives, hoping to meet here her tutor, a serious young theology student named Spitta. She in her turn is forced to flee from her father, who also has a rendezvous, and a rather less innocent one, with a Viennese actress, whose fame, he hopes, will help him once again to a position as director. And the following acts bring the varied characters together in similar ways.

The obstacles in the path of Spitta and Walburga do not prove to be insurmountable. The young man breaks with his father, a country pastor, because he decides to give up his studies and to become an actor. He irritates Hassenreuter, whom he chooses as his new teacher, by rejecting Schiller and upholding the principles of the new naturalist school—he has left oratory behind him in the pulpit and has no wish to practise it on the stage. Indeed when Hassenreuter discovers his daughter's affection for this infuriating young man, he forbids her to see him and locks her in her room. But Walburga alarms her parents by breaking out and running away. And Hassenreuter, having achieved his coveted directorship in Strassburg, decides to be tolerant. If

[20]In his *Erkner im Leben und Werk Gerhart Hauptmanns* Walter Requardt presents interesting evidence that Hauptmann hoped to work out the two stories, although separately and in narrative form, at a very early date. In a fragment written in 1887, entitled "Der Buchstabe tötet," the dramatist described the visit of a servant girl to a married couple who seem to have adopted her child and who are uneasy when she appears. Also a list of projected works, made not later than 1889, includes among possible subjects "Hessler—Maskenverleihamt." Hessler was the name of the actor with whom Hauptmann took lessons.

Spitta is willing to work hard and to wait, his beloved will some day be his.

The story of Frau John is more complicated and is deeply tragic. When Pipercarcka's baby is born she passes it off as her own, and not even her rejoicing husband, away from home for long periods, doubts her word. But presently Pipercarcka changes her mind and claims the child. She has registered the birth, she tells Frau John, and told the authorities that the Johns are looking after the baby; she will be back the next day with an inspector from the welfare department. Still guarding her secret Frau John disappears for a few days, allegedly to visit a sister-in-law. On the following afternoon Selma Knobbe, daughter of a highly disreputable neighbour, "happens" to leave her sickly infant brother in the John apartment, and Pipercarcka, who has never seen her child, believes that it is her own. But Frau Knobbe arrives, and while the two women dispute the wretched baby breathes its last. A day or so later Frau John returns, weary and apprehensive. Then Bruno appears. His sister has instructed him to try to keep Pipercarcka away from the house. Days and nights of roistering have been followed by a struggle under a lilac bush in the Tiergarten. Pipercarcka will never interfere again. By now the police are alarmed and the house is surrounded. John, home again, is perplexed by strange tales and rumours. His wife, he discovers, has not been with his sister, but has been seen among shacks near the Spree. He thinks at first that Bruno must be the father of Pipercarcka's child and that she has been helping the pair dispose of it. Horrified, he prepares to remove his own child from such a mother. Then Selma, who has carried the baby from the loft where it was born, at last tells the truth, and Frau John, all hope of keeping the baby gone, rushes to her death in the heavy traffic of the street below.

Dramatists who wish to portray a cross-section of society too often bring together an assortment of typical characters, on a boat, or in a country house, and let them act out before us their typical fates. Hauptmann's tenement house, his varied characters, and his separate and very different stories are used, in a similar manner, to give us a true representation of the mixed life of Germany's greatest city. But there is nothing conventional or facile about the setting, the people, or the action. There is an element of arbitrariness in placing a story of young and idealistic love beside that of a woman driven by her desire for a child down dark paths to murder and suicide. And there is a certain coincidence of events which makes us conscious of the hand of the author. But the fact that Hassenreuter, for example, as he pronounces his eulogies on classical tragedy, remains serenely unconscious of what is going on in his own loft, contributes to the impression that Hauptmann wishes to make of a heterogeneous society whose members associate only at the most superficial levels, ignorant of one another and unconcerned. The juxtaposition of the two stories has the same function as the predominance of chance in the closely related *Peter Brauer*. Yet it is only the simplest and most obvious of the means which Hauptmann uses to portray his tragicomic world. To appreciate *Die Ratten* we need to examine in detail the incidents and characters, in their variety and in the way they reflect and colour one another.

There are moments of pure comedy in the play, of comedy as care-free as Hauptmann ever wrote. When Hassenreuter, for example, lays hold of Spitta, and bends his recalcitrant scholarly limbs in a vain attempt to make him resemble an awe-inspiring member of the tragic chorus of Schiller's *Braut von Messina*, we feel nothing but amusement at the older man's irritability and the serious, perplexed clumsiness of Spitta. And there are moments of pure tragedy. When Frau John, cutting bread for the hungry Selma as though she were mesmerized and performing the familiar task in a trance, lets bread and knife slip to the table and cries, "Angst! Sorge!—Da wisst ihr nischt von!" we think of nothing but her fear; and we are filled with a pity that is almost unendurable as she bends frantically, in the last act, to pick up the baby clothes on which she has sewn for so long and which her husband, in his impious rage, has thrown

to the floor, begging him, as she does so, not to tear the rags
from her naked body.

More frequently, however, we see one incident in the light of
another: the comedy is darkened by the shadow of tragedy, and
the tragedy is broken by irony, by a sense of the ridiculous and
the grotesque. Walburga scrambles up the loft stairs, in fear of
being discovered by papa; only a few moments ago Pipercarcka
has retreated the same way, her terrified eyes fixed on the repellent Bruno. Hassenreuter, having brought out a bottle of wine
to drink with his Viennese love, and noticing after a moment's
absence that some of it has gone, rushes into the next room,
expecting to find her happily tippling; the wine has just vanished,
in the anxious hand of Frau John, to strengthen the servant girl
in the first pangs of child-birth. Or again, the incidents are in
themselves a blend of the comic and the tragic. At the end of
the third act Pipercarcka and Frau Knobbe almost come to
blows over the dying baby. We may recall a similar incident
from an earlier play—the moment when Hanne and Eveline
fight over the bed of Schilling. But in *Schilling* we experience
sheer repulsion. There is no such unmitigated reaction here.
For at one moment Frau Knobbe holds a handkerchief to her
allegedly aristocratic nose to mark her superiority to the plebeian,
and at the next raises her parasol to strike. And Pipercarcka
swears a solemn and circumstantial oath that she is the true
mother on the rather flimsy evidence that the baby is sufficiently
like her own—"janz jenug identisch"—to confirm her claim.

Towards the end, as the lighter comedy fades into the background, the atmosphere of cheap and sordid crime throws a
macabre light on the most sombre and alarming events. The
police close in to search the house, jamming the funeral procession of the baby into the filthy corridor, and, in their general
clean-up of unsavoury characters—"dufte Kunden"—arrest two
of the pallbearers. As Bruno is reporting to his sister in the fourth
act, the church bells ring out, for it is Sunday morning, and he
has to put down the sprig of lilac picked from the tree under
which the dead girl lies and press to his nose, which has suddenly

begun to bleed, a vinegar-soaked towel. He has been describing, in snatches, his attempts to divert Pipercarcka, their wanderings, as a popular song of the day would seem to have it, "Von det eene Ristorang in det andre Ristorang." Now, reflecting that at half-past three that morning she might still have heard the bells, he comes to the climax of his story: "Und da fuhr se mit eemal nach meine Jurjel, det ick denke . . . det ick jleich denke, det ick soll alle werden! Na, und da . . . da war ick nu ooch 'n bissken frisch—und denn war et halt so jekomm"—one of the most effectively understated accounts of a murder, one would think, in all literature. And the whole scene, which ends in Frau John's collapse, evokes in the spectator the utmost in horror, fascination, pity, and aversion that the human heart can experience in one and the same moment.

The same complexity of emotional effects is aroused by the characters. Here again, some are merely amusing, the actress, for example, with her straight, light Viennese chatter: "I möcht' lieber bei dir spielen, und das musst mir versprechen, wann's du wieder eine Direktion übernehmen tust . . . das versprichst mir, dass i augenblickli kontraktbrüchig werden kann! . . . Berlin mag i net! Und a Hoftheater schon lang net. Jessas die Leit!" And John, in the main, awakens only our sympathy and respect. He is something of a lighter urban equivalent of Henschel, a man who is restless enough, as an industrial worker, that he has once thought of emigrating to America, but who is shrewd, industrious, good-natured, proud of his honesty and of his good name, and content, now that he has a son, to work and save for him in his native city. Nor is there much difference between, let us say, Crampton's daughter Gertrud and Walburga, neither of them, like many young girls, being particularly distinguished in character. Yet Gertrud's worship of her father is a more or less routine characteristic, and Walburga has a quality which we might not expect, a coolness and presence of mind which enable her to stand up to Hassenreuter in time of need. From her refuge in the loft she has become aware of her father's *amour*. When he threatens that, if she will not give up Spitta, she will have to make her own way in the world, she turns on him with the retort that women have been known to do so, the Viennese actress, for example. She is well aware that her "denke doch mal an Alice Rütterbusch" will make him think of more than the point they are openly discussing. She wins the round, and the somewhat neutral benevolence with which we have regarded her hitherto takes on a note of startled and amused respect.

We find a like mixture of qualities, in a much higher degree, in her beloved Spitta. He says himself, with great perspicacity, that he is a "Kauz"—a queer bird— and in many respects, as we consider his stooped shoulders, his sharp features, his spectacles, and his burning scorn for all who are Pharisees in word and deed, we are inclined to agree with him. He has, moreover, not a glimmer of a sense of humour. A twelve-page letter brings his father to Berlin, and in it, he assures us, he has traced point by point the inner struggle that has led him to renounce theology in favour of the stage. Yet he too has a coolness and a measure of his own ability which are highly impressive. His glasses are broken and his clothes covered with dust when he undertakes to rescue a woman who has fallen in the path of an approaching tram. The woman, it develops, is Frau Knobbe, and it is more likely than not that she was drunk. He is unperturbed. Years ago, he tells Walburga, his father drove his sister into the streets after a youthful misfortune; society is to blame for such transgressors. He counters Hassenreuter's anti-naturalist salvoes with dry and cutting persistence, upholding Lessing against Schiller and reminding his adversary that oratory will never prove him wrong. And he is determined to go his way with all risks calculated and without heroics. "Ich habe Mut!" he says in the last act, "Ich denke auch nicht daran, etwa als Lebensmüder feige zu endigen! . . . Dass ich vorläufig arm bin und meine Suppe hie und da in der Volksküche essen muss, untergräbt meinen Glauben an mich und an eine bessere Zukunft nicht." All in all he has the stamp, not of the usual romantic rebel, but of the unusual reformer, and we end by recognizing in him an idealist without illusions, a doctrinarian with a passion for practical action, and as nearly a Shavian a figure as has ever come from Hauptmann's pen.

Other characters provoke the same varied reaction because, consciously or unconsciously, they are acting—not a strange phenomenon, certainly, in a play which is partly about theatrical people, nor the first time we have found Hauptmann's men and women living on illusions. But the number of people who act in *Die Ratten* is remarkable, and the laymen are sometimes quite as good as the professionals. Hassenreuter manages to play several roles at once: *père de famille*, temperamental director, and patriotic Prussian, and when Alice is present he fancies himself as Egmont. He manages also to orate in all of them, rather more effectively on the virtues of sterilized milk than on those of German classical drama, though he has a touch of Crampton's eloquence and terms Spitta's dramatic theories, nimbly enough, "eine Pharaphrase des Willens zum Blödsinn." The stocky, well-fed Pastor Spitta is not perhaps quite as good in his part of a simple country priest, broken by his son's waywardness and horrified at the evil ways of the metropolis, where he cannot move without an offer of "etwas Pikantes . . .?" But Frau Knobbe is excellent as an interesting tragic heroine with memories of her innocent girlhood and of her ejection by a stern father, as a woman pursued by fate, a crushed worm, a deceived romantic, and a lady still, whose fine instincts have to be dulled continually by morphine and alcohol as a precaution against despair and insanity. It may occur to the spectator, as he listens to her tale, that its inspiration is partly literary. But if Hauptmann was parodying in her the false pathos of Sudermann's *Sodoms Ende*, the parody is truer than the original, and we see in Frau Knobbe the real tragedy of a woman fallen from the upper classes to become a street-walker and the mother of debased and cruelly neglected children. As a final example we may cite Pipercarcka, who plays a somewhat simpler version of an innocent woman betrayed. "Ick stürze mir Landwehrkanal!" she recites to Frau John, ignoring the older woman's offers of help, "Ick schreibe Zettel, ick lasse

Zettel in mein Jackett zurück: du hast mit deine verfluchte Schlechtigkeit deine Pauline im Wasser jetrieben!" And her subsequent realization that she is an affectionate mother is explained by her, "Nu jerade! Nu muss er mir heiraten!"— "Now he will have to marry me!" It is a shocking and yet not inappropriate ending that the little servant girl, frivolous and woebegone, meets her death under a lilac tree while her beloved, not far away, dances at his wedding, having given the honour of bearing his name to a woman who owns a merry-go-round.

But with Pipercarcka and Frau Knobbe it is not only the fact that they are acting that causes us to regard them with mixed feelings, for as the action leads to murder and imprisonment, so several of the characters, and these two among them, are stamped by a degeneration so marked as to verge on the criminal or the pathological. Selma and Quaquaro, the caretaker, belong to this group and so do Bruno and Frau John. Quaquaro is an ex-convict, hired by the army, which owns the tenement, to watch over the potential criminals within its walls. Bruno has been brought up by Frau John, and she may well have helped to pervert him by lavishing on him the same inordinate affection that she displays towards the baby of Pipercarcka. But the disposition to crime must also have been strong in him from the beginning, and for a long time he has walked crooked paths, the undistinguished and sordidly crooked paths of the degenerate of low mentality. We see in him a loiterer in the underworld, weak and vicious, and redeemed only, if this is not too strong a word, by his attachment to his sister and by the "Galgenhumor" which gives a bizarre touch to his already colourful jargon. "Bruno, wenn se dir aber festsetzen?" asks his sister anxiously, when she has heard his story, and he answers, "Na jut, denn mache ick Bammelmann, und denn ha'm se uff Charité wieder ma wat zum Sezieren." We may take it, since he is arrested before the end of the play, that his grim prediction comes true.

The case of Frau John is of course more complicated, and in her Hauptmann gives us a full-length study of a woman whose environment combines with an innate instability to destroy qualities that are sound and good. With a husband working in Altona, because the pay is better, she has sat alone, through the greater part of her married life, in a house that hides much that is beyond the law, scraping together money in good lower-middle-class fashion, and longing for a child with a desire which, natural as it is, is somewhat overwrought. There was a screw loose when she had her first, says Quaquaro, and now, with the second, there are two. And when her own baby dies, the life in the house cannot but suggest to her that she acquire another by illegal means. She makes an uncanny impression on us from the beginning, pleading feverishly with Pipercarcka in the dark studio, and threatening Bruno—though perhaps in the only language that he can understand—that she will make a corpse of him if he says a word to anyone about the girl's visit. For a while, when we first see her with the baby, she seems relaxed—gentle and weary, Hauptmann notes, like a woman who has just given physical birth. But she makes her husband uneasy by her concern about a mistake in registering the birth and by wanting to name the living child after the dead. She puzzles Spitta by her great joy at the discovery that the hair of the two is of the same colour and texture. And as her fear of losing the baby grows she becomes obsessed with the idea that the first child has returned to life in the second, that the two are one, manifestations, it would seem, of the life that she has once felt within her and will never cease to feel. "I, wenn een Kindchen meinsweejen jeboren is," she explains, "denn is et jedennoch noch in de Mutter, und wenn et meinsweejen jestorben is, denn is et immer noch in de Mutter." Her last actions, the blind flight and the setting of Bruno on Pipercarcka, are clearly no longer those of a sane woman. Yet she not only claims our sympathy but—such is the world she lives in—she is right. We have noted that she is a good housekeeper, a good business woman, and that she is respected by all whom we see with her. But these are not the only factors to be considered. The father of the baby, says Quaquaro, cares nothing for it, the mother was a loose woman, and in the city-approved home to which it will now be sent it will probably die—ten out of a dozen do. True, Hassenreuter has a momentary impulse to adopt it, but he is off to his director-ship in Strassburg, to introduce Schiller, no doubt, to Germany's new French citizens, and the thought of red tape deters him. In a word, not only has Frau John risked her life for the child, but it would have had a better chance with her than anywhere else. Yet no one understands until too late. Even John, though the end of the play finds him rushing after her with the cry, "Mutter! Uffhalten!" fails her at the critical moment when she needs his support, thinking only of his pride as a man and a father, lashing her with bitter words, and welcoming the police, the agents of the law.

At the end of the play Frau John and Pipercarcka lie dead, Bruno is facing trial for murder, Frau Knobbe is to be sent to a reformatory, there is one baby's coffin on its way to the cemetery and every prospect that another will shortly follow. Hauptmann had not, since his early work, written quite such a public play, a play in which his characters, in life and in death, are affected by the official guardians of the land. And, except perhaps in *Quint*, he had never written such a sweeping condemnation of the life of his day. The action and the characters, proceeding their several ways in the dark, airless house teeming with life, speak for themselves. But the dramatist underlined his indictment by the comments of his people, some of them casually spoken and some of them not. At an early point Hassenreuter gives a vivid picture of the house: "Was so hier in diesem alten Kasten mit schmutzigen Unterröcken die Treppe fegt und überhaupt schleicht, kriecht, ächzt, seufzt, schwitzt, schreit, flucht, lallt . . . ," he exclaims, "treppauf treppab allerhand dunkle Gewerbe treibt, was hier an lichtscheuem Volke nistet, Zither klimpert, Harmonika spielt—was hier an Not, Hunger, Elend existiert und an lasterhaftem Lebenswandel geleistet wird, das ist auf keine Kuhhaut zu schreiben." And John, striking the walls and floor as he does so, supplements the director's somewhat picturesque outburst by passing drastic judgment on the building and all that it contains: "Horchen Se ma, wie det knackt, wie

Putz hinter de Tapete runterjeschoddert kommt! Allens is hier morsch! Allens faulet Holz! Allens unterminiert, von Unjexiefer, von Ratten und Mäuse zerfressen! . . . Allens schwankt! Allens kann jeden Oojenblick bis in Keller durchbrechen." Hassenreuter, of course, is in the building only during a period of misfortune, and it looks as though Strassburg has saved him. But most of those who come under its eaves—and they come from various classes and from various parts of the land—are condemned. The house with its occupants becomes a symbol for the dangerous aspects of metropolitan life, for the herding together of uprooted and unfortunate people in a hopelessness and poverty that can only heighten degeneracy and promote crime.

But there is abundant evidence that the house represented to Hauptmann not only the life of Berlin but the whole civilization of the Germany of his day. The nature of the two rooms in which the action takes place, the studio above with its fading, dust-covered costumes for classical plays, and the lower-middle-class room below, where basically sound instincts take on a twisted and perverted form, would suggest this wider reference. And if rats, in the opinion of John, are undermining the house, they are equally busy, according to Hassenreuter, gnawing at the foundations of the Reich. "Sie sind ein Sympton . . . ," he charges Spitta, in the course of their argument about drama, "Sie sind eine Ratte! Aber diese Ratten fangen auf dem Gebiete der Politik—Rattenplage!—unser herrliches neues geeinigtes Deutsches Reich zu unterminieren an. Sie betrügen uns um den Lohn unserer Mühe und im Garten der deutschen Kunst—Rattenplage!—fressen sie die Wurzeln des Baumes des Idealismus ab: sie wollen die Krone durchaus in den Dreck reissen." We may not agree with Hassenreuter's definition of a rat, or see the danger where he sees it, but we can hardly fail to take his words as further evidence that in Hauptmann's mind the house and society are one, that the Empire is disintegrating from within and its theatrical upper floor about to crash on its crumbling foundations.

Most of the miscellaneous information which we gather about social and political conditions confirms this impression. Hassenreuter himself is—we should perhaps avoid the harsher term—a symptom, the spokesman of those official late-nineteenth-century attitudes which Hauptmann disliked so intensely and which he had already satirized in *Der rote Hahn*. The director is a good Prussian, and, as such, an admirer of the mighty hero Bismarck, a *Kulturkämpfer* and a staunch upholder of German family life. He has a son, named Otto, in the navy. He hopes that John will have the baby christened: "Sie werden den Bengel doch hoffentlich in die Gemeinschaft der christlichen Kirche aufnehmen lassen." And his literary tastes run not only to the more resounding works of the "giants" of Weimar, but to romantic and patriotic song. Somewhere in the house, he says, he has heard the fine voices of young men singing "Deutschland Deutschland über alles," and "Wer hat dich du schöner Wald...." The fine young voices, incidentally, belong to members of a gang among whom not even Quaquaro ventures without his bull-dog. Hauptmann, it is true, does not distort his characters so that they become mere mouthpieces of certain opinions, and Hassenreuter is so jovial and pompous and hot-tempered and kindly withal that we may be unaware of all his sentiments at a first reading. Alice too is so charming that we may read her gay account of walking arm in arm with a nice old prince in the Tiergarten and of a still higher personage who rode by in a carriage and wagged his finger in mock disapproval, and think no more about it than the persons concerned. Pastor Spitta is not quite honest and it may be some time before we realize that, whether he is genuinely shocked or not, shop windows filled with pictures of the royal family and of naked actresses and dancers are not a sign of national health. And we interpret Frau Knobbe's charge that the aristocratic circles of her origin are without refinement or decency in the first analysis as part of the role she is playing. But a little reflection convinces us that the characters are condemning both themselves and their world, and we feel that the bitterness of the young Spitta is justified, who, after his break with his father, spent the night in the Tiergarten, thinking, as certain figures prowled around him, that his sister may well have sat there night after night, reflecting on the love and humanity of this highly Christian world, "um in ihrer Verlassenheit, Ausgestossenheit und Entwürdigung darüber nachzudenken, wie triefend von Menschenliebe, triefend von Christentum zweitausend Jahre nach Christi Geburt diese allerchristlichste Welt sich manifestiert."

The play is not without its elements of hope, the greatest of which is Spitta himself. And John too has cautious opinions of his own. Hassenreuter sees in the baby a future German soldier, "Acht Pfund zehn Gramm frisches deutsch-nationales Menschenfleisch." But John is not enthusiastic. He came home from the war, he says, eager for a son who should join the army; now that he has one he does not want him used as cannon-fodder. Or again, when Hassenreuter asks, "Sind Sie nicht Bismarckverehrer, John?" he answers carefully, "Det kann ick nu so jenau nich sachen; aber wat meine Jenossen in't Mauerjewerbe sind, die sind et nich." But the work is written with a mixture of bitterness and ironic reserve that make it, in a way, the most hopeless and tragic of all Hauptmann's prose dramas. We have known anger and pain and biting satire, and we have heard cries as despairing as Frau John's "Jerechtigkeit is noch nich ma oben in Himmel." What we have not heard is a phrase like "das ganze skurrile Menschheitsintermezzo." What we have not known, though we have had a foretaste of it in *Peter Brauer*, is the attempt to stress the nonchalant indifference of society to the destruction that is going on in its midst by the juxtaposition of comedy and tragedy or by the portrayal of the tragedy as a play within a play—both he and Frau John, says Spitta, would be interesting figures on the stage. And what we have not known also is the strong impression with which *Die Ratten* leaves us of illness, of crime and of decadence.

Hauptmann once wrote that at some time every object revealed its immanent beauty, and it was a generalization, of course, to which he found many exceptions. But in the main his efforts were directed to feeling his way so deeply into the lives of his characters that the sense of anything merely cheap or repellent or degenerate vanishes, as the distortion vanishes from the dead face of Arnold Kramer. We do not cease to know his people as they are and we do not become blind to their weaknesses, but we accept them as we accept ourselves. It is not easy to do that here. Again and again, moreover, in spite of the increasing sharpness of his tragedy, and in spite of the feeling of loneliness that grips his protagonists, Hauptmann had introduced into his plays characters—Käthe and Anna, the older Kramer, Siebenhaar, Mäurer, August—who can feel with the sufferers, and who if they cannot prevent the tragedy can provide an adequate reverberation and some sense of reconciliation. Reconciliation is as lacking here as it is in *Florian Geyer*. But where the end of *Geyer* is brutal, the end of *Die Ratten* is trite. We find, if we turn to the last pages, that Spitta indeed remarks that the baby has lost its true mother in Frau John, and Quaquaro agrees. But then Hassenreuter joins in with a pious platitude, "Sofern es nämlich bei dem Vater dort oben, der alles sieht, nicht anders beschlossen ist." Quaquaro, misunderstanding, answers "Meen Se Pauln? den Mauerpolier! Nu nich mehr! Dem kenn ick, wo der uff'n Ehrenpunkt kitzlich is." And Spitta tops off the whole with the academic, "Finden Sie nicht, dass hier ein wahrhaft tragisches Verhängnis wirksam gewesen ist?"

There is probably some danger in pushing such observations too far, the danger of losing sight entirely of the outlines of Hauptmann's usual world, which are still just perceptible in *Die Ratten*, and of suggesting that he has lost his way and his standards. His first play was partly inspired by Tolstoi's *The Power of Darkness*. It helps us to keep a just perspective on *Die Ratten* if we look at it for a moment in the light of another Russian play, Gorki's *The Lower Depths*. The German play contains no character whose views approach the nihilism of Gorki's Satin, no one as cruelly aggressive as the landlady Vasilisa Karpovna, and no one as uprooted as the wanderer Luka, who comes from nowhere and vanishes into the beyond, preaching absolute redemption as the only alternative to absolute depravity. The action is still centred about three family groups. And the people are still aware of a definite social structure within which they live and to whose ideals, for better or worse, they pay some regard. Even the morphine-soaked body of Frau Knobbe is embellished with the rags of polite behaviour. Moreover Hauptmann manages, in the end, to find his moment of beauty, of sympathetic identification, not only in Frau John but even in such characters as Frau Knobbe and Bruno, and he finds it in a way that is typical of him, in an expression of natural affection towards those to whom nature has bound them. Bruno, as he leaves, puts a horseshoe on the table beside the lilac. "Wacht ma Jette:" he says to his sister, "hier is noch 'n Hufeisen! Det ha ick jefunden! Det bringt Glick! Ick brauche ihm nich." Frau Knobbe, at the sight of her dead baby, stuffs a handkerchief in her mouth and there is a rattle deep in her throat. But *Die Ratten* represents a limit of what can be encompassed by a combination of refined realism and humane sympathy. To portray a world still more uprooted and chaotic requires, perhaps, an author who is less involved in his material than Hauptmann, or whose brush is less realistic and who judges by more purely intellectual standards. And that impression is confirmed by Hauptmann's development from 1911 on, both by the novels and by the prose plays in which he attempts to deal with contemporary life.

VI. Epilogue

AFTER HE HAD WRITTEN *Die Ratten* Hauptmann turned his attention increasingly to verse drama and epic and to the novel. From 1911 until 1924 he wrote only one play in prose; and although there were seven more between 1924 and 1937 three of them are of one-act length only and one of the others is not fully worked out. The changing world, moreover, and his own declining power brought a deterioration in many of Hauptmann's late works which makes the task of discussing them a sad one, and the prose plays are no exception. They contain some interesting scenes, for his feeling for the stage did not desert him, he remained to some extent aware of contemporary and widely valid problems, and he still tried, at times, to set complex figures against a rich and detailed background. Indeed, it is not always easy to put one's finger precisely on what has gone wrong. But his sense of the irrational and of its power over human life, always strong, was heightened by events during and after the war, and although he communicated this new awareness successfully in some of his verse plays, through the medium of characters and events taken from historical or literary sources, he tried to express it also, and less fortunately, by means that we have already noted in *Elga* or *Und Pippa tanzt!* by illustrating some preconceived problem or mystery, some symbol or fancy. The influence of post-war literary movements, with their stress on subjective and unrealistic expression, helped to encourage him in his vagaries. And the cult of mythology and visions, of possessed men and daemonic women, which dominates his novels and his verse epics, played an increasingly important role in his prose plays. But even where he seems to be doing his best to penetrate and illuminate the immediate world, his pictures are pale and abstract beside the living representations of former years, and the settings are like scaffolds, deliberately erected, and giving insufficient support to the strange problems attached to them.

Almost any line of the dialogue, and this is a crucial point, will reveal this great inferiority, a fact that critics have not always been ready to admit. Carl Zuckmayer, for example, in an attempt to save *Herbert Engelmann*, speaks of the "gehobenen Nüchternheit"—the elevated sobriety—of the dialogue.[1] But Hauptmann's whole power lies in his ability to respond to concrete scenes or impressions and to the varying, impassioned voices of his fellowmen. He is not capable of adopting a cool and measured tone and of maintaining it, consciously and successfully, throughout a whole work. The language here, like the language in many of his novels, is not "sober" in a good sense, but laborious and banal, and we can trace the resemblance, if we wish, to details, to the excessive use of subordinate clauses, for example, or of prepositive participial constructions, or even to the strange clumsiness in the use of proper names which makes the author seem uncertain of his attitude to his characters and the characters themselves unhappy with one another. "Regen Sie sich nicht auf, bester Herbert," says the hero's future mother-in-law, "Es ist ein sehr grosser Fehler, dass Sie sich immer so in Harnisch bringen lassen, Herr Engelmann." And if the language is at some points stiff and flat it is at others forced and inflated. In discussing the late plays, as in discussing *Pippa* or *Die versunkene Glocke*, it is one thing to speculate about Hauptmann's intentions; it is another to record what he achieved.

The least impressive of the post-war works are two which owe their origin, in the main, to fantasy, with or without the help of the supernatural: *Hexenritt* (1929), and *Die goldene Harfe* (1933). The former is a short one-act play in which a Swedish explorer and his Berlin friend, camping for the night in the ruins of a castle on the south shore of Sweden, encounter the ghost of the former owner, an obscene female Bluebeard whom Hauptmann associates with the goddess Astarte. The sketch is one of the excursions into the occult to which he became in-

[1] In the *Nachwort* to his revision (Munich, 1952).

creasingly addicted in his late years, and it is aptly characterized
by the Berliner. "Don't keep on involving me," he begs his
friend, "in your distasteful ghost-story."

Die goldene Harfe, according to Behl, was inspired by a Mozart
andantino,[2] and something of the enchantment of Mozart's
music is caught in the descriptions of the eighteenth-century
park in which the action is set. But the mood is not maintained
by the characters and the incidents. Twin brothers, one pensive
and one dashing and gay, visit the family of a friend killed in the
Napoleonic Wars, and become rivals for the love of his sister,
summoning her back to the world which she has renounced since
his death. And it is not merely the suicide of the pensive twin
which upsets the balance of the play or the symbolic weight
which Hauptmann attaches to his heroine, in whom he sees the
introverted and problematic soul of Germany, but the awkward
attempt to blend harps and flutes with Korner's resounding
"Lützows wilde verwegene Jagd," and the awakened dreamer
tipping the hats of her cavaliers with her riding whip in a manner
reminiscent of musical comedy. Die goldene Harfe is less complex
and obscure than Pippa, but it is compounded of the same
elements, and Hauptmann's ability to handle them had not
improved in the intervening years.

Nor was he much more successful with the longer of the two
historical plays which he wrote in this late period. Magnus
Garbe, which was first contemplated in 1898, was intended as a
sequel to Florian Geyer, and its subject is the counter-revolutionary
witch-hunting in the sixteenth century. But it rested until 1914,
when the outbreak of the war, sharpening Hauptmann's sense
of the uncanny transformation of masses of men under the influence of fear and bloodshed—"Glaubt an die grausige Wandel-
barkeit der Menschennatur" says one of the characters—seems
to have moved him to attempt to work out his earlier plan.
There is horror enough in the play, as the young and beautiful
wife of Garbe, mayor of a German free-city, is snatched by
Dominican monks from her ancestral home, dragged through

[2]Wege zu Gerhart Hauptmann (Goslar, 1948), p. 132.

the streets as she writhes in the pangs of child-birth, tortured and condemned to the stake. But the characters and the milieu are painted in thin, representative colours; the patrician leaders of the city, for example, resemble the figures of a routine Dutch painting of a syndicate. And although one speech informs us that the hysteria of the mob is due not only to the fanaticism of the monks but to a drought which threatens to bring starvation, to a disease which is wiping out the cattle, and to the appearance in the town of the dreaded Black Death, Hauptmann is more concerned with a ball of fire which dances over the church than with the portrayal of the people. The play, moreover, is seriously disturbed by the introduction of a second motive. The mayor has such a fear of experiencing the suffering of his wife that when the hour comes for the birth of the child he forgets the situation in the city and retreats to an idyllic vineyard outside the walls, where, for the entire second act, he waits, while a series of messengers arrive to tell him of the disaster, but hesitate until too late. When he finally learns that his wife is in prison, he suffers a stroke, leaving the dramatist nothing to do in the third and final act but picture the death of the maimed and crippled pair. The play was not published until 1942, allegedly because Hauptmann did not wish to offend the Roman Catholic Church, but perhaps also because he knew that it was a series of sketches rather than an adequately realized work.

In 1929 however, in a one-act tragedy entitled *Die schwarze Maske*, he made a second and more successful attempt to paint a rapidly rising panic. The action this time is set in a Silesian city, in the year 1662 and in the house of the mayor Schuller—a name which was originally associated with the story of *Magnus Garbe*. The land is still stricken from the Thirty Years' War; starvation, ruins, plague, robbers, and a dark, cold February day surround the house. But Schuller has returned to his native province from a long sojourn in Holland, bringing with him a cultivated, philanthropic, and fabulously wealthy Dutch wife and has set himself to relieve the suffering of the townspeople and to establish a haven of culture and of religious tolerance within his own walls. Around his table, accordingly, we meet not only members of the local nobility, but a fiery little organist, a simple Protestant pastor, an austere and saintly young abbot, related to the house of Fugger, who is possessed by an unswerving ambition to enrich the church he serves, and a steady and humane Jewish merchant who has known the Schullers in Amsterdam and who visits them frequently in the course of his travels. The mixed group is served by a greedy and fanatical Jansenist butler and by a Huguenot refugee whom Schuller has saved from starvation on the highway. The characters give us a credible and fascinating glimpse of the shaken world of the seventeenth century, and indirectly, of the equally unsettled years in which the play was written. And the conversation reflects their varied interests and viewpoints, turning now to local affairs, to the misery of the people and the hostility between the confessions, and now to distant fields, to the prosperous cities of Holland or to a performance of a Shakespeare play on some far-off stage. The action, unfortunately, is unconvincing and arbitrary. For, while it was ingenious on Hauptmann's part to link the Black Death in the town with Frau Schuller's wealth, which comes from the slave-trade, and to have her struck down in the end, leaving us uncertain whether the cause is the plague or her sense of guilt, there is no connection between this story and the Silesian setting. And, worse still, her conscience is personified by a negro slave who was once her lover, and who, having found her out, steals into the house, terrifying the guests and transforming her, in an instant, from a gracious lady into what passes with Hauptmann as a sex-ridden maniac—a problem which need not delay us here, since it appears in a more aggravated form in *Dorothea Angermann*. Yet, story aside, Hauptmann recovered in *Die schwarze Maske* something of his old power, and when, at the end, a girl whom Schuller has rescued from the ashes of her father's farm joins hands with the Jewish merchant in an attempt to save the broken man, we feel once again the deep love and understanding which accompany his most valid and convincing portrayals.

The four remaining plays deal with the life of Hauptmann's own day, and it is here, where he had achieved his greatest triumphs, that the loss of his creative power and the difficulties presented by the post-war world are most apparent. *Herbert Engelmann*, which was written in 1924, and never fully worked out, is evidence of both. Its hero is a young soldier who, returning to Germany from Russia a year after the end of the war, shell-shocked, ill, and penniless, and finding his parents dead and the fatherland in a state of chaos, robs a *Geldbriefträger*—a postman entrusted with the delivery of money. The man, whom he has left gagged and bound—it is not clear where—dies before he is discovered. Engelmann, in a highly critical state and not fully conscious of what he has done, takes a room in a Berlin boarding-house run by a pastor's widow and her daughter, marries the girl after a time, and tries to free himself from his psychosis by retreating with her to a suburban villa and devoting himself to writing. But some months later he is arrested, and, although there is not sufficient evidence against him to convict him, he now remembers what has happened and commits suicide.

We realize as we read the play that Hauptmann had set himself tasks of no small magnitude: he was trying to paint a world dominated to a degree he had never known before by anti-bourgeois and anti-Christian standards; he was trying to show the psychological effect of war, and above all of slaughter, on those who engage in it; and he was trying, finally, to question the right of the state to urge men to kill. In all respects he got no further than an attempt. The Berlin pension, it is true, shelters a mixed group. There are secret police living there and a movie star, a homosexual nobleman and his friend, a veterinarian, who belong to a mystic order with great power in high places, and a young student who champions the restoration of the Germanic gods. "Man kann nie wissen, ob der oder jener ein Biedermann, Juwelendieb oder Agent der Sowjets ist," says one of the characters, aptly enough. But Hauptmann, who had always known his people, is not genuinely interested in characters who might be anything, and he has merely sketched these, assembled

what he has to say about them, it would appear, from newspaper
articles or from the talk of the day, and so clumsily that, for all
their flamboyant characteristics, they appear constructed and
dull.

Nor has he any clear picture of his hero. He gives us a few
details of his boyhood which remind us of what we have heard of
Johannes Vockerat, he makes use of the words "Kriegshysterie"
and "Kriegspsychose," and he describes the tormented man, in a
sudden panic, leaping into a taxi to avoid meeting a mailman.
Engelmann, moreover, is given to outbursts of anger or despair,
and has many bitter things to say about the war—that attacking
with hand-grenades, to give one instance, teaches men lessons
which they cannot get out of their blood. And once or twice,
as he speaks, the language suddenly begins to flow with pain and
anger. "Wenn nur das die Hauptsache wäre," he answers the
student, who has declared himself ready to die in the next war,
"aber die Hauptsache ist das nicht. Etwas ganz anderes ist die
Hauptsache. Die Blinden, die Verstümmelten, die körperlich
und seelisch Ruinierten sind die Hauptsache. . . ." But the pieces
never come together to form a living being, however storm-
tossed and shattered; and the dialogue, as we have already noted,
is for the most part strained and unnatural.

With his failure to portray his people Hauptmann fails also
in his argument. He might have made *Herbert Engelmann* effective
by concentrating his picture and raising the tone of the whole,
as he did in *Kramer* or in some of his verse plays, but he was not
master enough of his milieu to free himself from details even
when they were strange and meaningless to him. Or he might
have rounded and smoothed his scenes, and given greater promi-
nence to the tracking down of his hero by the police, as Zuckmayer has done, finishing the tale of the inverts, for example, with
a neatly macabre touch by having the veterinarian bite the nobleman, whereupon both are transported by the police to the Charité.
But Hauptmann—with all due respect to Zuckmayer—was never
merely a skilful craftsman. He wrote works of the highest
calibre, or he blundered. The fact that he did not finish his play

speaks for the sincerity of his intentions as well as for his failure to give real expression to the tragedy of the post-war scene.

If *Herbert Engelmann* shows Hauptmann baffled by the present, *Dorothea Angermann*, which appeared in 1925, indicates that he had lost his power of recreating the past. The play traces the fate of a pastor's daughter who is seduced by the cook of a hotel where she has been sent for training, forced by her father to marry him, and sent with him to the United States, where the pair sink quickly into the New York underworld. A year later a son of the hotel owner, who loves her, coming to America to visit a brother, finds her deserted by her husband and makes an attempt to save her. But it is too late. When the cook reappears she returns to him, and remains with him until, a few months later, he dies from an overdose of morphine. Then, broken in mind and body, she drags herself back to Germany, is rejected once again by her father, and kills herself. The very variety of the play's settings—it moves from the Preussische Krone to the pastor's apartment in Breslau, from there to America and then back again to Hamburg—is a key to its weakness. In earlier years Hauptmann had been so impressed by the scenes he remembered that a room or two, with perhaps a strip of beach or the edge of a field, can evoke and give life to a whole work. *Dorothea Angermann* is an attempt to construct a play out of a series of past scenes, none of which are fully apprehended and realized.

The characters, above all the heroine, are drawn with the same pallor and uncertainty. From the time he wrote *Elga* Hauptmann made periodic attempts to depict a type of seductress whom he intended to be at one and the same time pure and childlike and evil and perverse. He never succeeded. Dorothea, like *Bürgermeisterin* Schuller, is a variant of this type, with middle-class complications. There are moments when the dramatist has made us feel her as a reserved, sensitive girl, delivered into the cook's power by a strain of passionate blood and a hot, weary afternoon in the midst of a frantically busy season, but quietly resolved to sink no further into the cheap and repellent

world her feet have touched; and there are excellent scenes
between her and her coarse, sensuous father. But for the most
part even this aspect of her struggle is talked about rather than
experienced. And the other Dorothea, the debased slave of the
cook, is portrayed by a few details reminiscent of a gangster
film—Hauptmann's impressions of New York were painfully
naïve—and by turgid and melodramatic generalizations. "Mein
Vater," she says, "hat mich in die Höhlen und Gruben der
hungrigen wilden Tiere hinuntergestossen," or, "Jawohl, Sie
sehen in mir eine Gesunkene." Hanna Elias is both a real woman
and an effective embodiment of the absolute power of sex.
Dorothea is neither. She merely embarrasses us for the dramatist,
who might have persuaded us to pity her as an outcast had he
not also wished us to admire her as a sister of Wedekind's Lulu
and as an inhabitant of a morass of poisonous slime where life
is stark and naked and dreadful and inaccessible to mere middle-
class compassion or understanding.

Vor Sonnenuntergang, which appeared in 1932, is the last of
Hauptmann's full-length prose plays, and a more even work
than some of its predecessors, although here again the main
theme is laboured and unconvincing. It presents a credible
facsimile of a wealthy, cultivated, and philanthropic manufacturer,
Geheimrat Clausen, and of his somewhat weak and spoiled
children. Clausen's seventieth birthday is being celebrated, as
the play opens, by the whole town, and although deeply shaken
by the death of his wife three years before, he appears to have
regained his strength and stability. Yet he feels that he cannot
face a future which offers him no problem beyond deciding the
date of his retirement, and proposes to begin a new stage of
his existence by marrying a young kindergarten teacher named
Inken Peters. But the antagonism of his children, who finally
take legal steps to depose him on the grounds of senility, upsets
the balance he has struggled to regain, and he commits suicide.

Hauptmann took the background for this play and some of
the details from the life of a Jewish friend, Max Pinkus, head of a
great textile firm, whose collection of the works of Silesian

authors was one of the finest in the country, and who had already inspired the figure of the merchant in *Die schwarze Maske*. But it was shaped also by the centenary of the death of Goethe, and in Clausen and Inken the dramatist was intent on recalling the love of the seventy-four year old Goethe for the young Ulrike von Levetzow. The idea was not fortunate, for even Goethe, in the beautiful sweeping verses of the "Marienbader Elegie," where all is anticipation and recollection, where hope and passion and despair are evoked solely by the heart of the poet, found it all but impossible to portray his late love as a complete and self-evident tragedy, and for Hauptmann the framework of a detailed and realistic play made the attempt more difficult still. Goethe moreover knew the real tragedy involved: the inherent impossibility of the transformation he longed for. Hauptmann interprets Clausen's love for Inken as a natural phase in a life remarkable for its vitality and wisdom, and places the main responsibility for the catastrophe in the hands of the ungrateful children. The result is a work which, for all its careful detail, is essentially remote both from Goethe and from the life of the dramatist's own day, and in striking contrast to *Rose Bernd*, which, less consciously formed, is close to both.

The figure of Clausen, we have just noted, was in part a tribute to Max Pinkus. Hauptmann was to raise one more monument to his friend, who died in 1934 of a heart attack. By this time anti-Semitism in Germany had reached such heights that Pinkus and his family were isolated, and his death was not publicly announced. Hauptmann, at the age of seventy-two and after a decade of universal acclaim as Germany's greatest living poet, was in no state, morally or intellectually, to wage open war against the Nazis. But he and his wife were the only Gentiles present at Pinkus' funeral. And three years later, in a sketch called *Die Finsternisse*, he recorded his memories of a meal eaten with the family the night before.[3] There are moments in the little play when Hauptmann approaches his subject in a way

---

[3]Published by Walter A. Reichart (Ann Arbor, 1947). The above details of Max Pinkus' life are taken from Professor Reichart's accompanying essay.

that is awkward and painful, and through the whole, as in other late works, he shows a tendency to attribute to fate a suffering which he would formerly have portrayed as the outcome of human greed and prejudice. Yet for all these limitations *Die Finsternisse* is genuinely moving, first in its directness and intimacy, for the conversation turns in part on the details of the family life, and then in Hauptmann's portrayal of the age-old tragedy of a persecuted people, which leads him, as Professor Reichart has noted, to intensify the religious atmosphere of the play and to present his figures as reincarnations of characters in the Old Testament, as members of a distinctive and indomitable race.[4] And yet not of a race set apart entirely, for what affects the Jews, in Hauptmann's eyes, affects mankind. Early in the play there is a vision: the dead Pinkus appears, together with Ahasuerus, the prophet Elijah, and St. John, and the three sit down with him at the richly set table to give some account of themselves to the man who has just entered their kingdom. "Ich würge an der Speise des Lebens," says Ahasuerus, "Die unversöhnliche Grausamkeit stopft sie mir in den Mund. . . . Ich wandere von Grabstätte zu Grabstätte, gefoltert von lechzendem Todesdurst. Oft schwebt ein taubenflügliger Engel auf mich zu. Endlich! jauchzt es in mir, aber er bringt einem anderen den Tod." St. John, to be sure, explains that he is waiting for the return of Christ—"Ich warte geduldig der Rückkehr des allbarmherzigen Gottessohnes auf diese Erde." But when Pinkus then asks, "So bist du besser dran als Ahasver?" he casts down his eyes and does not answer. The play, on the whole, leaves us grateful that, for all the strange ways Hauptmann wandered in his late years, he was able, in this last brief prose drama, to meet the challenge offered him by the suffering of his friends, to see to some extent as he had seen in his best years, and to touch once more the heights in a realm that is pre-eminently his own.

There are, then, not more than one or two of the late works which add to Hauptmann's stature. Yet he is by no means the only author who, setting out to portray the life of his own day,

[4]*Ibid.*, p. 28.

could not continue to the end in the way he began—witness Keller's late *Martin Salander*, or, an almost exact parallel, the work of Shaw, who wrote most of his best plays, a round dozen, between 1892 and 1912 and only three—*Back to Methuselah, St. Joan* and *The Apple Cart*—from then until his death. And as Shaw expressed himself most effectively after the war through the medium of history or phantasy, so Hauptmann did his best work from 1913 on in his verse plays. His material here, history or legend or the tales of others, gave him, for one thing, a more immediate inspiration than the fading memories of his youth. And it gave him also, paradoxical as it may seem, the distance necessary to weigh his scenes, to consider contemporary problems through the medium of the past, and to reassert the values in which he believed most deeply and which were menaced by a too intimate preoccupation with life around him in the post-war world. Just how precisely he did this is evident if we compare for a moment *Herbert Engelmann* with *Die Winterballade*, which appeared in 1917, or with the *Iphigenie* cycle, which was begun in 1940 and completed in 1944. The problem in all three plays is the same—the effect of war on its participants—all three leading figures are driven to murder, and all three reach the same conclusion, that whether their actions have been voluntary or not, what they have done leaves them no choice but to take their own lives. But *Herbert Engelmann* remained a sketch. The *Iphigenie* plays, though they contain undigested mythological lumps, are much more fully and successfully realized. And *Die Winterballade* is as powerful a tragedy as Hauptmann ever wrote. It does much to compensate for the failure of the late prose plays that they are by no means Hauptmann's last word, even about the life of his own day.

The earlier plays, in the meantime, remain his finest single accomplishment, and if there have been frequent references to Ibsen and Shaw in these pages it is because he has no other rivals in modern literature in the field of realistic prose drama. In spite of the importance of Antoine's reform the French did their best work, in the decades before and after the turn of the century, in the novel. Strindberg, obsessed by the problem of the struggle between the sexes or by the futility of human existence, said what he had to say in a very few works. Chekhov produced fine and delicate analyses of the last days of the Russian upper classes. Gorki wrote intelligently and with a wide range, but his characters, except in three or four plays, lack individual life. O'Neill, coming later, experimented more often than he succeeded. Hauptmann's work has breadth, a unique power of creating men and environment, and an attitude which makes it as progressive as that of his often more argumentative contemporaries. His first service to his own and succeeding generations is his ability to paint human beings from many spheres of society, from the lower classes as well as the middle, and with equal understanding and concern for both. But his second service is that, though his plays lack the intellectual quality of those of Ibsen or Shaw, he touches in his own way on just as wide a range of problems, social and economic, religious and political. And his whole attitude implies a desire for reform wherever it appears to him that the society of his day has become rigid in its ideals, careless of the lives of its individual members, or blind to the inevitability of change.

He was, it is true, a man sensitive above all to pain, and a man whose deep longing for peace, strengthened by the pietist influences of his youth and of the province from which he came, made him intensely aware that conflict in all its forms means destruction as well as growth; and the stress in his plays, as we have repeatedly noted, is less on action or on strong-willed, aggressive characters than on the emotional states of those who suffer and are vanquished. It is also true that he would probably have agreed with Friedrich Hebbel that the need of his day was not for an entirely new society but for a better basis for that which existed. But the German middle class, fighting for its rights in the late eighteenth century, had fashioned not only certain specific precepts which the generation of 1860 was mechanically repeating, but powerful long-range weapons in the form of rational enquiry, tolerance, and concern for the well-being of one's fellow-man; and Hauptmann, inheriting the latter from Lessing and Keller and Fontane and his own father, was still able to use them to judge the society in which he lived and to hold himself receptive to new developments. The old Vockerats or Henschel may represent a past which seems to have been happier than the present, but Hauptmann never wrote the swan-songs of a Chekhov.

It never occurred to him, moreover, as it has occurred to many who have come after him, that the masses ought to be controlled in the interests of stability or that the findings of psychology are a proof of man's natural propensity to sin and point to the readoption of authoritarian standards, preferably ecclesiastical, as the only salvation for weak humanity. His compassion, being deeper than that of a Lessing or Keller, may sometimes be embodied in a figure like August Keil, who can provide only a last refuge for a broken life; but it is expressed also in Spitta, who burns with anger because, two thousand years after Christ, men have not yet heard His message. Hauptmann did not write drama because he had given up struggle, or tragedy because he had lost his ideals; he wrote because his ideals were ineradicable and because they were not realized in the world in which he lived.

There is some tendency at present to regard the prose plays as one of the last flowerings of liberalism or, as Werner Ziegenfuss terms it, bourgeois humanism,[5] that we are likely to see; a tendency, that is to say, to relegate them to the past and to consider their assumptions and conclusions no longer valid. This attitude, consciously or unconsciously, is reflected in the many recent discussions of his work in which the major stress is placed on the late fiction or on the verse epics. But it is reflected also in the opinions of those who value the earlier works, but with reservations. Critics on the west side of the Iron Curtain can accept plays like *Die Weber* or *Der Biberpelz* or *Die Ratten* only by arguing that Hauptmann is not concerned with immedi-

---

[5]*Gerhart Hauptmann: Dichtung und Gesellschaftsidee der bürgerlichen Humanität* (Berlin, 1948).

ate social or political problems; those on the east maintain that his concern, although great, is not great enough. Lukács has recently explained that the value of his observations is limited because his viewpoint is identical with that of the people he paints and because to him liberalism represents absolute rather than, as the Marxist believes, relative progress. And Brecht, in a revision of *Der Biberpelz* and *Der rote Hahn* which seems to reflect the tragic pressure of official opinion on a powerful and original dramatist, illustrated how Hauptmann's judgment can be corrected.

In *Der Biberpelz*, just before the end, Fleischer makes a statement of his principles in which he affirms his right to freedom of thought and association: "Ich bin keinem Menschen Rechenschaft schuldig. Was ich tu' und lasse, ist meine Sache. Mit wem ich umgehe, ist meine Sache. Was ich denke und schreibe, ist meine Sache." But according to Brecht the voice of liberalism is not nearly so brave. "Das ist nicht meine Sprache, Herr von Wehrhahn," says the new Fleischer, repudiating the authorship of a certain pamphlet, "Das ist eines dieser sozialdemokratischen Machwerke! Ich distanziere mich aufs schärfste von derlei rüden und im Grunde primitiven Folgerungen der Tagespolitik." And Brecht further improved the two plays by turning the constable Rauchhaupt into a worker of Marxist persuasions, by introducing another as the sweetheart of Leontine, by showing Fielitz as well as Motes engaged in informing, and by stressing, much more pointedly than in his own *Mutter Courage*, that if the people think to gain their own ends by conniving with their oppressors, they are deceived.[6]

The trouble with the revision is not that it is wrong at every point. But, taken as a whole, the theories it propounds have so regimented Hauptmann's observations, remodelled them according to a scheme of accepted truths, that the result is merely routine and rigid propaganda.[7] It is Hauptmann's world which

[6] *Theaterarbeit* (Dresden, 1952), pp. 171 ff.
[7] "Wir glauben, dass es weder erlaubt noch notwendig ist, Gerhart Hauptmann in seinem zeitkritischen Bemühen zu verstärken." Heinz Menzel, in *Blätter der Städtischen Bühne Heidelberg*, II, 1956–7.

leaves the doors open for progress; from that of the revision there is no exit.

But the trouble with both sides is that unless they regain the courage to be guided in their judgments by Fleischer's "Was ich denke und schreibe, ist meine Sache," we shall have no appreciation of Hauptmann's prose plays in the spirit in which they were written, and his example will inspire no successors. We may then have to admit that we have moved into a new era. We may even have to admit that we are happy with a new theatre dominated by journalistic *plaidoyers* of the status quo, by a revival of Calderon, and by moral and ontological allegories so tenuous and fantastic that they may safely be said to be harmless.

Index

ALBERTI, CONRAD, 7
Andersen, Hans Christian, 178
Anselm, Georg, 163n
Antoine, André, 7, 8, 230
Anzengruber, Ludwig, 5, 156, 161
Archer, William, 3
Aristotle, 53
Arnold, R. F., 5
Augier, Emile, 4, 6, 7

BAB, JULIUS, 165n
Baginski, Max, 67, 69–70, 109, 172–3
Balzac, Honoré de, 169
  Les Paysans, 7
Becque, Henri, 4
Beethoven, 117
Behl, C. F. W., 13, 15n, 16n, 28n, 60n,
  70n, 92n, 100n, 121n, 150, 151, 157n,
  179n, 180n, 191n, 221
Bennigsen, von, Rudolf 73
Bergson, Henri, 3
Bismarck, Otto von, 98, 162, 215, 216
Bleibtreu, Karl, 7
Boecklin, Arnold, 11, 102
Böhme, Jakob, 184
Bölsche, Wilhelm, 7
Bräuer, Albrecht, 110
Brahm, Otto, 9n
Brecht, Bertolt, 96
  Mutter Courage, 97, 233
  Adaptation of Der Biberpelz and Der
    rote Hahn, 233
Browning, Robert, 4
Büchner, Georg, 4, 11
Byron, 4, 14

CALDERON, 234
Campbell, T. M., 7n
Caprivi, Count Leo von, 162
Chapiro, J., 67n
Chaplin, Charles, 141
Chekhov, Anton, 3, 4, 149, 231, 232
Conrad, Georg, 7

DAHN, FELIX, 14
Darwin, Charles, 3, 35, 39, 45
Dauthendey, Maximilian, 176
Dickens, Charles
  A Tale of Two Cities, 7
Dickinson, T. H., 5n
Dosenheimer, Elise, 66n
Dostoievski, Feodor, 11
  Crime and Punishment, 7
Du Bois-Reymond, E., 9
Dumas fils, Alexandre, 4, 6, 7

ENDRES, FRITZ, 121n
Evans, M. Blakemore, 45

FAIRLEY, BARKER, 199n
Fechter, Paul, 27
Feise, Ernst, 19, 45, 51n
Fontane, Theodor, 232
Forel, Auguste, 3, 11, 34
Freud, Sigmund, 3, 187
Fry, Christopher, 154

GARTEN, HUGH, 165n
Glass, Emil, 186n
Glitschmann (painter, model for Peter
    Brauer), 136–7
Goethe, 45, 46, 50, 94, 102
  Egmont, 210
  Faust, 39, 135, 191, 197 ff.
  Götz von Berlichingen, 96
  Hermann und Dorothea, 194
  "Marienbader Elegie," 228
  Wilhelm Meister, 94, 102
Gorki, Maxim, 3, 231
  The Lower Depths, 217
  The Zykovs, 187
Goya, 130
Gregor, Joseph, 137n
Grelling, Richard, 68
Grillparzer, Franz, 4
  Die Jüdin von Toledo, 99
  Das Kloster bei Sendomir, 99

Grundmann, Anna, 191n
Gryphius, Andreas, 161

HAECKEL, ERNST, 10, 35, 45
Halbe, Max, 9n
Hardy, Thomas, 124
  The Return of the Native, 7
Hart, Heinrich, 7
Hart, Julius, 7
Hauptmann, Carl, 10 ff., 34, 45–6
Hauptmann, Georg, 10, 107, 110
Hauptmann, Gerhart
  Das Abenteuer meiner Jugend, 12–13,
    15, 45, 68, 110, 151, 179
  Anna, 191n
  Der arme Heinrich, 95, 178, 179
  Ausblicke, 20n, 41, 47, 180n, 185, 201–2
  Bahnwärter Thiel, 14, 102, 122, 124,
    151, 176, 187
  Der Biberpelz, 71, 76, 109, 140, 149,
    150–62, 164 ff., 177, 179 ff., 183,
    232–4.
  Das Buch der Leidenschaft, 33, 45, 122
  Das bunte Buch, 14, ("Wie eine Windes-
    harfe"), 172, ("Die Mondbraut"),
    172–3, 176
  Christiane Lawrenz, 99n
  Dorothea Angermann, 223, 226–7
  Einsame Menschen, 16, 27, 28, 31, 34,
    35–52, 53, 54, 59, 63, 65, 85, 98,
    99, 102, 110 ff., 117, 118, 122, 123,
    126, 129, 134, 148, 151, 171, 180,
    184, 196, 201, 217, 225, 232
  Elga, 99, 179, 199, 219, 226
  Fasching, 14
  Die Finsternisse, 228–9
  Florian Geyer, 75, 76–98, 102, 123, 129,
    144, 149, 150, 169, 177, 179, 187,
    217, 221
  Das Friedensfest, 16, 28–35, 37, 47, 50,
    59, 102, 107, 111, 117
  Fuhrmann Henschel, 103, 149, 179–90,
    194 208, 217, 232
  Gabriel Schillings Flucht, 103, 110,
    123–36, 146–8, 179, 184 ff., 190,
    193, 203, 207, 217
  Germanen und Römer, 14
  Die goldene Harfe, 220–1
  Griselda, 99–100, 101
  Der grosse Traum, 121
  Hanneles Himmelfahrt, 70, 75, 76, 98,
    149, 150, 169–78, 179

Herbert Engelmann, 99n, 220, 224–6, 230
Das Hermannslied, 14
Hexenritt, 220–1
Das Hirtenlied, 179
Die Insel der Grossen Mutter, 109
Iphigenie, 95, 123, 230
Die Jungfern vom Bischofsberg, 99, 109
Der Ketzer von Soana, 124
Kollege Crampton, 76, 99, 103–9, 110,
  137, 139 ff., 144, 147, 149, 165,
  178, 208, 210
Magnus Garbe, 221–2
Michael Kramer, 71, 95, 98, 101, 103,
  110–23, 124, 129, 134, 135, 142,
  143, 145, 146–8, 149, 164n, 179,
  184, 190, 201, 217, 225, 227
Der Narr in Christo Emanuel Quint, 16,
  65, 70, 71, 75, 124, 147, 169, 178,
  213
Peter Brauer, 101, 103, 136–44, 146–8,
  149, 162, 169, 203, 206, 216
Promethidenlos, 14
Die Ratten, 103, 137, 144, 149, 162,
  165, 169, 179, 203–18, 219, 232
Rose Bernd, 95, 98, 103, 144, 149, 186,
  187, 190, 191–203, 217, 228, 232
Der rote Hahn, 137n, 149, 152, 162–9,
  203, 215, 233
Die schwarze Maske, 222–3, 226, 228
Till Eulenspiegel, 121
Ulrich von Lichtenstein, 109
Und Pippa tanzt!, 99, 100–2, 219, 220,
  221
Veland, 95
Die versunkene Glocke, 95, 102, 110, 220
Vor Sonnenaufgang, 3, 8, 9, 15, 16–28,
  30–2, 34, 35, 45, 50, 61, 64, 71,
  102, 109, 141, 152, 171, 177, 188
Vor Sonnenuntergang, 227–8
Die Weber, 16, 53–76, 77, 79, 81, 83,
  85, 98, 102, 103, 109, 149, 150,
  168, 170, 177, 188, 190, 213, 232
Die Winterballade, 95, 230
Hauptmann, Lotte, 34
Hauptmann, Margarete (nee Marschalk),
  122n, 228
Hauptmann, Marie (the dramatist's
  mother), 11, 12, 34
Hauptmann, Marie (nee Thienemann), 10
Hauptmann, Martha (nee Thienemann),
  10, 43n
Hauptmann, Robert, 9, 12, 110

Hebbel, Friedrich, 4, 96, 231
  Maria Magdalene, 6, 187, 200–1
Heimann, Moritz, 163n, 179n
Heine, Heinrich, 14, 202
  "Die Schlesischen Weber," 53
Heise, Wilhelm, 40, 66, 92, 95, 101n, 156, 161
Henckell, Karl, 7
Hessler, Alexander, 204n
Heuser, F. W. J., 34n, 68n
Hofmannsthal, Hugo von, 3
Holz, Arno, 7, 9, 16, 18, 176
  Die Familie Selicke, 28
  Papa Hamlet, 8, 15, 28n
Houben, H. H., 68n, 73
Hülsen, Hans von, 110n
Hutten, Ulrich von, 11, 98
  "Von Wahrheit ich will nimmer lan," 87–8, 93
Huxley, Thomas, 3

Ibsen, 3, 4, 6, 11, 18, 20, 26, 50, 131, 149, 230, 231
  The Doll's House, 19, 201
  Ghosts, 7, 8
  Rosmersholm, 42–3

James, Henry, 50
Jones, Henry Arthur, 4, 7
Jordan, Wilhelm, 14

Keller, Gottfried, 11, 232
  Martin Salander, 230
Kerr, Alfred, 185
Kleist, Heinrich von, 4, 9, 50
  Das Käthchen von Heilbronn, 94
  Der zerbrochene Krug, 156
Klinger, Max, 148
Kodis-Krzyzanowska, Josepha, 11, 34
Körner, Karl Theodor
  "Lützows wilde verwegene Jagd," 221
Kotzebue, August von, 3
Krogmann, Willy, 13n
Kutscher, A., 34n

Lessing, 9, 209, 232
Litt (art student, model for Arnold Kramer), 110
Lukács, György, 233
Luther, 81, 84, 88

Maeterlinck, Maurice, 102

Mann, Heinrich, 168
Mann, Thomas, 148
  Der kleine Herr Friedemann, 120–1
Marschalk, Margarete, see Hauptmann, Margarete
Marshall, James, 103, 104, 137
Marx, Karl, 3
Marx, Paul, 66, 69, 74
Mebius, Lola, 165n
Meiningen, Duke Georg von, 4
Menzel, Heinz, 165n, 234n
  Moderne Dichtercharaktere, 8
Molière, 37, 108
  L'Avare, 103, 106, 107
Montesquieu, 75
Mozart, 221
Mühler, Robert, 101n
Müller, Max, 34
Murry, John Middleton, 191

Nietzsche, Friedrich, 3, 51

O'Neill, Eugene, 231
  Desire under the Elms, 187
Ostrovski, Alexander N., 4

Petsch, Robert, 41–2, 50
Pinero, Arthur Wing, 4, 7
Pinkus, Max, 227, 228
Plato, 102, 122
Ploetz, Alfred, 11

Rabl, Hans, 59
Rattigan, Terence, 3
Reichart, Walter A., 228, 229
Renan, Ernst, 3
Requardt, Walter, 14n, 16n, 163n, 204n
Rilke, Rainer Maria, 120, 148
Robertson, T. W., 4, 5
  Caste, 6
Rostand, Edmond, 3

Sardou, Victorien, 4
Scherer, Wilhelm, 9
Schiller, 9, 41, 50, 202, 209, 213
  Die Braut von Messina, 206
  Die Jungfrau von Orleans, 77
  Maria Stuart, 77
  Wilhelm Tell, 96
Schlaf, Johannes
  Die Familie Selicke, 28
  Papa Hamlet, 8, 15, 28n

Schlegel, Friedrich, 47
Schlenther, Paul, 9n, 15, 94n, 101, 106, 109n, 123, 156, 179
Schmidt, Hugo Ernst, 110, 123, 124n, 134, 136
Schnitzler, Arthur, 3, 8
Scholz, Albert, 97n
Scribe, Eugene, 3, 4, 18
Shakespeare, 37, 161, 191, 223
   As You Like It, 123
   Hamlet, 103, 177
   Henry IV, 107
   Lear, 103
   Macbeth, 103, 189
   Measure for Measure, 144
   Othello, 103
   Richard III, 177
   Twelfth Night, 123
Shaw, George Bernard, 3, 7, 26, 74, 149, 154–5, 161, 210, 231
   The Apple Cart, 230
   Back to Methuselah, 230
   Candida, 123, 201
   The Devil's Disciple, 123
   Pygmalion, 155
   Mrs. Warren's Profession, 43
   St. Joan, 97, 230
Shelley, 4
Stehr, Hermann, 184
   Der Graveur, 179n
Stirk, S. D., 66, 69, 74
Strauss, David Friedrich, 3, 77, 87n
Strindberg, August, 3, 50, 100, 231
   The Father, 7
   Miss Julie, 43
Sudermann, Hermann, 210

Sulger-Gebing, E., 121n
Synge, John, 161

Taine, Hippolyte, 3
Tennyson, 4, 5
Thienemann, Marie, *see* Hauptmann, Marie
Thienemann, Martha, *see* Hauptmann, Martha
Tolstoi, Alexei, 4
Tolstoi, Leo, 11, 18,
   The Power of Darkness, 7, 15, 26–7, 217
   War and Peace, 7
Treitschke, Heinrich von, 9

Voigt, F. A., 13n, 28n, 41, 70n, 137n, 170n

Wagner, Richard, 5
Wedekind, Frank, 3, 8, 34, 100
   Erdgeist, 227
   Frühlings Erwachen, 178
   Die junge Welt, 13
Weigand, Hermann, 77, 91, 93, 94n, 96
Wilde, Oscar, 3, 154
Wildenbruch, Ernst von
   Die Haubenlerche, 6
   Die Karolinger, 5
   König Heinrich, 97–8
Wilhelm II, 72, 98
Wolff, F. W., 70, 71

Ziegenfuss, Werner, 66, 232
Zimmermann, Alfred, 54, 64, 70, 75
Zola, Emile,
   L'Assommoir, 7
Zuckmayer, Carl, 220
   Adaptation of *Herbert Engelmann*, 225